# LONDON

## Hotels and Restaurants – Town Plans

## 1995

**MICHELIN TYRE Public Limited Company**
Tourism Department – The Edward Hyde Building
38 Clarendon Road – WATFORD Herts WD1 1SX
Tel. : (01923) 415000 – Fax : (01923) 415250

# Dear Reader

*This booklet "hotels and restaurants"
is an extract from the Michelin Guide
"GREAT BRITAIN and IRELAND" 1995
and has been created specially
for your visits to London.*

*Independently compiled by our inspectors,
the Guide provides travellers
with a wide choice of establishments
at all levels of comfort and price.*

*We are committed to providing readers
with the most up to date information
and this edition has been produced
with the greatest care.*

*That is why only this year's guide
merits your complete confidence.*

*Thank you for your comments,
which are always appreciated.*

*For a detailed tour of the city,
use the Michelin Green Guide "LONDON".*

*We wish you a pleasant stay
in the British capital !*

# Contents

# How to use this guide

CATEGORIES

PEACEFUL ATMOSPHERE AND SETTING

HOTEL FACILITIES

STARS

THE RED « **Meals** »

PRICES

LONDON

CAR, TYRES

TOWN PLANS

This guide offers a selection of hotels and restaurants to help the motorist on his travels. In each category establishments are listed in order of preference according to the degree of comfort they offer.

## CATEGORIES

| | | |
|---|---|---|
| | Luxury in the traditional style | XXXXX |
| | Top class comfort | XXXX |
| | Very comfortable | XXX |
| | Comfortable | XX |
| | Quite comfortable | X |
| | Other recommended accommodation, at moderate prices | |
| | Simple comfort | |
| without rest. | The hotel has no restaurant | |
| | The restaurant also offers accommodation | with rm |

## PEACEFUL ATMOSPHERE AND SETTING

Certain establishments are distinguished in the guide by the red symbols shown below.

Your stay in such hotels will be particularly pleasant or restful, owing to the character of the building, its decor, the setting, the welcome and services offered, or simply the peace and quiet to be enjoyed there.

| | |
|---|---|
| to | Pleasant hotels |
| XXXXX to X | Pleasant restaurants |
| « Riverside setting » | Particularly attractive feature |
| | Very quiet or quiet, secluded hotel |
| | Quiet hotel |
| ≤ London | Exceptional view |
| ≤ | Interesting or extensive view |

# HOTEL FACILITIES

In general the hotels we recommend have full bathroom and toilet facilities in each room. However, this may not be the case for certain rooms in categories , ,  and .

| | |
|---|---|
| **30 rm** | Number of rooms |
| | Lift (elevator) |
| | Air conditioning |
| | Television in room |
| | Establishment either partly or wholly reserved for non-smokers |
| | Telephone in room: outside calls connected by the operator |
| | Telephone in room: direct dialling for outside calls |
| | Rooms accessible to disabled people |
| | Outdoor or indoor swimming pool |
| | Exercise room - Sauna |
| | Garden |
| 18 | Hotel tennis court - Golf course and number of holes |
| 150 | Equipped conference hall: maximum capacity |
| | Hotel garage (additional charge in most cases) |
| P | Car park for customers only |
| | Dogs are not allowed in all or part of the hotel |
| Fax | Telephone document transmission |
| *closed Saturday and August* | Dates when closed as indicated by the restaurateur |
| LL35 OSB | Postal code |
| (Forte) | Hotel Group (See list on page 48) |

**Animals**

It is forbidden to bring domestic animals (dogs, cats...) into Great Britain and Ireland.

## STARS

Certain establishments deserve to be brought to your attention for the particularly fine quality of their cooking. **Michelin stars** are awarded for the standard of meals served.

For each of these restaurants we indicate three culinary specialities typical of their style of cooking to assist you in your choice.

✿✿✿ **Exceptional cuisine, worth a special journey**
Superb food, fine wines, faultless service, elegant surroundings. One will pay accordingly !

✿✿ **Excellent cooking, worth a detour**
Specialities and wines of first class quality. This will be reflected in the price.

✿ **A very good restaurant in its category**
The star indicates a good place to stop on your journey.
But beware of comparing the star given to an expensive « de luxe » establishment to that of a simple restaurant where you can appreciate fine cooking at a reasonable price.

## THE RED « Meals »

Whilst appreciating the quality of the cooking in restaurants with a star, you may, however, wish to find some serving a perhaps less elaborate but nonetheless always carefully prepared meal.

Certain restaurants seem to us to answer this requirement. We bring them to your attention by marking them with a red « **Meals** » in the text of the Guide.

### Alcoholic beverages-conditions of sale

The sale of alcoholic drinks is governed in Great Britain and Ireland by licensing laws which vary greatly from country to country.

Allowing for local variations, restaurants may stay open and serve alcohol with a bona fide meal during the afternoon. Hotel bars and public houses are generally open between 11am and 11pm at the discretion of the licensee. Hotel residents, however, may buy drinks outside the permitted hours at the discretion of the hotelier.

Children under the age of 14 are not allowed in bars.

# PRICES

Prices quoted are valid for autumn 1994. Changes may arise if goods and service costs are revised.

*Your recommendation is self-evident if you always walk into a hotel guide in hand.*

Hotels and restaurants in bold type have supplied details of all their rates and have assumed responsibility for maintaining them for all travellers in possession of this guide.

Prices are given in £ sterling.

Where no mention **s., t.,** or **st.** is shown, prices may be subject to the addition of service charge, V.A.T., or both.

### Meals

| | |
|---|---|
| **Meals** 13.00/24.00 | **Set meals** - Lunch 13.00, dinner 24.00 - including cover charge, where applicable |
| **Meals** 15.00/25.00 | See page 12 |
| **s. - t.** | Service only included - V.A.T. only included |
| **st.** | Service and V.A.T. included |
| 🍾 6.00 | Price of 1/2 bottle or carafe of house wine |
| **Meals** a la carte 20.00/25.00 | **A la carte meals** - The prices represent the range of charges from a simple to an elaborate 3 course meal and include a cover charge where applicable |
| ☕ 8.50 | Charge for full cooked breakfast (i.e. not included in the room rate)<br>Continental breakfast may be available at a lower rate |

⌂ : Dinner in this category of establishment will generally be offered from a fixed price menu of limited choice, served at a set time to residents only. Lunch is rarely offered. Many will not be licensed to sell alcohol.

### Rooms

| | |
|---|---|
| **rm** 80.00/150.00 | Lowest price 80.00 per room for a comfortable single and highest price 150.00 per room for the best double |
| **rm** ☕ 85.00/155.00 | Full cooked breakfast (whether taken or not) is included in the price of the room |

### Short breaks

Many hotels now offer a special rate for a stay of two or more nights which comprises dinner, room and breakfast usually for a minimum of two people. Please enquire at hotel for rates.

### Deposits - Credit cards

Some hotels will require a deposit, which confirms the commitment of customer and hotelier alike. Make sure the terms of the agreement are clear.

| | |
|---|---|
| AE VISA JCB | Credit cards accepted by the establishment:<br>Access (MasterCard, Eurocard) - American Express - Diners Club - Visa - Japan Card Bank |

# LONDON

| | |
|---|---|
| ✉ Fulham | Postal address |
| ☏ | STD dialling code. Omit 0 when dialling from abroad |
| BX **A** | Letters giving the location of a place on the town map |
| ⛳18 | Golf course and number of holes (handicap usually required, telephone reservation strongly advised) |
| ☀, ⋞ | Panoramic view, viewpoint |
| ✈ | Airport |
| 🚗 ✆ 0345 090700 | Motorail connection; further information from telephone number listed |
| ℹ | Tourist Information Centre |

## Sights-Star rating

| | |
|---|---|
| ★★★ | Worth a journey |
| ★★ | Worth a detour |
| ★ | Interesting |

## Standart Time

In winter standard time throughout the British Isles is Greenwich Mean Time (G.M.T.). In summer British clocks are advanced by one hour to give British Summer Time (B.S.T.). The actual dates are announced annually but always occur over weekends in March and October.

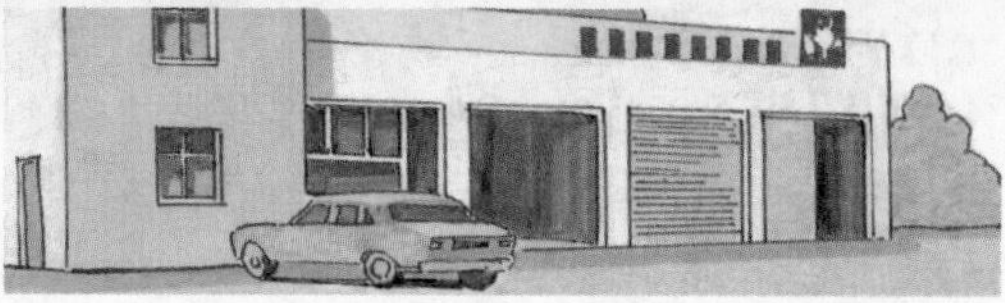

# CAR, TYRES

The wearing of seat belts in Great Britain is obligatory for drivers, front seat passengers and rear seat passengers where seat belts are fitted. It is illegal for front seat passengers to carry children on their lap.

## MICHELIN TYRE SUPPLIERS

The address of the nearest ATS tyre dealer can be obtained by contacting the address below between 9am and 5pm.

ATS HOUSE
180-188 Northolt Rd.
Harrow,
Middlesex HA2 OED
(0181) 423 2000

## MOTORING ORGANISATIONS

The major motoring organisations in Great Britain are the Automobile Association and the Royal Automobile Club. Each provides services in varying degrees for non-resident members of affiliated clubs.

AUTOMOBILE ASSOCIATION
Fanum House
BASINGSTOKE, Hants., RG21 2EA
✆ (01256) 20123

ROYAL AUTOMOBILE CLUB
RAC House, Lansdowne Rd.
CROYDON, Surrey CR9 2JA
✆ (0181) 686 2525

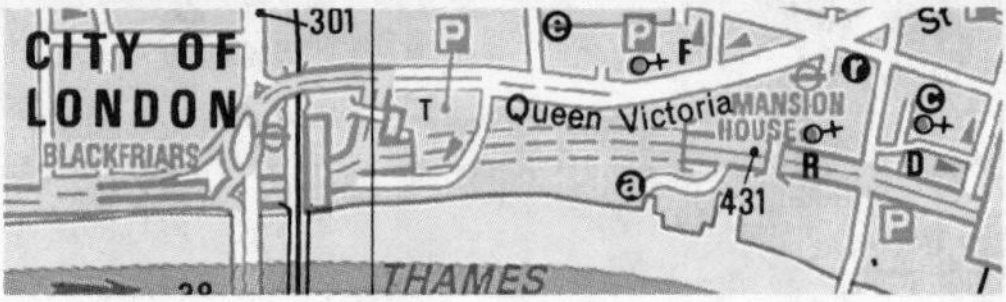


# TOWN PLANS

**Hotels – Restaurants**

## Sights

Place of interest and its main entrance
Interesting place of worship

## Roads

M 1 — Motorway
Interchanges : complete, limited
Dual carriageway with motorway characteristics
Main traffic artery
A 2 — Primary route
(network currently being reclassified)
One-way street – Unsuitable for traffic, street subject to restrictions
Pedestrian street
Piccadilly — Shopping street – Car park
Gateway – Street passing under arch – Tunnel
15'5 — Low headroom (16'6" max.) on major through routes
Station and railway
Funicular – Cable-car
B — Lever bridge – Car ferry

## Various signs

Tourist Information Centre
Mosque – Synagogue
Communications tower or mast – Ruins
Garden, park, wood – Cemetery
Stadium – Racecourse – Golf course
Golf course (with restrictions for visitors)
View – Panorama
Monument – Fountain – Hospital
Pleasure boat harbour – Lighthouse
Airport – Underground station
Ferry services :
passengers and cars
Main post office with poste restante, telephone
Public buildings located by letter :
C H — County Council Offices – Town Hall
M T U — Museum – Theatre – University, College
POL. — Police (in large towns police headquarters)

## London

BRENT SOHO — Borough – Area
Borough boundary – Area boundary

North is at the top on all town plans.

# Ami lecteur

*Cette plaquette « hôtels et restaurants »*
*réalisée d'après le guide Michelin*
*« GREAT BRITAIN and IRELAND » 1995*
*a été conçue spécialement*
*pour vos voyages à Londres.*

*Réalisée en toute indépendance*
*par nos inspecteurs,*
*elle offre au voyageur de passage*
*un large choix d'adresses*
*à tous les niveaux de confort et de prix.*

*Toujours soucieux d'apporter à nos lecteurs*
*l'information la plus récente,*
*nous avons mis à jour cette édition*
*avec le plus grand soin.*

*C'est pourquoi, seul,*
*le Guide de l'année en cours*
*mérite votre confiance.*

*Merci de vos commentaires*
*toujours appréciés*

*Pour une visite détaillée de la ville,*
*utilisez le guide Vert Michelin « LONDRES ».*

*Bon séjour*
*dans la capitale britannique !*

# Sommaire

# Comprendre

CATÉGORIES

AGRÉMENT ET TRANQUILLITÉ

L'INSTALLATION

LES ÉTOILES

« **Meals** »

LES PRIX

LONDRES

LA VOITURE, LES PNEUS

LES PLANS

Ce guide vous propose une sélection d'hôtels et restaurants établie à l'usage de l'automobiliste de passage. Les établissements, classés selon leur confort, sont cités par ordre de préférence dans chaque catégorie.

## CATÉGORIES

| | | |
|---|---|---|
| | Grand luxe et tradition | XXXXX |
| | Grand confort | XXXX |
| | Très confortable | XXX |
| | De bon confort | XX |
| | Assez confortable | X |
| | Simple mais convenable | |
| | Autre ressource hôtelière conseillée, à prix modérés | |
| Without rest. | L'hôtel n'a pas de restaurant | |
| | Le restaurant possède des chambres | with rm |

## AGRÉMENT ET TRANQUILLITÉ

Certains établissements se distinguent dans le guide par les symboles rouges indiqués ci-après. Le séjour dans ces hôtels se révèle particulièrement agréable ou reposant.
Cela peut tenir d'une part au caractère de l'édifice, au décor original, au site, à l'accueil et aux services qui sont proposés, d'autre part à la tranquillité des lieux.

| | |
|---|---|
| à | Hôtels agréables |
| XXXXX à X | Restaurants agréables |
| « Riverside setting » | Élément particulièrement agréable |
| | Hôtel très tranquille ou isolé et tranquille |
| | Hôtel tranquille |
| < London | Vue exceptionnelle |
| < | Vue intéressante ou étendue. |

# L'INSTALLATION

Les chambres des hôtels que nous recommandons possèdent, en général, des installations sanitaires complètes. Il est toutefois possible que dans les catégories , , et , certaines chambres en soient dépourvues.

| | |
|---|---|
| **30 ch** | Nombre de chambres |
| | Ascenseur |
| | Air conditionné |
| | Télévision dans la chambre |
| | Établissement entièrement ou en partie réservé aux non-fumeurs |
| | Téléphone dans la chambre relié par standard |
| | Téléphone dans la chambre, direct avec l'extérieur |
| | Chambres accessibles aux handicapés physiques |
| | Piscine : de plein air ou couverte |
| | Salle de remise en forme – Sauna |
| | Jardin de repos |
| 18 | Tennis à l'hôtel – Golf et nombre de trous |
| 150 | Salles de conférences : capacité maximum |
| | Garage dans l'hôtel (généralement payant) |
| | Parking réservé à la clientèle |
| | Accès interdit aux chiens (dans tout ou partie de l'établissement) |
| Fax | Transmission de documents par télécopie |
| *closed Saturday and August* | Fermeture communiquée par le restaurateur |
| LL35 OSB | Code postal de l'établissement |
| (Forte) | Chaîne hôtelière (voir liste p. 48) |

**Animaux**

L'introduction d'animaux domestiques (chiens, chats...) est interdite en Grande-Bretagne et en Irlande.

# LES ÉTOILES

Certains établissements méritent d'être signalés à votre attention pour la qualité de leur cuisine. Nous les distinguons par **les étoiles de bonne table**.

Nous indiquons, pour ces établissements, trois spécialités culinaires qui pourront orienter votre choix.

✿✿✿ **Une des meilleures tables, vaut le voyage**
Table merveilleuse, grands vins, service impeccable, cadre élégant... Prix en conséquence.

✿✿ **Table excellente, mérite un détour**
Spécialités et vins de choix... Attendez-vous à une dépense en rapport.

✿ **Une très bonne table dans sa catégorie**
L'étoile marque une bonne étape sur votre itinéraire.
Mais ne comparez pas l'étoile d'un établissement de luxe à prix élevés avec celle d'une petite maison où à prix raisonnables, on sert également une cuisine de qualité.

# « Meals »

Tout en appréciant les tables à « étoiles », on peut souhaiter trouver sur sa route un repas plus simple mais toujours de préparation soignée. Certaines maisons nous ont paru répondre à cette préoccupation.

Le mot « Meals » rouge les signale à votre attention dans le texte de ce guide.

## La vente de boissons alcoolisées

En Grande-Bretagne et en Irlande, la vente de boissons alcoolisées est soumise à des lois pouvant varier d'une région à l'autre.

D'une façon générale, les hôtels, les restaurants et les pubs peuvent demeurer ouverts l'après-midi et servir des boissons alcoolisées dans la mesure où elles accompagnent un repas suffisamment consistant. Les bars ferment après 23 heures.

Néanmoins, l'hôtelier a toujours la possibilité de servir, à sa clientèle, des boissons alcoolisées en dehors des heures légales.

Les enfants au-dessous de 14 ans n'ont pas accès aux bars.

# LES PRIX

Les prix que nous indiquons dans ce guide ont été établis en automne 1994. Ils sont susceptibles de modifications, notamment en cas de variations des prix des biens et services.

*Entrez à l'hôtel le guide à la main, vous montrerez ainsi qu'il vous conduit là en confiance.*

Les prix sont indiqués en livres sterling (1 L = 100 pence). Lorsque les mentions **s.**, **t.**, ou **st.** ne figurent pas, les prix indiqués peuvent être majorés d'un pourcentage pour le service, la T.V.A., ou les deux.

Les hôtels et restaurants figurent en gros caractères lorsque les hôteliers nous ont donné tous leurs prix et se sont engagés, sous leur propre responsabilité, à les appliquer aux touristes de passage porteurs de notre guide.

## Repas

| | |
|---|---|
| **Meals** 13.00/24.00 | **Repas à prix fixe** - Déjeuner 13.00, diner 24.00. Ces prix s'entendent couvert compris |
| Meals 15.00/25.00 | Voir page 22 |
| **s. - t.** | Service compris - T.V.A. comprise |
| **st.** | Service et T.V.A. compris (prix nets) |
| 🍷 6.00 | Prix de la 1/2 bouteille ou carafe de vin ordinaire |
| **Meals** à la carte 20.00/25.00 | **Repas à la carte** - Le 1er prix correspond à un repas simple mais soigné, comprenant : petite entrée, plat du jour garni, dessert. Le 2e prix concerne un repas plus complet, comprenant : hors-d'œuvre, plat principal, fromage ou dessert. Ces prix s'entendent couvert compris |
| ☕ 8.50 | Prix du petit déjeuner à l'anglaise, s'il n'est pas compris dans celui de la chambre. Un petit déjeuner continental peut être obtenu à moindre prix |

⌂: Dans les établissements de cette catégorie, le dîner est servi à heure fixe exclusivement aux personnes ayant une chambre. Le menu, à prix unique, offre un choix limité de plats. Le déjeuner est rarement proposé. Beaucoup de ces établissements ne sont pas autorisés à vendre des boissons alcoolisées.

## Chambres

| | |
|---|---|
| **rm** 80.00/150.00 | Prix minimum 80.00 d'une chambre pour une personne et prix maximum 150.00 de la plus belle chambre occupée par deux personnes |
| **rm** ☕ 85.00/155.00 | Le prix du petit déjeuner à l'anglaise est inclus dans le prix de la chambre, même s'il n'est pas consommé |

## Short Breaks

Certains hôtels proposent des conditions avantageuses ou Short Break pour un séjour minimum de 2 nuits. Ce forfait, calculé par personne pour deux personnes au minimum, comprend la chambre, le dîner et le petit déjeuner. Se renseigner auprès de l'hôtelier.

## Les arrhes - Cartes de crédit

Certains hôteliers demandent le versement d'arrhes. Il s'agit d'un dépôt-garantie qui engage l'hôtelier comme le client. Bien faire préciser les dispositions de cette garantie.

| | |
|---|---|
| AE VISA JCB | Cartes de crédit acceptées par l'établissement : Access (Eurocard) - American Express - Diners Club - Visa - Japan Card Bank |

# LONDRES

| | |
|---|---|
| ✉ Fulham | Bureau de poste desservant la localité |
| ✆ | Indicatif téléphonique interurbain (de l'étranger, ne pas composer le 0) |
| BX **A** | Lettres repérant un emplacement sur le plan |
| ⛳ 18 | Golf et nombre de trous (Handicap généralement demandé, réservation par téléphone vivement recommandée) |
| ✵, ⋖ | Panorama, point de vue |
| ✈ | Aéroport |
| 🚗 ✆ 0345 090700 | Localité desservie par train-auto. Renseignements au numéro de téléphone indiqué |
| **i** | Information touristique |

## Les curiosités

| | |
|---|---|
| ★★★ | Vaut le voyage |
| ★★ | Mérite un détour |
| ★ | Intéressant |

## Heure légale

Les visiteurs devront tenir compte de l'heure officielle en Grande-Bretagne : une heure de retard sur l'heure française.

# LA VOITURE, LES PNEUS

En Grande-Bretagne, le port de la ceinture de sécurité est obligatoire pour le conducteur et le passager avant ainsi qu'à l'arrière, si le véhicule en est équipé. La loi interdit au passager avant de prendre un enfant sur ses genoux.

## PNEUS MICHELIN

Des renseignements sur le plus proche point de vente de pneus ATS pourront être obtenus en s'informant entre 9 h et 17 h à l'adresse indiquée ci-dessous.

ATS HOUSE — 180-188 Northolt Rd.
Harrow,
Middlesex HA2 OED
(0181) 423 2000

Dans nos agences, nous nous faisons un plaisir de donner à nos clients tous conseils pour la meilleure utilisation de leurs pneus.

## AUTOMOBILE CLUBS

Les principales organisations de secours automobile dans le pays sont l'Automobile Association et le Royal Automobile Club, toutes deux offrant certains de leurs services aux membres de clubs affilés.

AUTOMOBILE ASSOCIATION
Fanum House
BASINGSTOKE, Hants., RG21 2EA
✆ (01256) 20123

ROYAL AUTOMOBILE CLUB
RAC House, Lansdowne Rd,
CROYDON, Surrey CR9 2JA
✆ (0181) 686 2525

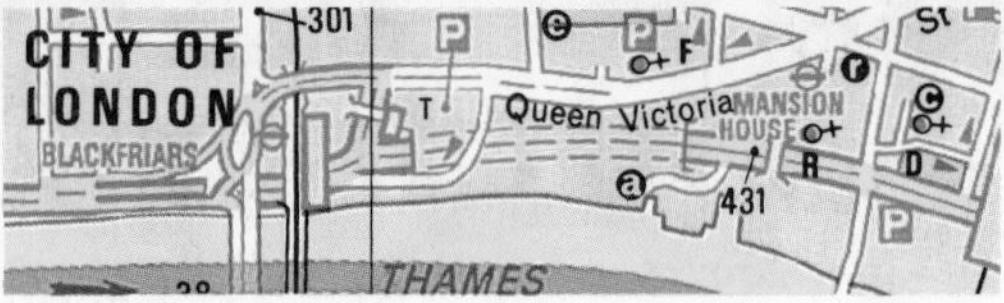


# LES PLANS

| | |
|---|---|
| | **Hôtels – Restaurants** |
| | **Curiosités** |
| | Bâtiment intéressant et entrée principale |
| | Édifice religieux intéressant |
| | **Voirie** |
| M 1 | Autoroute |
| | échangeurs : complet, partiel |
| | Route à chaussées séparées de type autoroutier |
| | Grand axe de circulation |
| A 2 | Itinéraire principal (Primary route) |
| | réseau en cours de révision |
| | Sens unique – Rue impraticable, réglementée |
| | Rue piétonne |
| Piccadilly | Rue commerçante – Parc de stationnement |
| | Porte – Passage sous voûte – Tunnel |
| 15'5 | Passage bas (inférieur à 16'6") sur les grandes voies de circulation |
| | Gare et voie ferrée |
| | Funiculaire – Téléphérique, télécabine |
| B | Pont mobile – Bac pour autos |
| | **Signes divers** |
| | Information touristique |
| | Mosquée – Synagogue |
| | Tour ou pylône de télécommunication – Ruines |
| | Jardin, parc, bois – Cimetière |
| | Stade – Hippodrome – Golf |
| | Golf (réservé) |
| | Vue – Panorama |
| | Monument – Fontaine – Hôpital |
| | Port de plaisance – Phare |
| | Aéroport – Station de métro |
| | Transport par bateau : |
| | passagers et voitures |
| | Bureau principal de poste restante, téléphone |
| | Bâtiment public repéré par une lettre : |
| C H | Bureau de l'Administration du Comté – Hôtel de ville |
| M T U | Musée – Théâtre – Université, grande école |
| POL. | Police (commissariat central) |
| | **Londres** |
| BRENT SOHO | Nom d'arrondissement (borough) – de quartier (area) |
| | Limite de « borough » – d'« area » |

Les plans de villes sont disposés le Nord en haut.

# Amico Lettore

*Questa pubblicazione alberghi e ristoranti*
*ricavata dalla guida Michelin*
*« GREAT BRITAIN and IRELAND » 1995,*
*è stata realizzata appositamente*
*per i vostri viaggi a Londra.*

*Realizzata dai nostri ispettori*
*in piena autonomia offre al viaggiatore*
*di passaggio un'ampia scelta*
*a tutti i livelli di comfort e prezzo.*

*Con l'intento di fornire*
*ai nostri lettori l'informazione più recente,*
*abbiamo aggiornato questa edizione*
*con la massima cura.*

*Per questo solo la Guida dell'anno*
*in corso merita pienamente*
*la vostra fiducia.*

*Grazie delle vostre segnalazioni*
*sempre gradite.*

*Per una visita turistica della città utilizzate*
*la guida verde Michelin « LONDON »,*
*disponibile in inglese ed in francese.*

*Buon soggiorno nella capitale britannica !*

# Sommario

# Come servirsi della Guida

Questa guida Vi propone una selezione di alberghi e ristoranti stabilita ad uso dell'automobilista di passaggio. Gli esercizi, classificati in base al confort che offrono, vengono citati in ordine di preferenza per ogni categoria.

## CATEGORIE

| | | |
|---|---|---|
| | Gran lusso e tradizione | XXXXX |
| | Gran confort | XXXX |
| | Molto confortevole | XXX |
| | Di buon confort | XX |
| | Abbastanza confortevole | X |
| | Semplice, ma conveniente | |
| | Altra risorsa, consigliata per prezzi contenuti | |
| without rest. | L'albergo non ha ristorante | |
| | Il ristorante dispone di camere | with rm |

## AMENITÀ E TRANQUILLITÀ

Alcuni esercizi sono evidenziati nella guida dai simboli rossi indicati qui di seguito. Il soggiorno in questi alberghi dovrebbe rivelarsi particolarmente ameno o riposante.
Ciò può dipendere sia dalle caratteristiche dell'edifico, dalle decorazioni non comuni, dalla sua posizione e dal servizio offerto, sia dalla tranquillità dei luoghi.

| | |
|---|---|
| a | Alberghi ameni |
| XXXXX a X | Ristoranti ameni |
| « Riverside setting » | Un particolare piacevole |
| | Albergo molto tranquillo o isolato e tranquillo |
| | Albergo tranquillo |
| ← London | Vista eccezionale |
| ← | Vista interessante o estesa |

# INSTALLAZIONI

Le camere degli alberghi che raccomandiamo possiedono, generalmente, delle installazioni sanitarie complete. È possibile tuttavia che nelle categorie 🏨, 🏠, ⛱ e ⌂ alcune camere ne siano sprovviste.

| | |
|---|---|
| **30 rm** | Numero di camere |
| [ascensore] | Ascensore |
| [aria] | Aria condizionata |
| TV | Televisione in camera |
| [non fumatori] | Esercizio riservato completamente o in parte ai non fumatori |
| [telefono] | Telefono in camera collegato con il centralino |
| ☎ | Telefono in camera comunicante direttamente con l'esterno |
| ♿ | Camere di agevole accesso per i minorati fisici |
| [piscina] [piscina coperta] | Piscina : all'aperto, coperta |
| [palestra] [sauna] | Palestra - Sauna |
| [giardino] | Giardino da riposo |
| [tennis] [golf] 18 | Tennis appartenente all'albergo - Golf e numero di buche |
| [conferenze] 150 | Sale per conferenze : capienza massima |
| [garage] | Garage nell'albergo (generalmente a pagamento) |
| P | Parcheggio riservato alla clientela |
| [cani] | Accesso vietato ai cani (in tutto o in parte dell'esercizio) |
| Fax | Trasmissione telefonica di documenti |
| *closed Saturday and August* | Periodo di chiusura, comunicato dall'albergatore |
| LL35 OSB | Codice postale dell' esercizio |
| (Forte) | Catena alberghiera (Vedere la lista p. 48) |

**Animali**

L'introduzione di animali domestici (cani, gatti...), in Gran Bretagna e in Irlanda, è vietata.

# LE STELLE

Alcuni esercizi meritano di essere segnalati alla Vostra attenzione per la qualità tutta particolare della loro cucina. Noi li evidenziamo con le « **stelle di ottima tavola** ».

Per questi ristoranti indichiamo tre specialità culinarie e alcuni vini locali che potranno aiutarVi nella scelta.

✿✿✿ **Una delle migliori tavole, vale il viaggio**
Tavola meravigliosa, grandi vini, servizio impeccabile, ambientazione accurata... Prezzi conformi.

✿✿ **Tavola eccellente, merita una deviazione**
Specialità e vini scelti... AspettateVi una spesa in proporzione.

✿ **Un'ottima tavola nella sua categoria**
La stella indica una tappa gastronomica sul Vostro itinerario.
Non mettete però a confronto la stella di un esercizio di lusso, dai prezzi elevati, con quella di un piccolo esercizio dove, a prezzi ragionevoli, viene offerta una cucina di qualità.

# « Meals »

Pur apprezzando le tavole a « stella », si desidera alle volte consumare un pasto più semplice ma sempre accuratamente preparato.

Alcuni esercizi ci son parsi rispondenti a tale esigenza e sono contraddistinti nella guida con « **Meals** » in rosso.

## La vendita di bevande alcoliche

In Gran Bretagna e Irlanda la vendita di bevande alcoliche è soggetta a leggi che possono variare da una regione all'altra.

In generale gli alberghi, i ristoranti e i pubs possono restare aperti il pomeriggio e servire bevande alcoliche nella misura in cui queste accompagnano un pasto abbastanza consistente. I bar chiudono dopo le ore 23.00.

L'albergatore ha tuttavia la possobilità di servire alla clientela bevande alcoliche anche oltre le ore legali.

Ai ragazzi inferiori ai 14 anni è vietato l'accesso ai bar.

## I PREZZI

I prezzi che indichiamo in questa guida sono stati stabiliti nel l'autunno 1994. Potranno pertanto subire delle variazioni in relazione ai cambiamenti dei prezzi di beni e servizi.

*Entrate nell'albergo o nel ristorante con la guida in mano, dimostrando in tal modo la fiducia in chi vi ha indirizzato.*

Gli alberghi e i ristoranti vengono menzionati in carattere grassetto quando gli albergatori ci hanno comunicato tutti i loro prezzi e si sono impegnati, sotto la propria responsabilità, ad applicarli ai turisti di passaggio, in possesso della nostra guida.

I prezzi sono indicati in lire sterline (1 £ = 100 pence).

Quando non figurano le lettere **s.**, **t.**, o **st.** i prezzi indicati possono essere maggiorati per il servizio o per l'I.V.A. o per entrambi.

### Pasti

| | |
|---|---|
| **Meals** 13.00/24.00 | **Prezzo fisso** – Pranzo 13.00, cena 24.00. |
| Meals 15.00/25.00 | Vedere p. 32 |
| **s. - t.** | Servizio compreso – I.V.A. compresa |
| **st.** | Servizio ed I.V.A. compresi (prezzi netti) |
| 6.00 | Prezzo della mezza bottiglia o di una caraffa di vino |
| **Meals** a la carte 20.00/25.00 | **Alla carta** – Il 1° prezzo corrisponde ad un pasto semplice comprendente : primo piatto, piatto del giorno con contorno, dessert. Il 2° prezzo corrisponde ad un pasto più completo comprendente : antipasto, piatto principale, formaggio e dessert |
| 8.50 | Prezzo della prima colazione inglese se non è compreso nel prezzo della camera. Una prima colazione continentale può essere ottenuta a minor prezzo |

: Negli alberghi di questa categoria, la cena viene servita, ad un'ora stabilita, esclusivamente a chi vi allogia. Il menu, a prezzo fisso, offre una scelta limitata di piatti. Raramente viene servito anche il pranzo. Molti di questi esercizi non hanno l'autorizzazione a vendere alcolici.

### Camere

| | |
|---|---|
| **rm** 80.00/150.00 | Prezzo minimo 80.00 per una camera singola e prezzo massimo 150.00 per la camera più bella per due persone |
| **rm** 85.00/155.00 | Il prezzo della prima colazione inglese è compreso nel prezzo della camera anche se non viene consumata |

### « Short Breaks »

Alcuni alberghi propongono delle condizioni particolarmente vantaggiose o short break per un soggiorno minimo di due notti. Questo prezzo, calcolato per persona e per un minimo di due persone, comprende : camera, cena e prima colazione. Informarsi presso l'albergatore.

### La caparra – Carte di credito

Alcuni albergatori chiedono il versamento di una caparra. Si tratta di un deposito-garanzia che impegna tanto l'albergatore che il cliente. Vi raccomandiamo di farVi precisare le norme riguardanti la reciproca garanzia.

| | |
|---|---|
| AE VISA JCB | Carte di credito accettate dall'esercizio : Access (Eurocard) American Express – Diners Club – Visa – Japan Card Bank |

# LONDRA

| | |
|---|---|
| ✉ Fulham | Sede dell'ufficio postale |
| ☎ | Prefisso telefonico interurbano. Dall'estero non formare lo 0 |
| BX **A** | Lettere indicanti l'ubicazione sulla pianta |
| ⚑18 | Golf e numero di buche (handicap generalmente richiesto, prenotazione telefonica vivamente consigliata) |
| ☼, ← | Panorama, punto di vista |
| ✈ | Aeroporto |
| 🚗 ☎ 0345 090700 | Località con servizio auto su treno. Informarsi al numero di telefono indicato |
| ℹ | Ufficio informazioni turistiche |

## Le curiosità

| | |
|---|---|
| ★★★ | Vale il viaggio |
| ★★ | Merita una deviazione |
| ★ | Interessante |

## Ora legale

I visitatori dovranno tenere in considerazione l'ora ufficiale in Gran Bretagna : un'ora di ritardo sull'ora italiana.

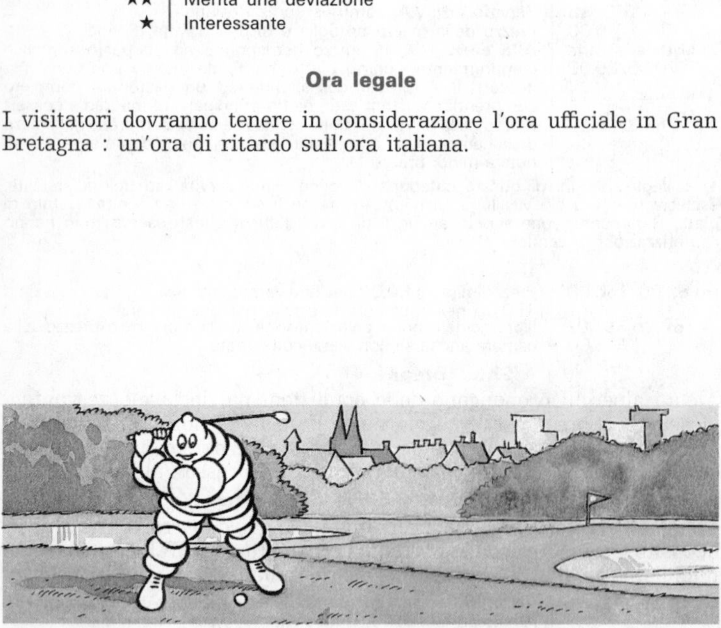

# L'AUTOMOBILE, I PNEUMATICI

In Gran Bretagna, l'uso delle cinture di sicurezza è obbligatorio per il conducente e il passeggero del sedile anteriore, nonchè per i sedili posteriori, se ne sono equipaggiati. La legge non consente al passaggero seduto davanti di tenere un bambino sulle ginocchia.

## PNEUMATICI MICHELIN

Potrete avere delle informazioni sul più vicino punto vendita di pneumatici ATS, rivolgendovi, tra le 9 e le 17, all'indirizzo indicato qui di seguito :

ATS HOUSE
180-188 Northolt Rd.
Harrow,
Middlesex HA2 OED
(0181) 423 2000

Le nostre Succursali sono in grado di dare ai nostri clienti tutti i consigli relativi alla migliore utilizzazione dei pneumatici.

## AUTOMOBILE CLUBS

Le principali organizzazioni di soccorso automobilistico sono l'Automobile Association ed il Royal Automobile Club : entrambe offrono alcuni loro servizi ai membri dei club affiliati.

AUTOMOBILE ASSOCIATION
Fanum House
BASINGSTOKE, Hants., RG21 2EA
✆ (01256) 20123

ROYAL AUTOMOBILE CLUB
RAC House, Lansdowne Rd,
CROYDON, Surrey CR9 2JA
✆ (0181) 686 2525

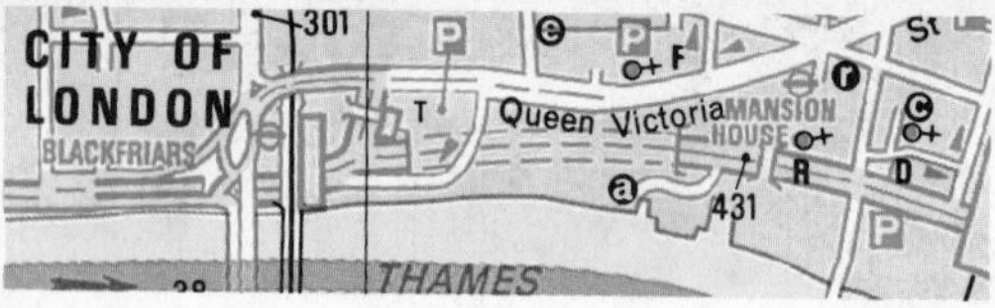


# LE PIANTE

Alberghi – Ristoranti

## Curiosità

Edificio interessante ed entrata principale
Costruzione religiosa interessante

## Viabilità

M 1 — Autostrada
svincoli : completo, parziale,
Strada a carregiate separate di tipo autostradale
Asse principale di circolazione
A 2 — Itinerario principale
(« Primary route », rete stradale in corso di revisione)
Senso unico – Via impraticabile, a circolazione regolamentata
Via pedonale
Piccadilly — Via commerciale – Parcheggio
Porta – Sottopassaggio – Galleria
15'5 — Sottopassaggio (altezza inferiore a 16'6") sulle grandi vie di circolazione
Stazione e ferrovia
Funicolare – Funivia, Cabinovia
Ponte mobile – Battello per auto

## Simboli vari

Ufficio informazioni turistiche
Moschea – Sinagoga
Torre o pilone per telecomunicazione – Ruderi
Giardino, parco, bosco – Cimitero
Stadio – Ippodromo – Golf
Golf riservato
Vista – Panorama
Monumento – Fontana – Ospedale
Porto per imbarcazioni da diporto – Faro
Aeroporto – Stazione della Metropolitana
Trasporto con traghetto :
passeggeri ed autovetture
Ufficio centrale di fermo posta, telefono
Edificio pubblico indicato con lettera :
C H — Sede dell'Amministrazione di Contea – Municipio
M T U — Museo – Teatro – Università, grande scuola
POL — Polizia (Questura, nelle grandi città)

## Londra

**BRENT** SOHO — Nome del distretto amministrativo (borough) – del quartiere (area)
Limite del « borough » – di « area »

Le piante topografiche sono orientate col Nord in alto.

# Lieber Leser

*Speziell für Ihren London-Besuch ist dieser Auszug aus dem Michelin-Führer « Great Britain and Ireland » 1995 gedacht.*

*Von unseren unabhängigen Hotelinspektoren ausgearbeitet, bietet der Hotelführer dem Reisenden eine große Auswahl an Hotels und Restaurants in jeder Kategorie sowohl was den Preis als auch den Komfort anbelangt.*

*Stets bemüht, unseren Lesern die neueste Information anzubieten, wurde diese Ausgabe mit größter Sorgfalt erstellt.*

*Deshalb sollten Sie immer nur dem aktuellen Hotelführer Ihr Vertrauen schenken.*

*Ihre Kommentare sind uns immer willkommen.*

*Eine detaillierte Stadtbeschreibung finden Sie im Grünen Michelin-Reiseführer « London » (in englischer und französischer Ausgabe).*

*Wir wünschen Ihnen einen angenehmen Aufenthalt in der Hauptstadt von Großbritannien.*

# Inhaltsverzeichnis

# Zum Gebrauch des Führers

KATEGORIEN

ANNEHMLICHKEITEN

EINRICHTUNG

DIE STERNE

« **Meals** »

PREISE

LONDON

DAS AUTO, DIE REIFEN

STADTPLÄNE

Die Auswahl der in diesem Führer aufgeführten Hotels und Restaurants ist für Durchreisende gedacht. In jeder Kategorie drückt die Reihenfolge der Betriebe (sie sind nach ihrem Komfort klassifiziert) eine weitere Rangordnung aus.

## KATEGORIEN

| | | |
|---|---|---|
| | Großer Luxus und Tradition | XXXXX |
| | Großer Komfort | XXXX |
| | Sehr komfortabel | XXX |
| | Mit gutem Komfort | XX |
| | Mit ausreichendem Komfort | X |
| | Bürgerlich | |
| | Preiswerte, empfehlenswerte Gasthäuser und Pensionen | |
| without rest. | Hotel ohne Restaurant | |
| | Restaurant vermietet auch Zimmer | with rm |

## ANNEHMLICHKEITEN

Manche Häuser sind im Führer durch rote Symbole gekennzeichnet (s. unten). Der Aufenthalt in diesen Hotels ist wegen der schönen, ruhigen Lage, der nicht alltäglichen Einrichtung und Atmosphäre und dem gebotenen Service besonders angenehm und erholsam.

| | |
|---|---|
| bis | Angenehme Hotels |
| XXXXX bis X | Angenehme Restaurants |
| « Riverside setting » | Besondere Annehmlichkeit |
| | Sehr ruhiges, oder abgelegenes und ruhiges Hotel |
| | Ruhiges Hotel |
| London | Reizvolle Aussicht |
| | Interessante oder weite Sicht |

# EINRICHTUNG

Die meisten der empfohlenen Hotels verfügen über Zimmer, die alle oder doch zum größten Teil mit einer Naßzelle ausgestattet sind. In den Häusern der Kategorien , ,  und  kann diese jedoch in einigen Zimmern fehlen.

| | |
|---|---|
| **30 rm** | Anzahl der Zimmer |
| | Fahrstuhl |
| | Klimaanlage |
| TV | Fernsehen im Zimmer |
| | Hotel ganz oder teilweise reserviert für Nichtraucher |
| | Zimmertelefon mit Außenverbindung über Telefonzentrale |
| ☎ | Zimmertelefon mit direkter Außenverbindung |
| ♿ | Für Körperbehinderte leicht zugängliche Zimmer |
| | Freibad, Hallenbad |
| | Fitneßcenter – Sauna |
| | Liegewiese, Garten |
| 18 | Hoteleigener Tennisplatz – Golfplatz und Lochzahl |
| 150 | Konferenzräume : Höchstkapazität |
| | Hotelgarage (wird gewöhnlich berechnet) |
| Ⓟ | Parkplatz reserviert für Gäste |
| | Hunde sind unerwünscht (im ganzen Haus bzw. in den Zimmern oder im Restaurant) |
| Fax | Telefonische Dokumentenübermittlung |
| *closed Saturday and August* | Schließungszeit, vom Hotelier mitgeteilt |
| LL35 OSB | Angabe des Postbezirks (hinter der Hoteladresse) |
| (Forte) | Hotelkette (Liste Seite 48) |

**Tiere**

Das Mitführen von Haustieren (Hunde, Katzen u. dgl.) ist bei der Einreise in Großbritannien und Irland untersagt.

## DIE STERNE

Einige Häuser verdienen wegen ihrer überdurchschnittlich guten Küche Ihre besondere Beachtung. Auf diese Häuser weisen die Sterne hin.

Bei den mit « **Stern** » ausgezeichneten Betrieben nennen wir drei kulinarische Spezialitäten, die Sie probieren sollten.

✿✿✿ **Eine der besten Küchen : eine Reise wert**
Ein denkwürdiges Essen, edle Weine, tadelloser Service, gepflegte Atmosphäre ... entsprechende Preise.

✿✿ **Eine hervorragende Küche : verdient einen Umweg**
Ausgesuchte Menus und Weine ... angemessene Preise.

✿ **Eine sehr gute Küche : verdient Ihre besondere Beachtung**
Der Stern bedeutet eine angenehme Unterbrechung Ihrer Reise.
Vergleichen Sie aber bitte nicht den Stern eines sehr teuren Luxusrestaurants mit dem Stern eines kleineren oder mittleren Hauses, wo man Ihnen zu einem annehmbaren Preis eine ebenfalls vorzügliche Mahlzeit reicht.

## « Meals »

Wir glauben, daß Sie neben den Häusern mit « Stern » auch solche Adressen interessieren werden, die einfache, aber sorgfältig zubereitete Mahlzeiten anbieten.

« **Meals** » im Text weist auf solche Haüser hin.

## Ausschank alkoholischer Getränke

In Großbritannien und Irland unterliegt der Ausschank alkoholischer Getränke gesetzlichen Bestimmungen, die in den einzelnen Gegenden verschieden sind.

Generell können Hotels, Restaurants und Pubs nachmittags geöffnet sein und alkoholische Getränke ausschenken, wenn diese zu einer entsprechend gehaltvollen Mahlzeit genossen werden. Die Bars schließen nach 23 Uhr.

Hotelgästen können alkoholische Getränke jedoch auch außerhalb der Ausschankzeiten serviert werden.

Kindern unter 14 Jahren ist der Zutritt zu den Bars untersagt.

# PREISE

Die in diesem Führer genannten Preise wurden uns im Herbst 1994 angegeben. Sie können sich mit den Preisen von Waren und Dienstleistungen ändern.
*Halten Sie beim Betreten des Hotels den Führer in der Hand. Sie zeigen damit, daß Sie aufgrund dieser Empfehlung gekommen sind.*
Die Preise sind in Pfund Sterling angegeben (1 £ = 100 pence).

*Wenn die Buchstaben* **s.**, **t.**, oder **st.** nicht hinter den angegebenen Preisen aufgeführt sind, können sich diese um den Zuschlag für Bedienung und/oder MWSt erhöhen.
Die Namen der Hotels und Restaurants, die ihre Preise genannt haben, sind fett gedruckt. Gleichzeitig haben sich diese Häuser verpflichtet, die von den Hoteliers selbst angegebenen Preise den Benutzern des Michelin-Führers zu berechnen.

## Mahlzeiten

| | |
|---|---|
| **Meals** 13.00/24.00 | **Feste Menupreise** - Mittagessen 13.00, Abendessen 24.00 |
| **Meals** 15.00/25.00 | Siehe Seite 42 |
| **s. - t. - st.** | Bedienung inkl. - MWSt inkl. - Bedienung und MWSt inkl. |
| 6.00 | Preis für 1/2 Flasche oder eine Karaffe Tafelwein |
| **Meals** a la carte 20.00/25.00 | **Mahlzeiten « à la carte »** - Der erste Preis entspricht einer einfachen aber sorgfältig zubereiteten Mahlzeit, bestehend aus kleiner Vorspeise, Tagesgericht mit Beilage und Nachtisch. Der zweite Preis entspricht einer reichlicheren Mahlzeit mit Vorspeise, Hauptgericht, Käse oder Nachtisch (inkl. Couvert) |
| 8.50 | Preis des englischen Frühstücks, wenn dieser nicht im Übernachtungspreis enthalten ist. Einfaches, billigeres Frühstück (Continental breakfast) erhältlich |

: In dieser Hotelkategorie wird ein Abendessen normalerweise nur zu bestimmten Zeiten für Hotelgäste angeboten. Es besteht aus einem Menu mit begrenzter Auswahl zu festgesetztem Preis. Mittagessen wird selten angeboten. Viele dieser Hotels sind nicht berechtigt, alkoholische Getränke auszuschenken.

## Zimmer

| | |
|---|---|
| **rm** 80.00/150.00 | Mindestpreis 80.00 für ein Einzelzimmer und Höchstpreis 150.00 für das schönste Doppelzimmer |
| **rm** 85.00/155.00 | Übernachtung mit englischem Frühstück, selbst wenn dieses nicht eingenommen wird |

## « Short Breaks »

Einige Hotels bieten Vorzugskonditionen für einen Mindestaufenthalt von zwei Nächten (Short Break). Der Preis ist pro Person kalkuliert, bei einer Mindestbeteiligung von zwei Personen und schließt das Zimmer, das Abendessen und das Frühstück ein.

## Anzahlung – Kreditkarten

Einige Hoteliers verlangen eine Anzahlung. Diese ist als Garantie sowohl für den Hotelier als auch für den Gast anzusehen.

| | |
|---|---|
| AE VISA JCB | Vom Haus akzeptierte Kreditkarten : Access (Eurocard) – American Express – Diners Club – Visa (Carte Bleue) – Japan Card Bank |

# LONDON

| | |
|---|---|
| ✉ Fulham | Zuständiges Postamt |
| ☎ | Vorwahlnummer (bei Gesprächen vom Ausland aus wird die erste Null weggelassen) |
| BX A | Markierung auf dem Stadtplan |
| ⛳18 | Öffentlicher Golfplatz und Lochzahl (Handicap erforderlich, telefonische Reservierung empfehlenswert) |
| ✻, ← | Rundblick, Aussichtspunkt |
| ✈ | Flughafen |
| 🚗 ☎ 0345 090700 | Ladestelle für Autoreisezüge – Nähere Auskünfte unter der angegebenen Telefonnummer |
| ℹ | Informationsstelle |

## Sehenswürdigkeiten

| | |
|---|---|
| ★★★ | Eine Reise wert |
| ★★ | Verdient einen Umweg |
| ★ | Sehenswert |

## Uhrzeit

In Großbritannien ist eine Zeitverschiebung zu beachten und die Uhr gegenüber der deutschen Zeit um 1 Stunde zurückzustellen.

# DAS AUTO, DIE REIFEN

In Großbritannien herrscht Anschnallpflicht für Fahrer, Beifahrer und auf dem Rücksitz, wenn Gurte vorhanden sind. Es ist verboten, Kinder auf den Vordersitzen auf dem Schoß zu befördern.

## LIEFERANTEN VON MICHELIN-REIFEN

Die Anschrift der nächstgelegenen ATS-Verkaufsstelle erhalten Sie auf Anfrage (9-17 Uhr) bei

ATS HOUSE
180-188 Northolt Rd.
Harrow,
Middlesex HA2 OED
(0181) 423 2000

## AUTOMOBILCLUBS

Die wichtigsten Automobilclubs des Landes sind die Automobile Association und der Royal Automobile Club, die den Mitgliedern der der FIA angeschlossenen Automobilclubs Pannenhilfe leisten und einige ihrer Dienstleistungen anbieten.

AUTOMOBILE ASSOCIATION
Fanum House
BASINGSTOKE, Hants., RG21 2EA
✆ (01256) 20123

ROYAL AUTOMOBILE CLUB
RAC House, Lansdowne Rd
CROYDON, Surrey CR9 2JA
✆ (0181) 686 2525

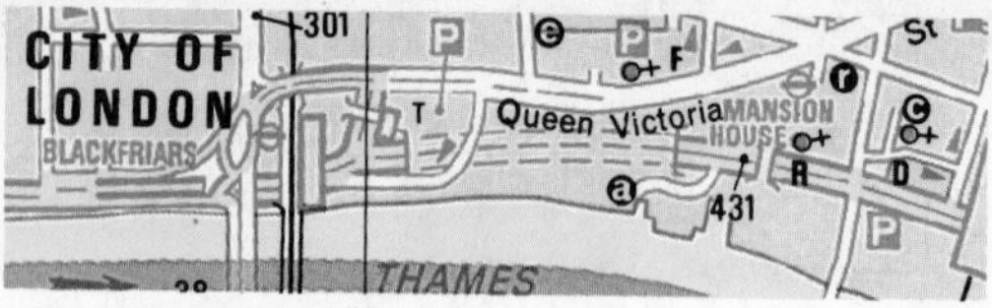


# STADTPLÄNE

| | |
|---|---|
| ⓐ ●a | **Hotels – Restaurants** |

## Sehenswürdigkeiten

Sehenswertes Gebäude mit Haupteingang
Sehenswerter Sakralbau

## Straßen

| | |
|---|---|
| M 1 | Autobahn |
| ❹ ④ | Anschlußstellen : Autobahneinfahrt und/oder-ausfahrt, |
| | Schnellstraße mit getrennten Fahrbahnen |
| | Hauptverkehrsstraße |
| A 2 | Fernverkehrsstraße (Primary route) Netz wird z.z. neu eingestuft |
| | Einbahnstraße – Gesperrte Straße, mit Verkehrsbeschränkungen |
| | Fußgängerzone |
| Piccadilly P | Einkaufsstraße – Parkplatz |
| | Tor – Passage – Tunnel |
| 15'5 | Unterführung (Höhe angegeben bis 15′5″) auf Hauptverkehrsstraßen |
| | Bahnhof und Bahnlinie |
| | Standseilbahn – Seilschwebebahn |
| B | Bewegliche Brücke – Autofähre |

## Sonstige Zeichen

| | |
|---|---|
| | Informationsstelle |
| | Moschee – Synagoge |
| | Funk-, Fernsehturm – Ruine |
| | Garten, Park, Wäldchen – Friedhof |
| 9 | Stadion – Pferderennbahn – Golfplatz |
| | Golfplatz (Zutritt bedingt erlaubt) |
| | Aussicht – Rundblick |
| | Denkmal – Brunnen – Krankenhaus |
| | Jachthafen – Leuchtturm |
| | Flughafen – U-Bahnstation |
| | Schiffsverbindungen : Autofähre |
| | Hauptpostamt (postlagernde Sendungen), Telefon |
| | Öffentliches Gebäude, durch einen Buchstaben gekennzeichnet : |
| C H | Sitz der Grafschaftsverwaltung – Rathaus |
| M T U | Museum – Theater – Universität, Hochschule |
| POL | Polizei (in größeren Städten Polizeipräsidium) |

## London

| | |
|---|---|
| BRENT SOHO | Name des Verwaltungsbezirks (borough) – des Stadtteils (area) |
| | Grenze des « borough » – des « area » |

Die Stadtpläne sind eingenordet (Norden = oben).

# Major hotel groups

Abbreviations used in the Guide and central reservation telephone numbers

# Principales chaînes hôtelières

Abréviations utilisées dans nos textes et centraux téléphoniques de réservation

# Principali catene alberghiere

Abbreviazoni utilizzate nei nostri testi e céntrali telefoniche di prenotazione

# Die wichtigsten Hotelketten

Im Führer benutzte Abkürzungen der Hotelketten und ihre Zentrale für telefonische Reservierung

| | | |
|---|---|---|
| COPTHORNE HOTELS | COPTHORNE | 0800 414741 (Freephone) |
| COUNTRY CLUB HOTEL GROUP *(Country Club Resorts – Lansbury Collection)* | COUNTRY CLUB | 01582 562256 |
| DE VERE HOTELS PLC | DE VERE | 01925 265050 |
| RADISSON EDWARDIAN HOTELS | RADISSON EDWARDIAN | 0800 191991 (Freephone) |
| FORTE HOTELS | FORTE | (0345) 404040 or 0800 404040 (Freephone) |
| TRAVELODGES | | 0800 850950 (Freephone) |
| FRIENDLY HOTELS | FRIENDLY | 0800 591910 (Freephone) |
| GRANADA HOTELS AND LODGES | GRANADA | 0800 555300 (Freephone) |
| HILTON HOTELS | HILTON | 0171 734 6000 |
| HOLIDAY INN WORLDWIDE | HOLIDAY INN | 0800 897121 (Freephone) |
| HYATT HOTELS | HYATT | 0171 580 8197 |
| INTERCONTINENTAL HOTELS LTD | INTER-CON | 0181 847 2277 or calls from outside London 0345 581444 |
| JARVIS HOTELS | JARVIS | (0345) 581811 |
| MARRIOTT HOTELS | MARRIOTT | 0800 221222 (Freephone) |
| MOUNT CHARLOTTE THISTLE HOTELS | MT. CHARLOTTE THISTLE | 0171 937 8033<br>01532 439111 |
| NOVOTEL | NOVOTEL | 0171 724 1000 |
| PREMIER LODGES & INNS | PREMIER | 0800 118833 (Freephone) |
| QUEENS MOAT HOUSES PLC | Q.M.H. | 0800 289330 (Freephone) or 01708 766677 |
| RAMADA INTERNATIONAL | RAMADA | 0800 181737 (Freephone) |
| SHERATON HOTELS | SHERATON | 0800 353535 (Freephone) |
| STAKIS HOTELS | STAKIS | 0800 262626 (Freephone) |
| SWALLOW HOTELS LTD | SWALLOW | 0191 529 4666 |
| TOBY HOTELS *(No central reservations – Contact Hotels direct)* | TOBY | |
| TRAVEL INNS | TRAVEL INN | 01582 414341 |

**London** 404 folds 42 to 44 – **London G.** – pop. 7 566 620 – ☎ 0171 or ☎ 0181 : see heading of each area.

✈ Heathrow, ☎ (0181) 759 4321, p. 8 AX – **Terminal :** Airbus (A1) from Victoria, Airbus (A2) from Paddington – Underground (Piccadilly line) frequent service daily.

✈ Gatwick, ☎ (01293) 535353, ☎ (0181) 763 2020, p. 9 : by A 23 EZ and M 23 – **Terminal :** Coach service from Victoria Coach Station (Flightline 777 hourly service) – Railink (Gatwick Express) from Victoria (24 h service).

✈ London City Airport ☎ (0171) 474 5555, p. 7 HV.

✈ Stansted at Bishop's Stortford, ☎ (01279) 680500, Fax 662066, NE : 34 m. p. 7 : by M 11 JT and A 120.

**British Airways, Victoria Air Terminal :** 115 Buckingham Palace Rd, SW1, ☎ (0171) 834 9411, Fax 828 7142, p. 32 BX.

🚘 Euston and Paddington ☎ 0345 090700.

ℹ British Travel Centre, 12 Regent St., Piccadilly Circus, SW1Y 4PQ ☎ (0171) 971 0026.
Selfridges, basement Service, Arcade, Selfridges Store, Oxford St. W1 ☎ (0171) 730 3488.
Victoria Station Forecourt SW1 ☎ (0171) 730 3488.

## Some practical advice

- **Parking** in central London, although available, is difficult to find and expensive. Public Transport - bus or Underground - is much more practical. Full details of these services can be obtained from London Transport Travel Enquiries, 55 Broadway, SW1, ☎ (0171) 222 1234.
- In most instances **taxi-cabs,** when showing the illuminated « For Hire » sign, will pick up passengers in the streets on demand. Alternatively they may be called by telephone. Consult your Hotel Porter.
- **Theatre bookings and car hire :** Your hotel can help you, either directly, or by giving agency addresses.

## Quelques renseignements pratiques

- Le **stationnement** dans le centre de Londres, bien que possible, est difficile et onéreux. Ainsi les transports en commun, bus ou métro, sont-ils beaucoup plus pratiques. Pour plus amples renseignements s'adresser au London Transport Travel Enquiries, 55 Broadway, SW1, ☎ (0171) 222 1234.
- Dans la plupart des cas, on peut héler les **taxis** munis du voyant lumineux « For Hire » mais il est possible de les appeler par téléphone. Se renseigner auprès des hôtels.
- **Places de théâtres et locations de voitures :** votre hôtel peut vous venir en aide, soit directement, soit en vous indiquant l'adresse d'une agence.

## Qualche consiglio pratico

- **Parcheggiare** nel centro di Londra è possibile, ma difficile e costoso. Perciò trasporti pubblici, autobus o metropolitana, sono assai più pratici. Per maggiori chiarimenti rivolgersi al London Transport Travel Enquiries, 55 Broadway, SW1, ☎ (0171) 222 1234.
- Generalmente è possibile fermare a voce un **taxi** che abbia l'indicazione « For Hire », ma si può anche chiamarlo per telefono. Informarsi all'albergo.
- Prenotazioni per **teatro e noleggio vetture :** il vostro hotel può provvedere sia direttamente, sia indicandovi l'indirizzo di un' agenzia.

## Nützliche hinweise für den aufenthalt

- Das **Parken** in der Londoner Innenstadt ist zwar möglich, aber teuer, und man findet schwer einen freien Platz. Die öffentlichen Verkehrsmittel wie Untergrundbahn und Autobus sind daher vorzuziehen. Nähere Auskünfte erteilt das Londoner Transport Travel Enquiries, 55 Broadway, SW1, ☎ (0171) 222 1234.
- **Taxis** mit der Leuchtschrift „For-Hire" können durch Herbeiwinken angehalten werden und nehmen Fahrgäste auf; sonst bestellt man sie telefonisch. Auskünfte gibt Ihr Hotel.
- Sie können die **Reservierung von Theaterplätzen** und das **Mieten eines Leihwagens** entweder direkt von Ihrem Hotel vornehmen lassen oder sich die Adressen der Agenturen und Autoverleihe geben lassen.

# Sights

## Curiosités – Le curiosità

## Sehenswürdigkeiten

### HISTORIC BUILDINGS AND MONUMENTS

Palace of Westminster★★★ : House of Lords★★, Westminster Hall★★ (hammerbeam roof★★★), Robing Room★, Central Lobby★, House of Commons★, Big Ben★, Victoria Tower★ p. 26 LY – Tower of London★★★ (Crown Jewels★★★, White Tower or Keep★★★, St. John's Chapel★★, Beauchamp Tower★, Tower Hill Pageant★) p. 27 PVX.

Banqueting House★★ p. 26 LX – Buckingham Palace★★ (Changing of the Guard★★, Royal Mews★★) p. 32 BVX – Kensington Palace★★ p. 24 FX – Lincoln's Inn★★ p. 33 EV – London Bridge★ p. 27 PVX – Royal Hospital Chelsea★★ p. 31 FU – St. James's Palace★★ p. 29 EP – South Bank Arts Centre ★★ (Royal Festival Hall★, National Theatre★, County Hall★) p. 26 MX – The Temple★★ (Middle Temple Hall★) p. 22 MV – Tower Bridge★★ p. 27 PX.

Albert Memorial★ p. 30 CQ – Apsley House★ p. 28 BP – Burlington House★ p. 29 EM – Charterhouse★ p. 23 NOU – Commonwealth Institute★ p. 24 EY – Design Centre★ p. 29 FM – George Inn★, Southwark p. 27 PX – Gray's Inn★ p. 22 MU – Guildhall★ (Lord Mayor's Show★★) p. 23 OU – Imperial College of Science and Technology★ p. 30 CR – Dr Johnson's House★ p. 23 NUV **A** – Lancaster House★ p. 29 EP – Leighton House★ p. 24 EY – Linley Sambourne House★★ p. 24 EY – Lloyds Building★★ p. 23 PV – Mansion House★ (plate and insignia★★) p. 23 PV **P** – The Monument★ (✻★) p. 23 PV **G** – Old Admiralty★ p. 26 KLX – Royal Exchange★ p. 23 PV **V** – Royal Opera Arcade★ (New Zealand House) p. 29 FGN – Royal Opera House★ (Covent Garden) p. 33 DX – Somerset House★ p. 33 EXY – Spencer House★★ p. 29 DP – Staple Inn★ p. 22 MU **Y** – Theatre Royal★ (Haymarket) p. 29 GM – Westminster Bridge★ p. 26 LY.

### CHURCHES

**The City Churches**

St. Paul's Cathedral★★★ (Dome ⩽★★★) p. 23 NOV.

St. Bartholomew the Great★★ (choir★) p. 23 OU **K** – St. Dunstan-in-the-East★★ p. 23 PV **F** – St. Mary-at-Hill★★ (woodwork★★, plan★) p. 23 PV **B** – Temple Church★★ p. 22 MV.

All Hallows-by-the-Tower (font cover★★ brasses★) p. 23 PV **Y** – Christ Church★ p. 23 OU **E** – St. Andrew Undershaft (monuments★) p. 23 PV **A** – St. Bride★ (steeple★★) p. 23 NV **J** – St. Clement Eastcheap (panelled interior★★) p. 23 PV **E** – St. Edmund the King and Martyr (tower and spire★) p. 23 PV **D** – St-Giles Cripplegate★ p. 23 OU **N** – St. Helen Bishopsgate★ (monuments★★) p. 23 PUV **R** – St. James Garlickhythe (tower and spire★, sword rests★) p. 23 OV **R** – St. Magnus the Martyr (tower★, sword rest★) p. 23 PV **K** – St. Margaret Lothbury★ (tower and spire★, woodwork★, screen★, font★) p. 23 PU **S** – St. Margaret Pattens (spire★, woodwork★) p. 23 PV **N** – St. Martin-within-Ludgate (tower and spire★, door cases★) p. 23 NOV **B** – St. Mary Abchurch★ (reredos★★, tower and spire★, dome★) p. 23 PV **X** – St. Mary-le-Bow (tower and steeple★★) p. 23 OV **G** – St. Michael Paternoster Royal (tower and spire★) p. 23 OV **D** – St. Nicholas Cole Abbey (tower and spire★) p. 23 OV **F** – St. Olave★ p. 23 PV **S** – St. Peter upon Cornhill (screen★) p. 23 PV **L** – St. Stephen Walbrook★ (tower and steeple★, dome★), p. 23 PV **Z** – St. Vedast (tower and spire★, ceiling★), p. 23 OU **E**.

**Other Churches**

Westminster Abbey★★★ (Henry VII Chapel★★★, Chapel of Edward the Confessor★★, Chapter House★★, Poets' Corner★) p. 26 LY.

Southwark Cathedral★★ p. 27 PX.

Queen's Chapel★ p. 29 EP – St. Clement Danes★ p. 33 EX – St. James's★ p. 29 EM – St. Margaret's★ p. 26 LY **A** – St. Martin-in-the-Fields★ p. 33 DY – St. Paul's★ (Covent Garden) p. 33 DX – Westminster Roman Catholic Cathedral★ p. 26 KY **B**.

## PARKS

Regent's Park★★★ p. 21 HI (terraces★★), Zoo★★★.

Hyde Park – Kensington Gardens★★ (Orangery★) pp. 24 and 25 St. James's Park★★ p. 26 KXY.

## STREETS AND SQUARES

The City★★★ p. 23 NV.

Bedford Square★★ p. 22 KLU – Belgrave Square★★ p. 32 AVX – Burlington Arcade★★ p. 29 DM – The Mall★★ p. 29 FP – Piccadilly★ p. 29 EM – The Thames★★ pp. 25-27 – Trafalgar Square★★ p. 33 DY – Whitehall★★ (Horse Guards★) p. 26 LX.

Barbican★ p. 23 OU – Bond Street★ pp. 28-29 CK-DM – Canonbury Square★ p. 23 NS – Carlton House Terrace★ p. 29 GN – Cheyne Walk★ p. 25 GHZ – Covent Garden★ p. 33 DX – Fitzroy Square★ p. 22 KU – Jermyn Street★ p. 29 EN – Merrick Square★ p. 27 OY – Montpelier Square★ p. 31 EQ – The Piazza★(Covent Garden) p. 33 DX – Piccadilly Arcade★ p. 29 DEN – Portman Square★ p. 28 AJ – Queen Anne's Gate★ p. 26 KY – Regent Street★ p. 29 EM – Piccadilly Circus★ p. 29 FM – St. James's Square★ p. 29 FN – St. James's Street★ p. 29 EN – Shepherd Market★ p. 28 CN – Soho★ p. 29 – Trinity Church Square★ p. 27 OY – Victoria Embankment gardens★ p. 33 DEXY – Waterloo Place★ p. 29 FN.

## MUSEUMS

British Museum★★★ p. 22 LU – National Gallery★★★ p. 29 GM – Science Museum★★★ p. 30 CR – Tate Gallery★★★ p. 26 LZ – Victoria and Albert Museum★★★ p. 31 DR.

Courtauld Institute Galleries★★ (Somerset House) p. 33 EXY – Museum of London★★ p. 23 OU **M** – National Portrait Gallery★★ p. 29 GM – Natural History Museum★★ p. 30 CS – Queen's Gallery★★ p. 32 BV – Wallace Collection★★ p. 28 AH.

Clock Museum★ (Guildhall) p. 22 OU – Imperial War Museum★ p. 27 NY – London Transport Museum★ p. 33 DX – Madame Tussaud's★ p. 21 IU **M** – Museum of Mankind★ p. 29 DM – National Army Museum★ p. 31 FU – Percival David Foundation of Chinese Art★ p. 22 KLT **M** – Sir John Soane's Museum★ p. 22 MU **M** – Wellington Museum★ p. 28 BP.

## OUTER LONDON

**Blackheath** p. 11 HX terraces and houses★, Eltham Palace★ **A** – **Brentford** p. 8 BX Syon Park★★, gardens★ – **Bromley** p. 10 GY The Crystal Palace Park★ – **Chiswick** p. 9 CV Chiswick Mall★★, Chiswick House★ **D**, Hogarth's House★ **E** – **Dulwich** p. 10 Picture Gallery★ FX **X** – **Greenwich** pp. 10 and 11 : Cutty Sark★★ GV **F**, Footway Tunnel(⋞ ★★) – National Maritime Museum★★ (Queen's House★★) GV **M**, Royal Naval College★★ (Painted Hall★, the Chapel★) GV **G**, The Park and Old Royal Observatory★ (Meridian Building : collection★★) HV **K**, Ranger's House★ GX **N** – **Hampstead** Kenwood House★★ (Adam Library★★, paintings★★) p. 5 EU **P**, Fenton House★, The Benton Fletcher Collection★ p. 20 ES – **Hampton Court** p. 8 BY (The Palace★★★, gardens★★★, Fountain Court★, The Great Vine★) – **Kew** p. 9 CX Royal Botanic Gardens★★★ : Palm House★★, Temperate House★, Kew Palace or Dutch House★★, Orangery★, Pagoda★, Japanese Gateway★ – **Hendon**★ p. 5, Royal Air Force Museum★★ CT **M** – **Hounslow** p. 8 BV Osterley Park★★ – **Lewisham** p. 10 GX Horniman Museum★ **M** – **Richmond** pp. 8 and 9 : Richmond Park★★, ⁂★★★ CX, Richmond Hill⁂★★ CX, Richmond Bridge★★ BX **R**, Richmond Green★★ BX **S** (Maids of Honour Row★★, Trumpeter's House★), Asgill House★ BX **B**, Ham House★★ BX **V** – **Shoreditch** p. 6 FU Geffrye Museum★ **M** – **Tower Hamlets** p. 6 GV Canary Wharf★ St. Katharine Dock★ **Y** – **Twickenham** p. 8 BX Marble Hill House★ **Z**, Strawberry Hill★ **A** .

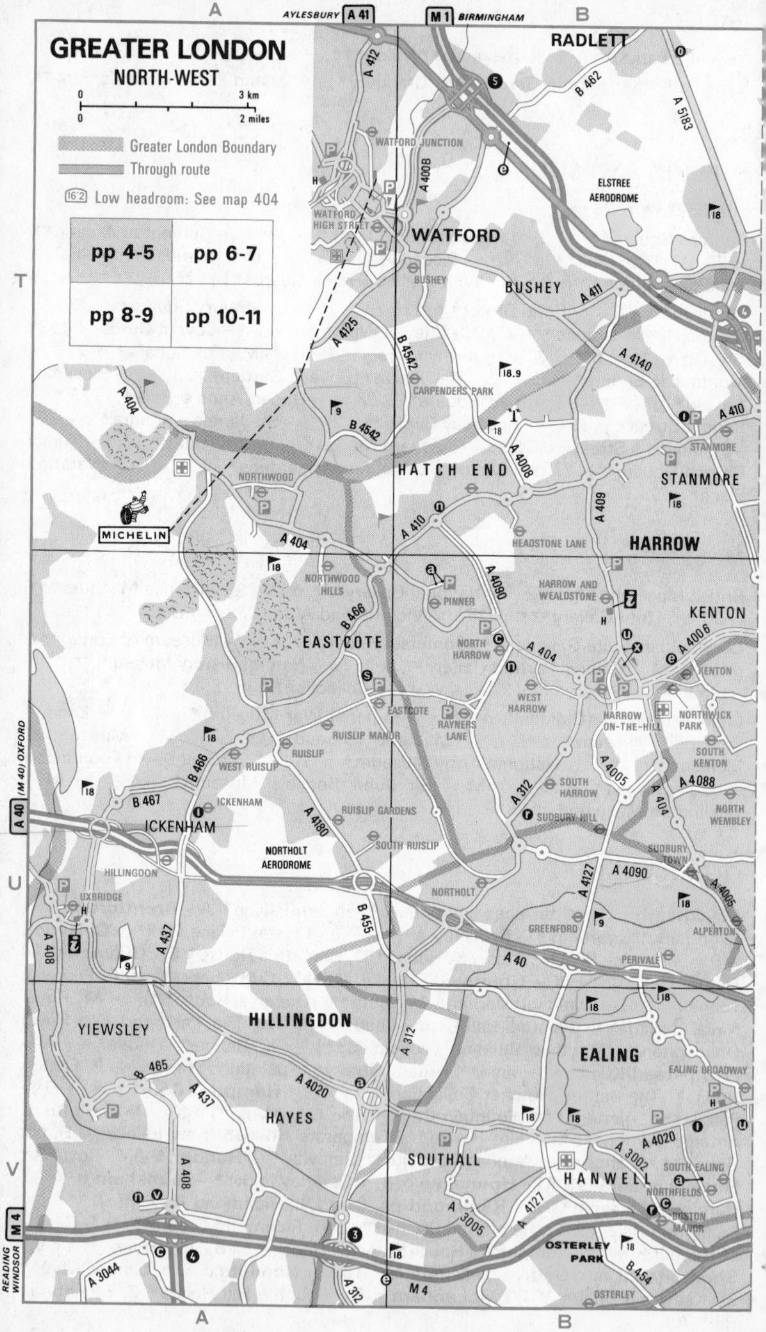
GREATER LONDON
NORTH-WEST
0 3 km
0 2 miles
Greater London Boundary
Through route
16'2 Low headroom: See map 404
pp 4-5
pp 6-7
pp 8-9
pp 10-11
A
B
T
U
V
AYLESBURY A 41
M 1 BIRMINGHAM
RADLETT
A 412
B 462
A 5183
WATFORD JUNCTION
A 4008
ELSTREE
AERODROME
WATFORD
HIGH STREET
WATFORD
BUSHEY
BUSHEY
A 411
A 4125
B 4542
A 4140
18.9
CARPENDERS PARK
A 404
A 410
STANMORE
B 4542
HATCH END
A 4008
STANMORE
NORTHWOOD
A 409
MICHELIN
A 404
A 410
HEADSTONE LANE
HARROW
NORTHWOOD
HILLS
PINNER
A 4090
HARROW AND
WEALDSTONE
KENTON
B 466
EASTCOTE
NORTH
HARROW
A 404
A 4006
KENTON
EASTCOTE
RAYNERS
LANE
WEST
HARROW
HARROW
ON-THE-HILL
NORTHWICK
PARK
RUISLIP MANOR
RUISLIP
B 466
WEST RUISLIP
SOUTH
KENTON
A 4005
A 4088
A 40 (M 40) OXFORD
B 467
ICKENHAM
A 4180
RUISLIP GARDENS
A 312
SOUTH
HARROW
A 404
NORTH
WEMBLEY
ICKENHAM
SUDBURY HILL
SOUTH RUISLIP
NORTHOLT
AERODROME
SUDBURY
TOWN
HILLINGDON
A 4127
A 4090
UXBRIDGE
NORTHOLT
A 4005
B 455
A 437
GREENFORD
ALPERTON
A 408
A 40
PERIVALE
YIEWSLEY
HILLINGDON
A 312
EALING
B 465
A 4020
EALING BROADWAY
A 437
HAYES
A 4020
A 3002
A 408
SOUTHALL
SOUTH EALING
HANWELL
NORTHFIELDS
A 3005
A 4127
BOSTON
MANOR
M 4
READING
WINDSOR
OSTERLEY
PARK
B 454
A 3044
A 312
M 4
OSTERLEY

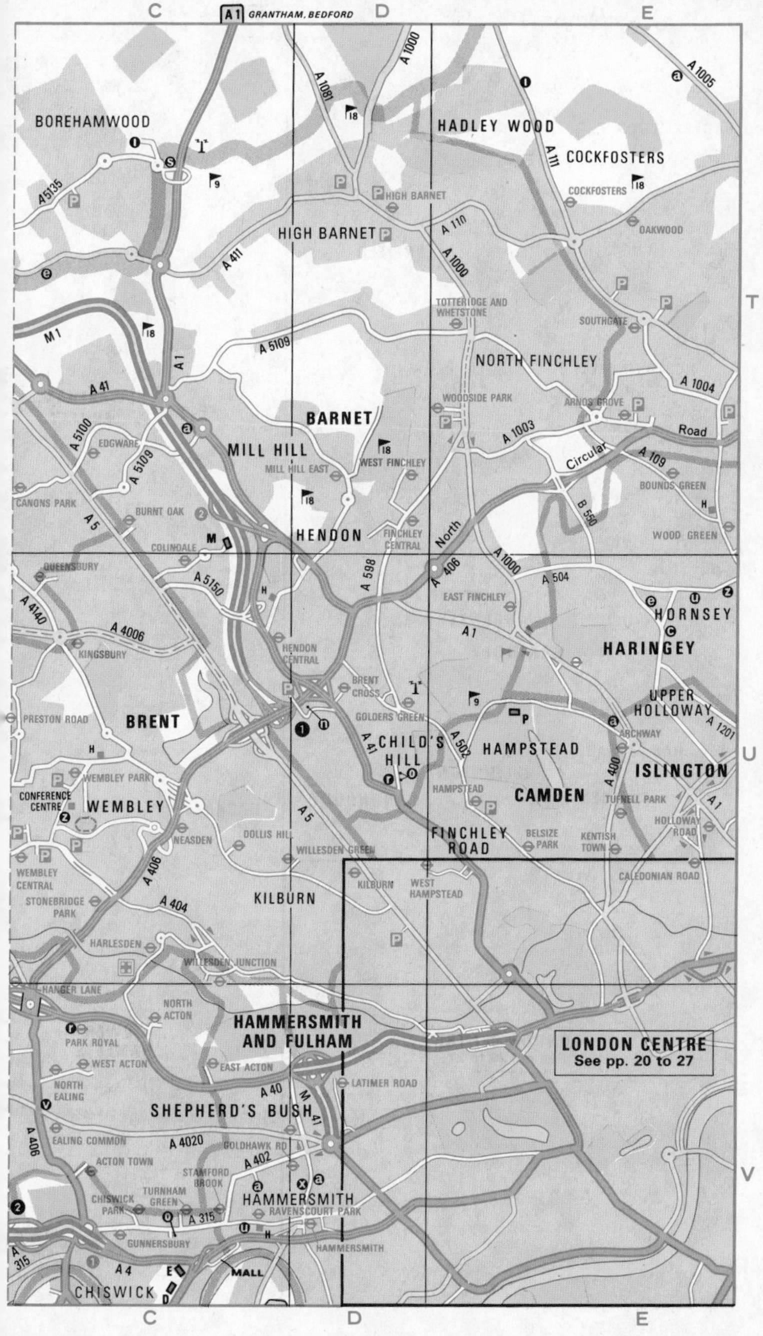
C
D
E
A 1 GRANTHAM, BEDFORD
T
U
V
BOREHAMWOOD
A 5135
A 1081
A 1000
A 1005
HADLEY WOOD
A 111
COCKFOSTERS
HIGH BARNET
A 110
A 411
OAKWOOD
M 1
A 1
A 5109
TOTTERIDGE AND WHETSTONE
SOUTHGATE
NORTH FINCHLEY
A 41
A 1004
WOODSIDE PARK
ARNOS GROVE
BARNET
A 1003
Road
Circular
A 109
A 5100
EDGWARE
MILL HILL
WEST FINCHLEY
MILL HILL EAST
BOUNDS GREEN
CANONS PARK
BURNT OAK
B 550
A 5
HENDON
FINCHLEY CENTRAL
North
WOOD GREEN
COLINDALE
QUEENSBURY
A 5150
A 598
A 406
A 1000
A 504
A 4140
EAST FINCHLEY
HORNSEY
A 4006
A 1
HARINGEY
KINGSBURY
HENDON CENTRAL
BRENT CROSS
UPPER HOLLOWAY
PRESTON ROAD
BRENT
GOLDERS GREEN
A 1201
A 41
CHILD'S HILL
A 502
HAMPSTEAD
ARCHWAY
ISLINGTON
A 400
WEMBLEY PARK
HAMPSTEAD
CAMDEN
TUFNELL PARK
CONFERENCE CENTRE
WEMBLEY
A 1
A 5
HOLLOWAY ROAD
FINCHLEY ROAD
NEASDEN
DOLLIS HILL
BELSIZE PARK
KENTISH TOWN
WILLESDEN GREEN
WEMBLEY CENTRAL
A 406
KILBURN
WEST HAMPSTEAD
CALEDONIAN ROAD
STONEBRIDGE PARK
KILBURN
A 404
HARLESDEN
WILLESDEN JUNCTION
HANGER LANE
NORTH ACTON
HAMMERSMITH AND FULHAM
PARK ROYAL
LONDON CENTRE
See pp. 20 to 27
WEST ACTON
EAST ACTON
LATIMER ROAD
NORTH EALING
A 40
M 41
SHEPHERD'S BUSH
A 406
EALING COMMON
A 4020
GOLDHAWK RD
ACTON TOWN
A 402
STAMFORD BROOK
TURNHAM GREEN
HAMMERSMITH
CHISWICK PARK
A 315
RAVENSCOURT PARK
GUNNERSBURY
HAMMERSMITH
A 315
A 4
MALL
CHISWICK

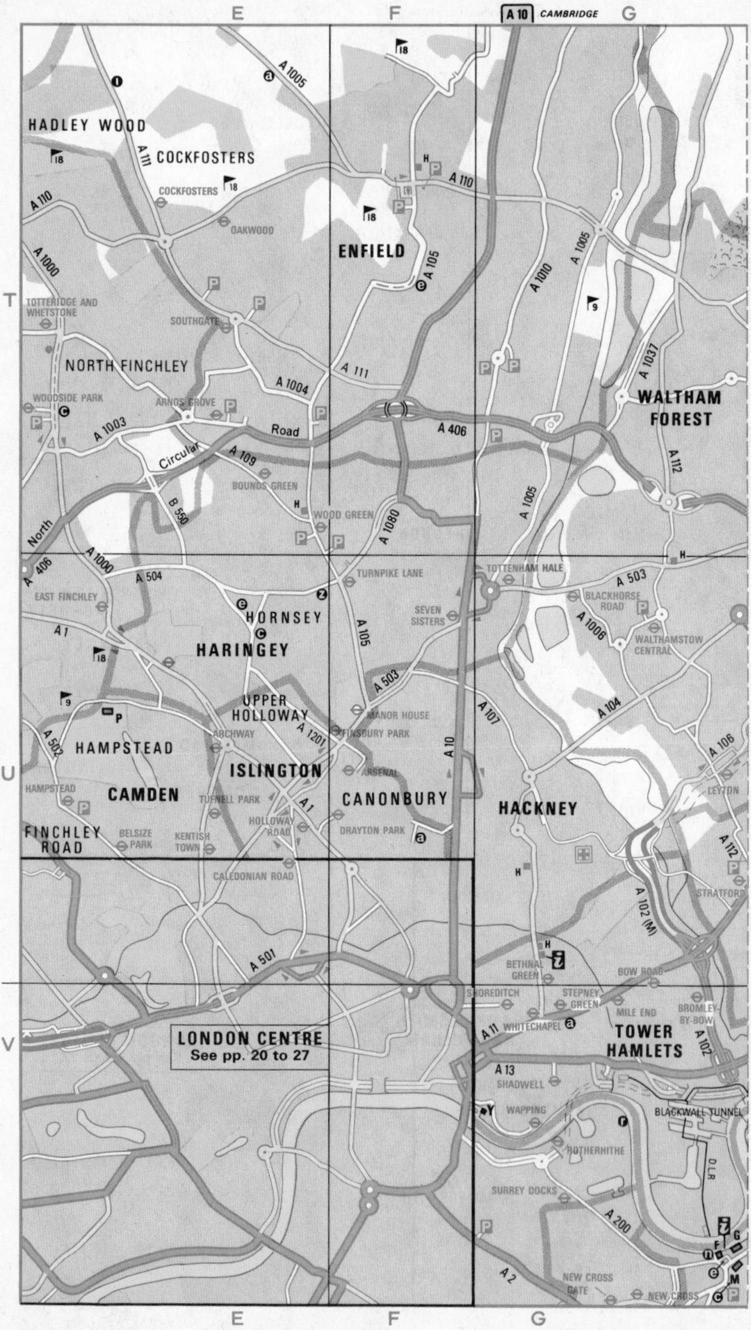

E
F
A 10 CAMBRIDGE
G
HADLEY WOOD
COCKFOSTERS
ENFIELD
WALTHAM FOREST
TOTTERIDGE AND WHETSTONE
SOUTHGATE
NORTH FINCHLEY
WOODSIDE PARK
ARNOS GROVE
OAKWOOD
A 406
A 109
BOUNDS GREEN
WOOD GREEN
Circular
Road
North
B 550
A 1080
A 1005
A 1010
A 1037
A 112
A 110
A 111
A 1000
A 1004
A 1003
A 105
T
EAST FINCHLEY
A 504
TURNPIKE LANE
TOTTENHAM HALE
A 503
BLACKHORSE ROAD
A 1006
WALTHAMSTOW CENTRAL
SEVEN SISTERS
HORNSEY
HARINGEY
A 1
UPPER HOLLOWAY
MANOR HOUSE
FINSBURY PARK
ARCHWAY
A 1201
A 104
A 106
A 107
A 10
HAMPSTEAD
ISLINGTON
ARSENAL
LEYTON
U
CAMDEN
TUFNELL PARK
CANONBURY
HACKNEY
FINCHLEY ROAD
BELSIZE PARK
KENTISH TOWN
HOLLOWAY ROAD
DRAYTON PARK
A 502
CALEDONIAN ROAD
STRATFORD
A 102 (M)
A 501
BETHNAL GREEN
BOW ROAD
SHOREDITCH
STEPNEY GREEN
MILE END
BROMLEY-BY-BOW
V
LONDON CENTRE
See pp. 20 to 27
A 11
WHITECHAPEL
TOWER HAMLETS
A 13
SHADWELL
A 102
WAPPING
BLACKWALL TUNNEL
ROTHERHITHE
D.L.R.
SURREY DOCKS
A 200
A 2
NEW CROSS GATE
NEW CROSS
E
F
G

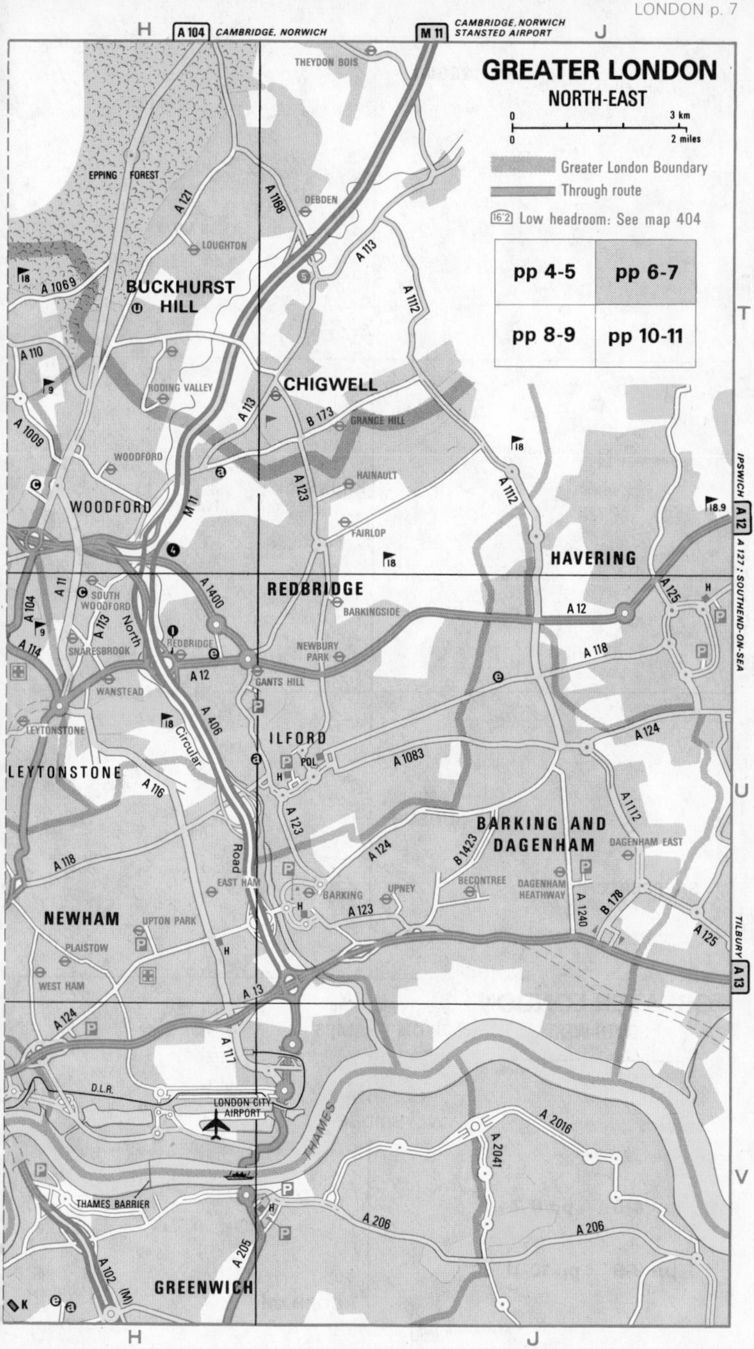
GREATER LONDON
NORTH-EAST
0 3 km
0 2 miles
Greater London Boundary
Through route
16'2 Low headroom: See map 404
pp 4-5
pp 6-7
pp 8-9
pp 10-11
A 104 CAMBRIDGE, NORWICH
M 11 CAMBRIDGE, NORWICH STANSTED AIRPORT
THEYDON BOIS
EPPING FOREST
DEBDEN
LOUGHTON
BUCKHURST HILL
CHIGWELL
RODING VALLEY
GRANGE HILL
WOODFORD
HAINAULT
FAIRLOP
HAVERING
REDBRIDGE
SOUTH WOODFORD
BARKINGSIDE
SNARESBROOK
NEWBURY PARK
GANTS HILL
WANSTEAD
LEYTONSTONE
ILFORD
POL
North Circular Road
BARKING AND DAGENHAM
DAGENHAM EAST
EAST HAM
BARKING
UPNEY
BECONTREE
DAGENHAM HEATHWAY
NEWHAM
UPTON PARK
PLAISTOW
WEST HAM
D.L.R.
LONDON CITY AIRPORT
THAMES
THAMES BARRIER
GREENWICH
IPSWICH A 12
A 127 ; SOUTHEND-ON-SEA
TILBURY A 13
A 1069
A 110
A 1009
A 121
A 1168
A 113
A 1112
B 173
A 123
M 11
A 11
A 104
A 114
A 1400
A 12
A 406
A 116
A 118
A 125
A 124
A 1083
B 1423
A 1240
B 178
A 13
A 117
A 2016
A 2041
A 206
A 205
A 102 (M)
H
J
T
U
V

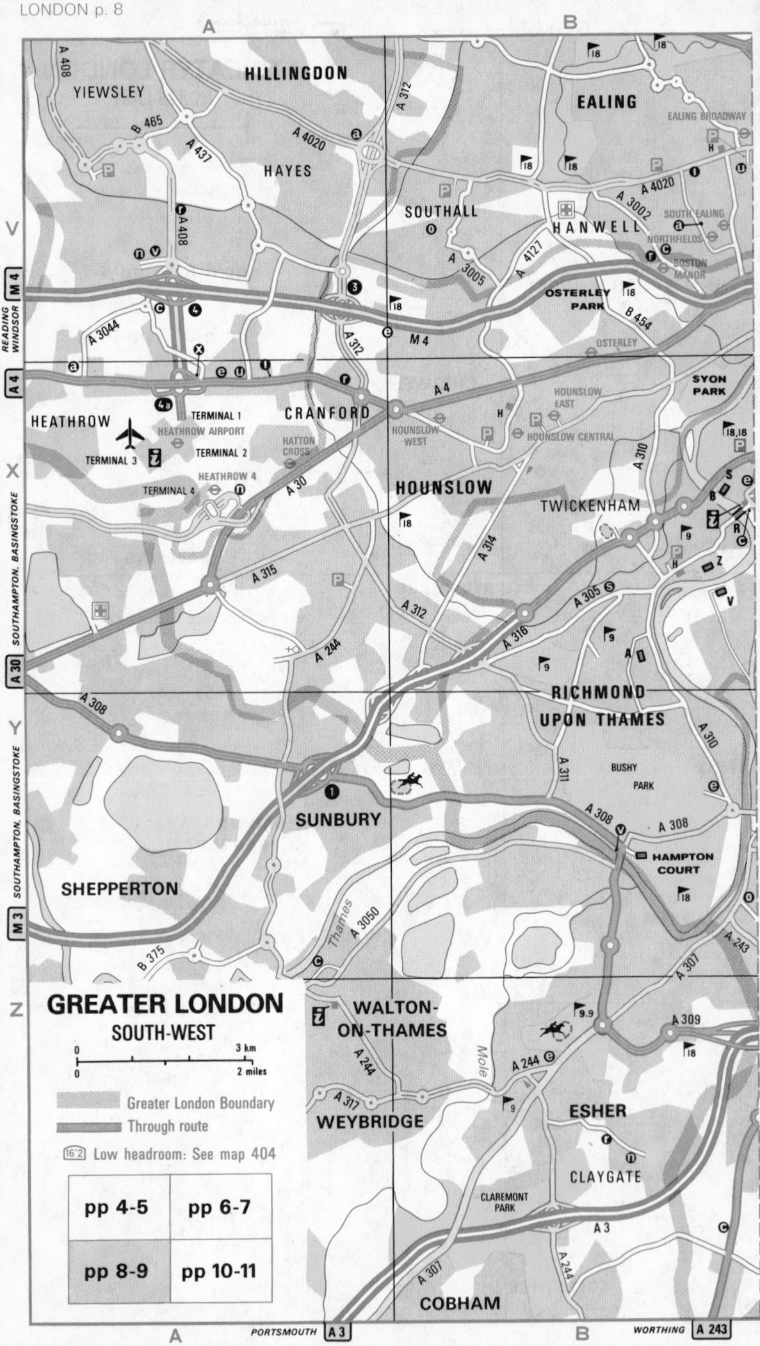
A
B
HILLINGDON
YIEWSLEY
EALING
HAYES
SOUTHALL
HANWELL
EALING BROADWAY
SOUTH EALING
NORTHFIELDS
BOSTON MANOR
OSTERLEY PARK
OSTERLEY
SYON PARK
HOUNSLOW EAST
HOUNSLOW CENTRAL
HOUNSLOW WEST
HEATHROW
TERMINAL 1
HEATHROW AIRPORT
TERMINAL 2
TERMINAL 3
TERMINAL 4
HEATHROW 4
HATTON CROSS
CRANFORD
HOUNSLOW
TWICKENHAM
RICHMOND UPON THAMES
BUSHY PARK
HAMPTON COURT
SUNBURY
SHEPPERTON
Thames
WALTON-ON-THAMES
Mole
WEYBRIDGE
ESHER
CLAYGATE
CLAREMONT PARK
COBHAM
V
X
Y
Z
M 4
READING WINDSOR
A 4
A 30
SOUTHAMPTON, BASINGSTOKE
M 3
PORTSMOUTH
A 3
WORTHING
A 243
A 408
B 465
A 437
A 4020
A 312
A 3002
A 4127
A 3005
B 454
A 3044
A 310
A 314
A 315
A 305
A 316
A 244
A 308
A 311
A 3050
B 375
A 307
A 309
A 317
GREATER LONDON
SOUTH-WEST
0 3 km
0 2 miles
Greater London Boundary
Through route
16'2 Low headroom: See map 404
pp 4-5
pp 6-7
pp 8-9
pp 10-11

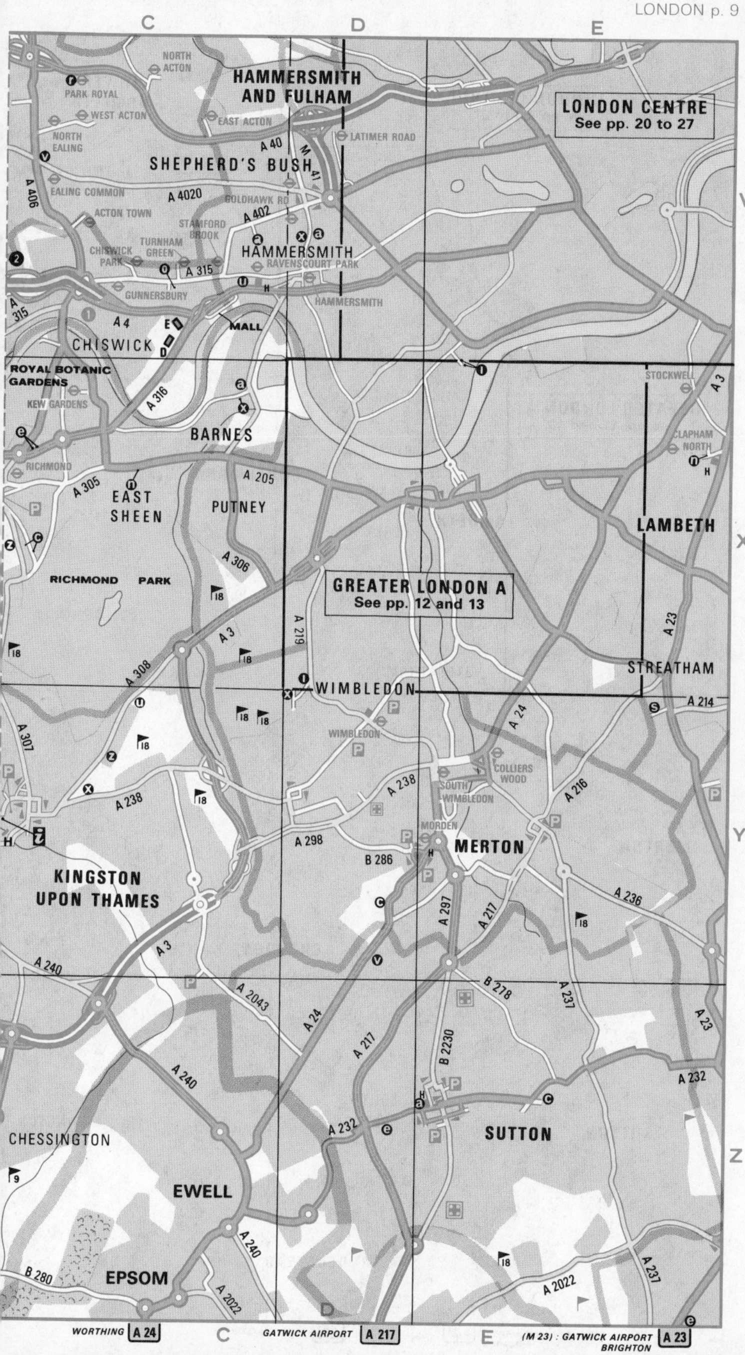
C
D
E
V
X
Y
Z
HAMMERSMITH AND FULHAM
LONDON CENTRE See pp. 20 to 27
NORTH ACTON
PARK ROYAL
WEST ACTON
EAST ACTON
LATIMER ROAD
NORTH EALING
SHEPHERD'S BUSH
A 40
M 41
A 406
EALING COMMON
A 4020
GOLDHAWK RD
ACTON TOWN
A 402
STAMFORD BROOK
TURNHAM GREEN
CHISWICK PARK
HAMMERSMITH
RAVENSCOURT PARK
A 315
GUNNERSBURY
A 4
CHISWICK
MALL
ROYAL BOTANIC GARDENS
KEW GARDENS
A 316
BARNES
RICHMOND
A 305
EAST SHEEN
A 205
PUTNEY
STOCKWELL
A 3
CLAPHAM NORTH
LAMBETH
A 306
RICHMOND PARK
GREATER LONDON A See pp. 12 and 13
A 219
A 308
WIMBLEDON
STREATHAM
A 23
A 214
A 307
A 24
COLLIERS WOOD
A 238
SOUTH WIMBLEDON
A 216
A 298
MORDEN
MERTON
B 286
KINGSTON UPON THAMES
A 236
A 297
A 217
A 240
B 278
A 237
A 2043
B 2230
A 232
SUTTON
CHESSINGTON
EWELL
B 280
EPSOM
A 2022
WORTHING A 24
GATWICK AIRPORT A 217
(M 23) : GATWICK AIRPORT BRIGHTON A 23

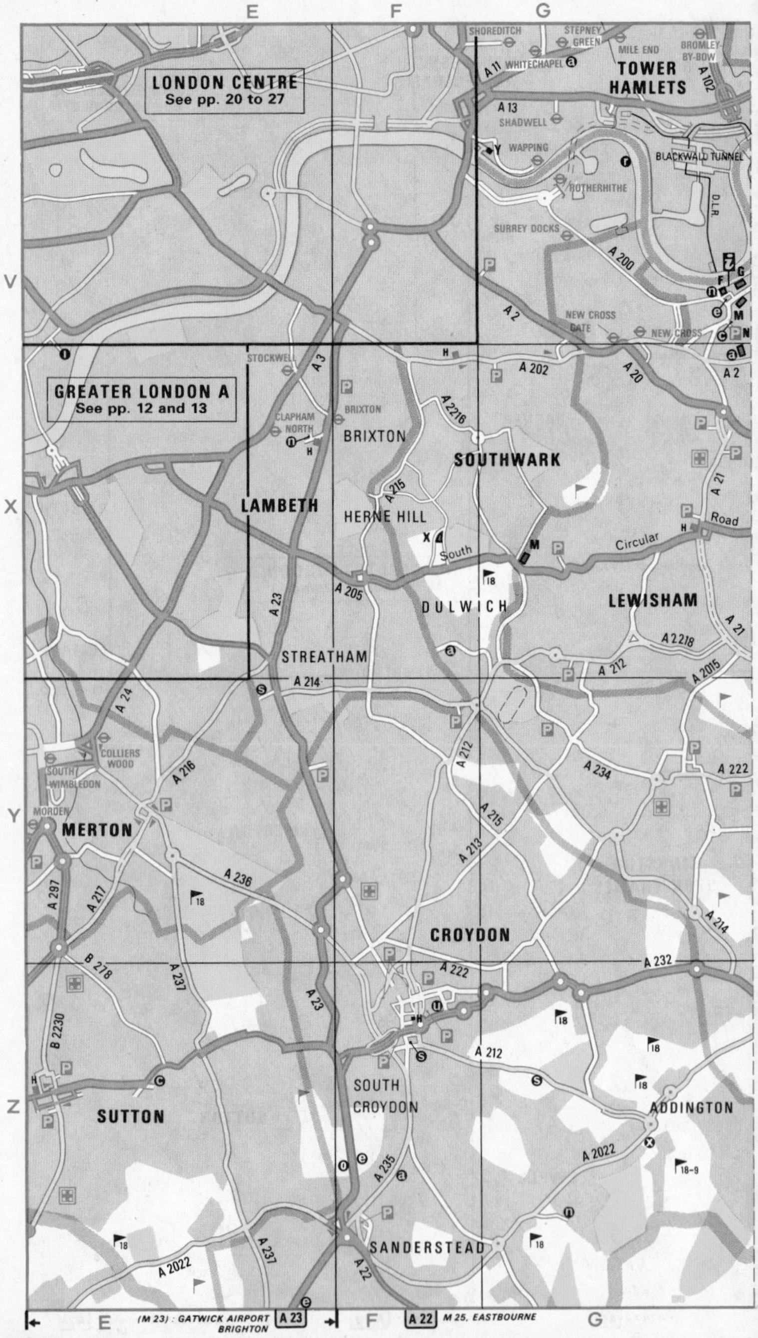
E
F
G
V
X
Y
Z
SHOREDITCH
STEPNEY GREEN
MILE END
BROMLEY-BY-BOW
A 11
WHITECHAPEL
TOWER HAMLETS
A 102
LONDON CENTRE
See pp. 20 to 27
A 13
SHADWELL
WAPPING
BLACKWALL TUNNEL
ROTHERHITHE
D.L.R.
SURREY DOCKS
A 200
A 2
NEW CROSS GATE
NEW CROSS
STOCKWELL
A 3
A 202
A 20
GREATER LONDON A
See pp. 12 and 13
CLAPHAM NORTH
BRIXTON
A 2216
SOUTHWARK
A 21
LAMBETH
A 215
HERNE HILL
Road
South
Circular
A 205
A 23
DULWICH
LEWISHAM
A 2218
STREATHAM
A 212
A 2015
A 214
A 24
COLLIERS WOOD
SOUTH WIMBLEDON
A 216
A 234
A 222
MORDEN
MERTON
A 213
A 236
A 297
A 217
CROYDON
B 278
A 237
A 232
B 2230
SOUTH CROYDON
ADDINGTON
SUTTON
A 2022
A 235
SANDERSTEAD
A 22
(M 23) : GATWICK AIRPORT
BRIGHTON
A 23
A 22
M 25, EASTBOURNE

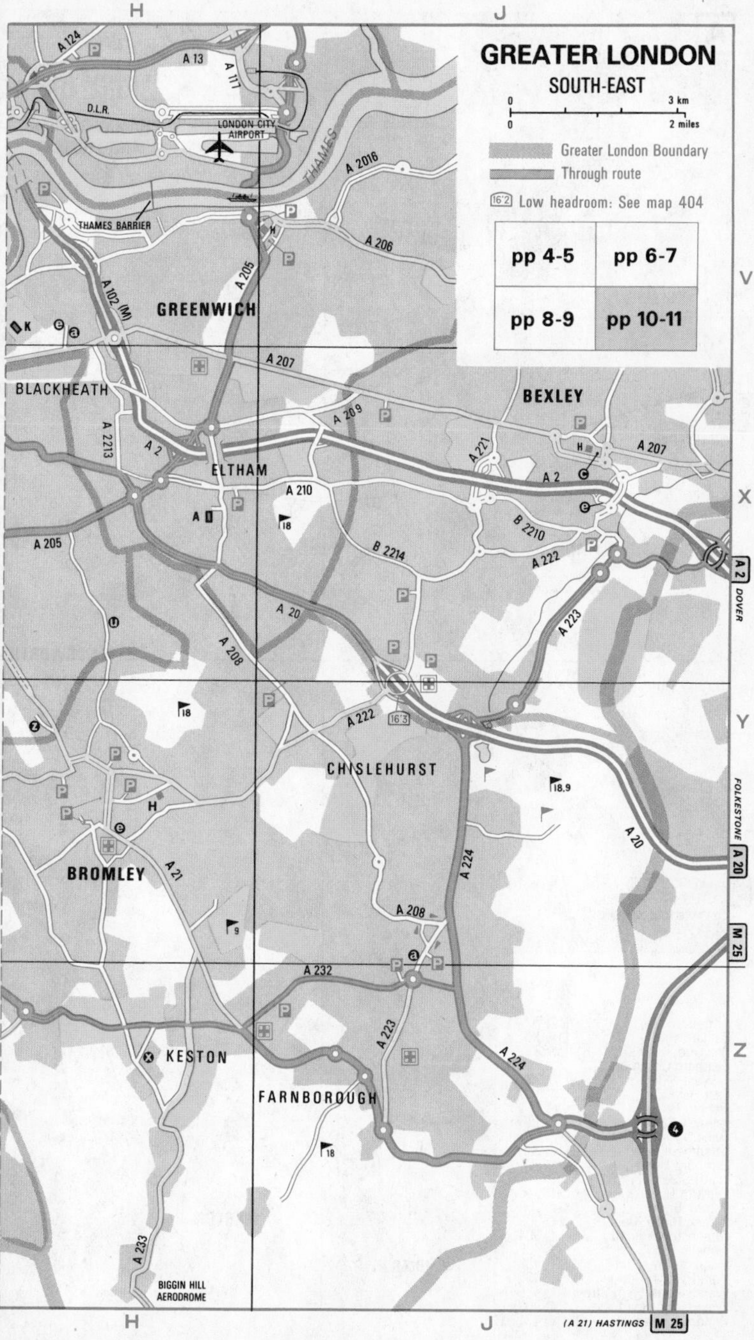
GREATER LONDON
SOUTH-EAST
0 3 km
0 2 miles
Greater London Boundary
Through route
16'2 Low headroom: See map 404
pp 4-5
pp 6-7
pp 8-9
pp 10-11
H
J
V
X
Y
Z
A 124
A 13
A 117
D.L.R.
LONDON CITY AIRPORT
THAMES
A 2016
THAMES BARRIER
A 206
A 205
A 102 (M)
GREENWICH
A 207
BLACKHEATH
A 2213
A 209
BEXLEY
A 2
A 221
A 207
ELTHAM
A 210
B 2210
A 205
B 2214
A 222
A 2 DOVER
A 20
A 223
A 208
A 222
16'3
CHISLEHURST
FOLKESTONE A 20
A 20
BROMLEY
A 21
A 224
A 208
M 25
A 232
A 223
A 224
KESTON
FARNBOROUGH
A 233
BIGGIN HILL AERODROME
(A 21) HASTINGS M 25

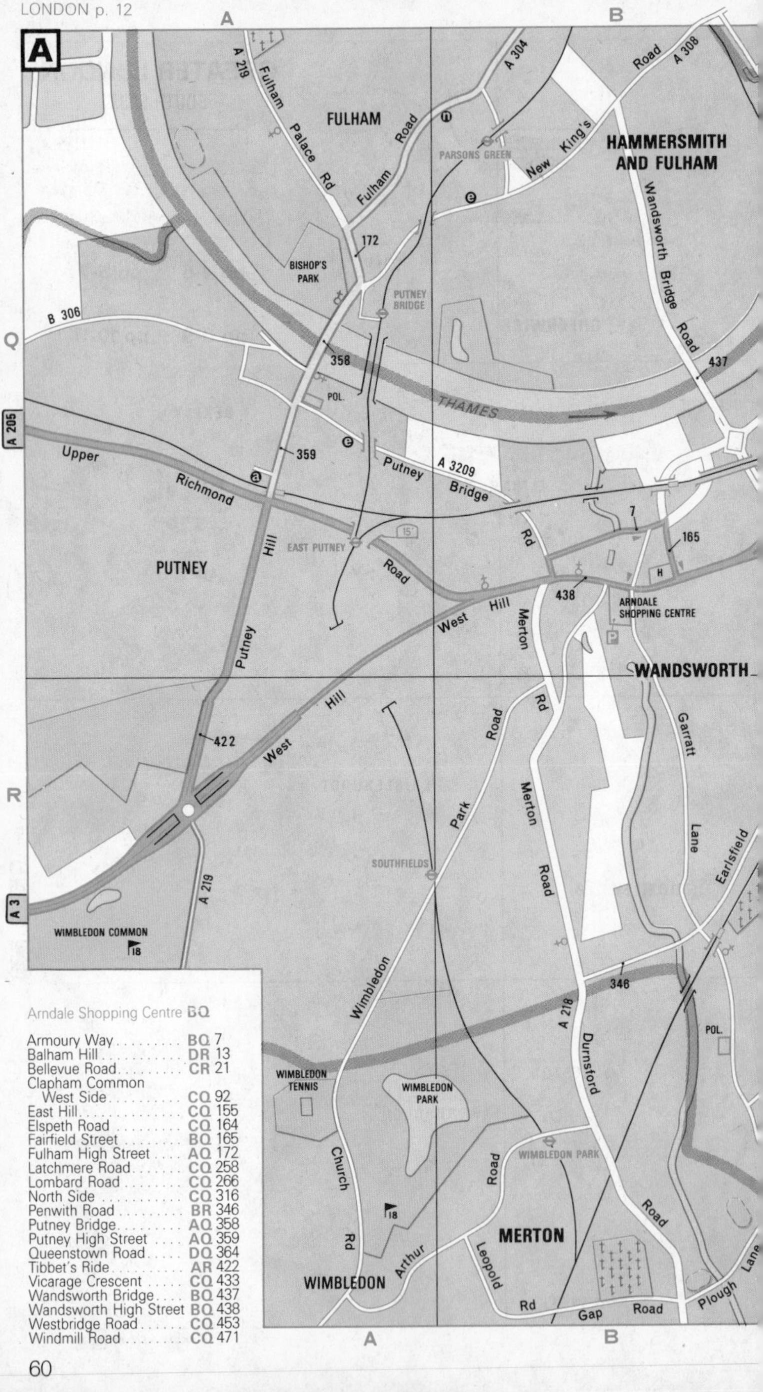
A
B
A
Q
R
A 205
A 3
A 219
Fulham Palace Rd
FULHAM
Fulham Road
A 304
New King's Road
A 308
PARSONS GREEN
HAMMERSMITH AND FULHAM
Wandsworth Bridge Road
172
BISHOP'S PARK
PUTNEY BRIDGE
B 306
358
437
THAMES
POL.
359
Upper Richmond Road
Putney Bridge Rd
A 3209
7
165
EAST PUTNEY
15'
PUTNEY
Putney Hill
West Hill
438
ARNDALE SHOPPING CENTRE
Merton Rd
WANDSWORTH
Garratt Lane
422
Park Road
Merton Road
Earlsfield
SOUTHFIELDS
A 219
WIMBLEDON COMMON
18
346
Wimbledon Park Road
A 218
Durnsford Road
POL.
WIMBLEDON TENNIS
WIMBLEDON PARK
Church Rd
WIMBLEDON PARK
18
MERTON
Arthur Rd
Leopold Rd
WIMBLEDON
Gap Road
Plough Lane
A
B

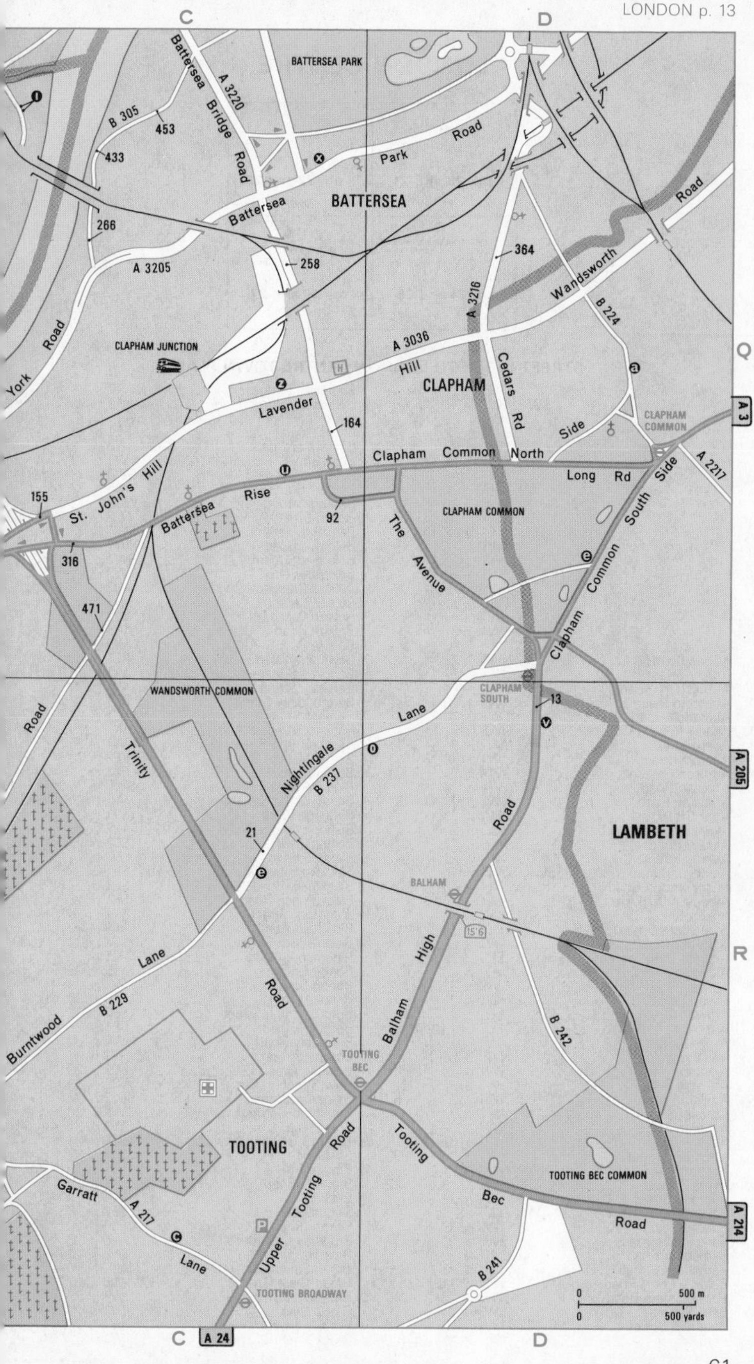
C
D
BATTERSEA PARK
Battersea Bridge Road
A 3220
B 305
453
433
Park Road
Battersea
BATTERSEA
266
258
A 3205
364
A 3216
Wandsworth Road
B 224
York Road
CLAPHAM JUNCTION
A 3036
Hill
Lavender
CLAPHAM
Cedars Rd
Q
A 3
CLAPHAM COMMON
Side
164
Clapham Common North
Long Rd
A 2217
St. John's Hill
155
Battersea Rise
92
The Avenue
CLAPHAM COMMON
South Side
316
471
Clapham Common
WANDSWORTH COMMON
CLAPHAM SOUTH
13
Lane
Nightingale
B 237
Trinity
A 205
Road
LAMBETH
21
BALHAM
High
15'6
R
Lane
Road
B 229
Burntwood
Balham
B 242
TOOTING BEC
TOOTING
Road
Tooting
TOOTING BEC COMMON
Garratt
A 217
Upper Tooting
Bec
Road
A 214
Lane
B 241
TOOTING BROADWAY
0
500 m
500 yards
C
A 24
D

# LONDON CENTRE

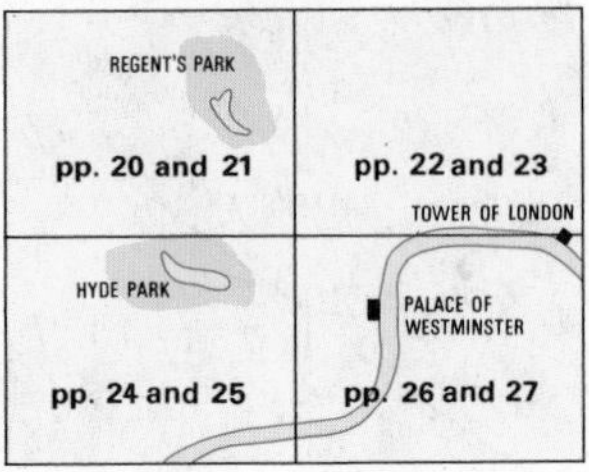


## STREET INDEX TO LONDON CENTRE TOWN PLANS

| | | | | |
|---|---|---|---|---|
| Brushfield Street | E1 | p. 23 | PU | |
| Bruton Street | W1 | p. 28 | CM | |
| Bryanston Square | W1 | p. 21 | HU | |
| Bryanston Street | W1 | p. 28 | AK | |
| Buckingham Gate | SW1 | p. 32 | CV | 56 |
| Buckingham Palace Road | SW1 | p. 32 | AY | |
| Bunhill Row | EC1 | p. 23 | PU | |
| Bury Street | SW1 | p. 29 | EN | |
| Bute Street | SW7 | p. 30 | CS | 59 |
| Byward Street | EC3 | p. 23 | PV | 62 |
| Cadogan Gardens | SW3 | p. 31 | FS | |
| Cadogan Place | SW1 | p. 31 | FR | |
| Cadogan Square | SW1 | p. 31 | FS | |
| Cadogan Street | SW3 | p. 31 | ET | |
| Caledonian Road | N1, N7 | p. 22 | MS | |
| Cale Street | SW3 | p. 31 | DT | |
| Calshot Street | N1 | p. 22 | MT | |
| Calthorpe Street | WC1 | p. 22 | MT | 65 |
| Camberwell New Road | SE5 | p. 27 | NZ | |
| Camberwell Road | SE5 | p. 27 | OZ | |
| Cambridge Circus | WC2 | p. 29 | GK | |
| Cambridge Square | W2 | p. 33 | EZ | 67 |
| Camden High Street | NW1 | p. 22 | JS | |
| Camden Road | E11 | p. 22 | KS | |
| Camden Street | NW1 | p. 22 | KS | |
| Camomile Street | EC3 | p. 23 | PU | 71 |
| Campden Hill Road | W8 | p. 24 | EX | |
| Cannon Street | EC4 | p. 23 | OV | |
| Canonbury Road | N1 | p. 23 | NS | |
| Canonbury Square | N1 | p. 23 | NS | |
| Carey Street | WC2 | p. 33 | EV | |
| Carlisle Place | SW1 | p. 32 | BX | |
| Carlos Place | W1 | p. 28 | BM | |
| Carlton Gardens | SW1 | p. 29 | FP | 74 |
| Carlton Hill | NW8 | p. 20 | FS | |
| Carlton House Terrace | SW1 | p. 29 | FN | |
| Carlton Vale | NW6 | p. 20 | ET | |
| Carriage Drive East | SW11 | p. 25 | IZ | |
| Carriage Drive North | SW11 | p. 25 | IZ | 75 |
| Carriage Road (the) | SW7, SW11 | p. 31 | EQ | |
| Castle Lane | SW1 | p. 32 | CX | |
| Cavendish Square | W1 | p. 28 | CJ | |
| Central Street | EC1 | p. 23 | OT | |
| Chalk Farm Road | NW1 | p. 21 | IS | |
| Chancery Lane | WC2 | p. 33 | EV | |
| Chandos Place | WC2 | p. 33 | DY | |
| Chandos Street | W1 | p. 28 | CH | |
| Chapel Market | N1 | p. 23 | NS | 78 |
| Chapel Street | SW1 | p. 32 | AV | |
| Chapter Road | SE17 | p. 27 | OZ | |
| Charlbert Street | NW8 | p. 21 | HT | 79 |
| Charles II Street | SW1 | p. 29 | FN | |
| Charles Street | W1 | p. 28 | CN | |
| Charing Cross | SW1 | p. 33 | DY | |
| Charing Cross Road | WC2 | p. 29 | GJ | |
| Charterhouse Square | EC1 | p. 23 | OU | 81 |
| Charterhouse Street | EC1 | p. 23 | NU | 83 |
| Cheapside | EC2 | p. 23 | OV | |
| Chelsea Bridge | SW1, SW8 | p. 25 | IZ | |
| Chelsea Bridge Road | SW1 | p. 25 | IZ | |
| Chelsea Embankment | SW3 | p. 25 | HZ | |
| Chelsea Manor Street | SW3 | p. 31 | EU | |
| Chelsea Square | SW3 | p. 31 | DU | |
| Cheltenham Terrace | SW3 | p. 31 | FT | |
| Chepstow Crescent | W11 | p. 32 | AZ | 84 |
| Chepstow Place | W2 | p. 32 | AZ | |
| Chepstow Road | W2 | p. 32 | AZ | |
| Chesham Place | SW2 | p. 31 | FR | |
| Chesham Street | SW1 | p. 31 | FS | |
| Chester Road | NW1 | p. 21 | IT | |
| Chester Row | SW1 | p. 32 | AY | |
| Chester Square | SW1 | p. 32 | AX | 88 |
| Chester Street | SW1 | p. 32 | AV | |
| Cheval Place | SW7 | p. 31 | ER | |
| Cheyne Walk | SW3, SW10 | p. 25 | GZ | |
| Chilworth Street | W2 | p. 32 | CZ | 90 |
| Chippenham Road | W9 | p. 20 | EU | |
| Chiswell Street | EC1 | p. 23 | OU | |
| Church Row | NW3 | p. 20 | ES | |
| Church Street | NW8, NW2 | p. 21 | GU | |
| Circus Road | NW8 | p. 21 | GT | |
| City Road | EC1 | p. 23 | NT | |
| Clapham Road | SW9 | p. 26 | MZ | |
| Clarendon Place | W2 | p. 33 | EZ | 93 |
| Clarendon Road | W11 | p. 24 | EX | |
| Claverton Street | SW1 | p. 26 | KZ | |
| Clayton Street | SE11 | p. 26 | MZ | |
| Clerkenwell Road | EC1 | p. 23 | NU | |
| Cleveland Gardens | W2 | p. 32 | CZ | 94 |
| Cleveland Square | W2 | p. 32 | CZ | |
| Cleveland Street | W1 | p. 22 | KU | |
| Cleveland Terrace | W2 | p. 32 | CZ | |
| Clifford Street | W1 | p. 29 | DM | |
| Cliveden Place | SW1 | p. 31 | FS | |
| Cockspur Street | SW1 | p. 29 | GN | |
| Collingham Gardens | SW5 | p. 30 | AT | 99 |
| Collingham Road | SW5 | p. 30 | AT | 101 |
| Commercial Street | E1 | p. 23 | PU | |
| Conduit Street | W1 | p. 29 | DL | |
| Connaught Square | W2 | p. 33 | EZ | 103 |
| Connaught Street | W2 | p. 33 | EZ | |
| Constantine Road | NW3 | p. 20 | ES | 106 |
| Constitution Hill | SW1 | p. 32 | AV | |
| Copenhagen Street | N1 | p. 22 | LS | |
| Cork Street | W1 | p. 29 | DM | |
| Cornwall Crescent | W11 | p. 20 | EV | 107 |
| Cornwall Gardens | SW7 | p. 30 | AR | |
| Cornwall Road | SE1 | p. 26 | MX | 108 |
| Corporation Row | EC1 | p. 23 | NT | 110 |
| Courtfield Gardens | SW5 | p. 30 | AT | |
| Courtfield Road | SW7 | p. 30 | BS | |
| Coventry Street | W1 | p. 29 | FM | |
| Cowcross Street | EC1 | p. 23 | NU | 113 |
| Cranbourn Street | WC2 | p. 33 | DX | 115 |
| Cranley Gardens | SW7 | p. 30 | CT | |
| Craven Hill | W2 | p. 32 | CZ | |
| Craven Road | W2 | p. 33 | DZ | |
| Craven Street | WC2 | p. 33 | DY | |
| Craven Terrace | W2 | p. 33 | DZ | |
| Crawford Place | W1 | p. 21 | HU | 116 |
| Crawford Street | W1 | p. 21 | HU | |
| Cromwell Crescent | SW5 | p. 24 | EZ | 119 |
| Cromwell Place | SW7 | p. 30 | CS | 120 |
| Cromwell Road | SW7, SW5 | p. 30 | CS | |
| Crowndale Road | NW1 | p. 22 | KS | |
| Crucifix Lane | SE1 | p. 27 | PX | 125 |
| Culross Street | W1 | p. 28 | AM | |
| Curtain Road | EC2 | p. 23 | PT | 126 |
| Curzon Street | W1 | p. 28 | BN | |
| Cut (The) | SE1 | p. 27 | NX | |
| Dante Road | SE11 | p. 27 | NZ | 129 |
| D'Arblay Street | W1 | p. 29 | EK | |
| Davies Street | W1 | p. 28 | BK | |
| Dawes Road | SW6 | p. 24 | EZ | |
| Dawson Place | W2 | p. 32 | AZ | |
| Deanery Street | W1 | p. 28 | BN | 132 |
| Dean Street | W1 | p. 29 | FJ | |
| De Beauvoir Road | N1 | p. 23 | PS | |
| Delancey Street | NW1 | p. 21 | JS | |
| Delaware Road | W9 | p. 20 | FT | |
| Denbigh Street | SW1 | p. 26 | KZ | |
| Denman Street | W1 | p. 29 | FM | 133 |
| Denmark Street | WC2 | p. 29 | GJ | 134 |
| De Vere Gardens | W8 | p. 30 | BQ | |
| Devonshire Street | W1 | p. 21 | IU | |
| Devonshire Terrace | W2 | p. 32 | CZ | 136 |
| Dorset Road | SW8 | p. 26 | LZ | |
| Dorset Street | W1 | p. 28 | AH | |
| Dovehouse Street | SW3 | p. 31 | DU | |
| Dover Street | W1 | p. 29 | DM | |
| Downham Road | N1 | p. 23 | PS | |
| Downing Street | SW1 | p. 26 | LX | 138 |
| Downshire Hill | NW3 | p. 20 | ES | 139 |
| Draycott Avenue | SW3 | p. 31 | ET | |
| Draycott Place | SW3 | p. 31 | ET | |
| Drayton Gardens | SW10 | p. 30 | BT | |
| Druid Street | SE1 | p. 27 | PY | |
| Drury Lane | WC2 | p. 33 | DV | |
| Dufferin Street | EC1 | p. 23 | OT | 141 |
| Duke of Wellington Place | SW1 | p. 32 | AV | 142 |
| Duke of York Street | SW1 | p. 29 | EN | 143 |
| Duke's Place | EC3 | p. 23 | PV | 145 |
| Duke Street | W1 | p. 28 | BK | |
| Duke Street ST. JAMES | SW1 | p. 29 | EN | 146 |
| Duncannon Street | WC2 | p. 33 | DY | 147 |
| Dunraven Street | W1 | p. 28 | AL | 149 |
| Dunton Road | SE1 | p. 27 | PZ | |
| Durham Street | SE11 | p. 26 | MZ | 150 |
| Eagle Wharf Road | N1 | p. 23 | OS | |
| Eardley Crescent | SW5 | p. 24 | EZ | 151 |
| Earlham Street | WC2 | p. 33 | DV | 153 |
| Earl's Court Road | W8, SW5 | p. 24 | EY | |
| Eastbourne Terrace | W2 | p. 33 | DZ | |
| Eastcastle Street | W1 | p. 29 | EJ | |
| Eastcheap | EC3 | p. 23 | PV | 154 |
| East Heath Road | NW3 | p. 20 | ES | |
| East Road | N1 | p. 23 | PT | |
| East Street | SE17 | p. 27 | PZ | |
| Eaton Place | SW1 | p. 32 | AX | |
| Eaton Square | SW1 | p. 32 | AX | |
| Ebury Bridge | SW1 | p. 25 | IZ | 156 |
| Ebury Street | SW1 | p. 32 | AY | |
| Ebury Bridge Road | SW1 | p. 25 | IZ | |
| Eccleston Bridge | SW1 | p. 32 | BY | 157 |
| Eccleston Square | SW1 | p. 32 | BY | |
| Eccleston Street | SW1 | p. 32 | AY | |

| Street | District | Page | Grid | No. |
|---|---|---|---|---|
| Hornton Street | W8 | p. 24 | FY | 229 |
| Houndsditch | EC3 | p. 23 | PU | |
| Howick Place | SW1 | p. 32 | CX | |
| Howland Street | W1 | p. 22 | KU | 232 |
| Hoxton Street | N1 | p. 23 | PT | |
| Hudson's Place | SW1 | p. 32 | BY | |
| Hugh Street | SW1 | p. 32 | BY | |
| Hunter Street | WC1 | p. 22 | LT | 233 |
| Hyde Park Gardens | W2 | p. 33 | DZ | |
| Hyde Park Square | W2 | p. 33 | EZ | 234 |
| Hyde Park Street | W2 | p. 33 | EZ | |
| Hyde Road | N1 | p. 23 | PS | 235 |
| Ifield Road | SW10 | p. 30 | AU | |
| Inverness Terrace | W2 | p. 32 | BZ | |
| Ixworth Place | NW6 | p. 31 | DT | |
| James Street | W1 | p. 28 | BJ | |
| James Street SOHO | WC2 | p. 29 | EL | |
| John Adam Street | WC2 | p. 33 | DY | |
| John Islip Street | SW1 | p. 26 | LZ | |
| John Ruskin Street | SE5 | p. 27 | OZ | |
| Jubilee Place | SW3 | p. 31 | ET | |
| Judd Street | WC1 | p. 22 | LT | |
| Keat's Grove | NW3 | p. 20 | ES | 236 |
| Kemble Street | WC2 | p. 33 | EV | |
| Kendal Street | W2 | p. 33 | EZ | |
| Kennington Lane | SE11 | p. 26 | MZ | |
| Kennington Oval | SE11 | p. 26 | MZ | |
| Kennington Park Road | SE11 | p. 27 | NZ | |
| Kennington Road | SE1, SE11 | p. 26 | MZ | |
| Kensal Road | W10 | p. 20 | ET | |
| Kensington Church Street | W8 | p. 32 | AZ | 238 |
| Kensington Court | W8 | p. 30 | AQ | 241 |
| Kensington Court Place | W8 | p. 30 | AR | 242 |
| Kensington Gardens Square | W2 | p. 32 | BZ | 243 |
| Kensington Gore | SW7 | p. 30 | CQ | |
| Kensington Palace Gardens | W8 | p. 24 | FX | |
| Kensington Park Road | W11 | p. 20 | EV | |
| Kensington Place | W8 | p. 32 | AZ | |
| Kensington Road | W8, SW7 | p. 30 | BQ | |
| Kensington Square | W8 | p. 30 | AQ | |
| Kentish Town Road | NW1, NW5 | p. 22 | JS | |
| Kenway Road | SW5 | p. 24 | FZ | 245 |
| Kilburn Lane | W10, W9 | p. 20 | ET | |
| Kilburn Park Road | NW6 | p. 20 | ET | |
| King Edward Street | EC1 | p. 23 | OU | 247 |
| Kingly Street | W1 | p. 29 | DK | |
| King's Cross Road | WC1 | p. 22 | LT | |
| Kingsland Road | E2, E8 | p. 23 | PT | |
| King Street ST. JAMES'S | SW1 | p. 29 | EN | |
| King Street STRAND | WC2 | p. 33 | DX | |
| Kingsway | WC2 | p. 33 | EV | |
| King William Street | EC4 | p. 23 | PV | 250 |
| Knaresborough Place | SW5 | p. 30 | AS | |
| Ladbroke Grove | W10, W11 | p. 20 | EU | |
| Lambeth Bridge | SW1, SE1 | p. 26 | LY | |
| Lambeth Palace Road | SE1 | p. 26 | MY | |
| Lambeth Road | SE1 | p. 26 | MY | |
| Lambeth Walk | SE11 | p. 26 | MZ | |
| Lancaster Gate | W2 | p. 32 | CDZ | 256 |
| Lancaster Grove | NW3, | p. 21 | GS | |
| Lancaster Place | SW19 | p. 33 | EX | |
| Lancaster Terrace | W2 | p. 33 | DZ | 257 |
| Lansdowne Walk | W11 | p. 24 | EX | |
| Lauderdale Road | W9 | p. 20 | FT | |
| Launceston Place | W8 | p. 30 | BR | 259 |
| Lawn Road | NW3 | p. 20 | ES | |
| Leadenhall Street | EC3 | p. 23 | PV | 260 |
| Lees Place | W1 | p. 28 | AL | |
| Leicester Square | WC2 | p. 29 | GM | 261 |
| Leinster Gardens | W2 | p. 32 | CZ | |
| Leinster Square | W2 | p. 32 | AZ | |
| Leinster Terrace | W2 | p. 32 | CZ | |
| Lennox Gardens | NW10 | p. 31 | ES | |
| Lennox Gardens Mews | SW3 | p. 31 | ES | 263 |
| Lever Street | EC1 | p. 23 | OT | |
| Lexham Gardens | W8 | p. 30 | AS | |
| Lexington Street | W1 | p. 29 | EL | |
| Lillie Road | SW6 | p. 24 | EZ | |
| Lincoln's Inn Fields | WC2 | p. 33 | EV | |
| Lisle Street | WC2 | p. 29 | GL | |
| Lisson Grove | NW1, NW8 | p. 21 | GT | |
| Little Boltons (The) | SW10 | p. 30 | BU | |
| Little Britain | EC1 | p. 23 | OU | 264 |
| Liverpool Road | N1, N7 | p. 22 | MS | |
| Liverpool Street | EC2 | p. 23 | PU | |
| Lloyd Baker Street | WC1 | p. 22 | MT | 265 |
| Lombard Street | EC3 | p. 23 | PV | 268 |
| London Bridge | SE1, EC4 | p. 27 | PX | |
| London Road | SE1 | p. 27 | NY | |
| London Street | W2 | p. 33 | DZ | |
| London Wall | EC2 | p. 23 | OU | |
| Long Acre | WC2 | p. 33 | DX | |
| Long Lane CITY | EC1 | p. 23 | OU | 270 |
| Long Lane SOUTHWARK | SE1 | p. 27 | PY | |
| Lothbury | EC2 | p. 23 | PU | 273 |
| Lots Road | SW10 | p. 24 | FZ | |
| Loudoun Road | NW8 | p. 20 | FS | |
| Lower Belgrave Street | SW1 | p. 32 | AX | |
| Lower Grosvenor Place | SW1 | p. 32 | BX | 274 |
| Lower Marsh | SE1 | p. 26 | MY | 277 |
| Lower Sloane Street | SW1 | p. 31 | FT | |
| Lower Terrace | NW3 | p. 20 | ES | |
| Lower Thames Street | EC3 | p. 23 | PV | 278 |
| Lowndes Square | SW1 | p. 31 | FQ | |
| Lowndes Street | SW1 | p. 31 | FR | |
| Luke Street | EC2 | p. 23 | PT | |
| Lupus Street | SW1 | p. 26 | JZ | |
| Lyall Street | SW1 | p. 31 | FR | |
| Lyndhurst Road | NW3 | p. 20 | ES | |
| Macklin Street | WC2 | p. 33 | DV | |
| Maddox Street | W1 | p. 29 | DK | |
| Maida Avenue | W2 | p. 20 | FU | |
| Maida Vale | W9 | p. 20 | FT | |
| Maiden Lane | WC2 | p. 33 | DY | |
| Mall (The) | SW1 | p. 29 | FP | |
| Malvern Road | NW6 | p. 20 | ET | |
| Manchester Square | W1 | p. 28 | AJ | 281 |
| Manchester Street | W1 | p. 28 | AH | |
| Manor Place | SE17 | p. 27 | OZ | |
| Manresa Road | SW3 | p. 31 | DU | |
| Mansell Street | E1 | p. 23 | PV | 282 |
| Marble Arch | W1 | p. 33 | EZ | |
| Margaret Street | W1 | p. 29 | DJ | |
| Market Place | W1 | p. 29 | DJ | 286 |
| Market Road | N7 | p. 22 | LS | |
| Markham Street | SW3 | p. 31 | ET | |
| Marlborough Place | NW8 | p. 20 | FT | |
| Marloes Road | W8 | p. 24 | FY | |
| Marshall Street | W1 | p. 29 | EK | |
| Marsham Street | SW1 | p. 26 | LY | |
| Marylebone High Street | W1 | p. 21 | IU | |
| Marylebone Lane | W1 | p. 28 | BJ | 287 |
| Marylebone Road | NW1 | p. 21 | HU | |
| Melbury Road | W14 | p. 24 | EY | |
| Merrick Square | SE1 | p. 27 | OY | |
| Merton Rise | NW3 | p. 21 | HS | |
| Midland Road | NW1 | p. 22 | LT | |
| Miles Street | SW8 | p. 26 | LZ | 290 |
| Millbank | SW1 | p. 26 | LY | |
| Milner Street | SW3 | p. 31 | ES | |
| Minories | EC3 | p. 23 | PV | |
| Monmouth Street | WC2 | p. 33 | DX | |
| Montagu Square | W1 | p. 28 | AH | |
| Montpelier Square | SW7 | p. 31 | EQ | |
| Montpelier Street | SW7 | p. 31 | ER | |
| Montpelier Walk | SW7 | p. 31 | DR | |
| Moore Street | SW3 | p. 31 | ES | |
| Moorgate | EC2 | p. 23 | PU | |
| Moreland Street | EC1 | p. 23 | OT | 293 |
| Mortimer Street | W1 | p. 22 | KU | |
| Moscow Road | W2 | p. 32 | BZ | |
| Mossop Street | SW3 | p. 31 | ES | |
| Mount Row | W1 | p. 28 | BM | |
| Mount Street | W1 | p. 28 | BM | |
| Munster Road | SW6 | p. 24 | EZ | |
| Musard Road | W6 | p. 24 | EZ | |
| Museum Street | WC1 | p. 33 | DV | 294 |
| Myddelton Street | EC1 | p. 23 | NT | 296 |
| Nassington Road | NW3 | p. 20 | ES | 297 |
| Neal Street | WC2 | p. 33 | DV | |
| Neate Street | SE5 | p. 27 | PZ | |
| Netherhall Gardens | NW3 | p. 20 | ES | |
| Nevern Place | SW5 | p. 24 | EZ | 298 |
| Nevern Square | SW5 | p. 24 | EZ | 299 |
| Neville Terrace | SW7 | p. 30 | CT | 300 |
| New Bridge Street | EC4 | p. 23 | NV | 301 |
| Newburn Street | SE11 | p. 26 | MZ | |
| New Cavendish Street | W1 | p. 28 | BH | |
| New Change | EC4 | p. 23 | OV | 304 |
| New Church Road | SE5 | p. 27 | PZ | |
| Newcomen Street | SE1 | p. 27 | PX | |
| New End Square | NW3 | p. 20 | ES | 305 |
| Newgate Street | EC1 | p. 23 | OU | |
| Newington Butts | SE1, SE11 | p. 27 | OZ | 306 |
| Newington Causeway | SE1 | p. 27 | OY | 307 |
| New Kent Road | SE1 | p. 27 | OY | |
| Newman Street | W1 | p. 22 | KU | |
| New North Road | N1 | p. 23 | OS | |
| New Oxford Street | WC1 | p. 33 | DV | 308 |
| New Row | WC2 | p. 33 | DX | |
| New Square | WC2 | p. 33 | EV | |
| Newton Road | W2 | p. 32 | BZ | |
| Newton Street | WC2 | p. 33 | DV | 309 |
| Nine Elms Lane | SW8 | p. 26 | KZ | |
| Noel Street | W1 | p. 29 | EJ | |

| | | | | |
|---|---|---|---|---|
| Norfolk Crescent | W2 | p. 33 | EZ | 310 |
| Norfolk Square | W2 | p. 33 | DZ | 313 |
| North Audley Street | W1 | p. 28 | AK | 314 |
| North Carriage Drive | W2 | p. 33 | EZ | |
| North End Road | W14, SW6 | p. 24 | EZ | |
| North Row | W1 | p. 28 | AL | |
| Northumberland Avenue | WC2 | p. 26 | LX | 317 |
| Notting Hill Gate | W11 | p. 32 | AZ | |
| Nutley Terrace | NW3 | p. 20 | ES | |
| Nuttall Street | N1 | p. 23 | PS | |
| Oakley Street | SW3 | p. 31 | DU | |
| Offord Road | N1 | p. 22 | MS | |
| Old Bailey | EC4 | p. 23 | NV | 318 |
| Old Broad Street | EC2 | p. 23 | PU | 319 |
| Old Brompton Road | SW7, SW5 | p. 30 | BT | |
| Old Burlington Street | W1 | p. 29 | DM | 322 |
| Old Church Street | SW3 | p. 30 | CU | |
| Old Compton Street | W1 | p. 29 | GK | 323 |
| Old Kent Road | SE1, SE15 | p. 27 | PZ | |
| Old Marylebone Road | NW1 | p. 21 | HU | 324 |
| Old Park Lane | W1 | p. 28 | BP | |
| Old Street | EC1 | p. 23 | OT | |
| Olympia Way | W14 | p. 24 | EY | 326 |
| Onslow Gardens | SW7 | p. 30 | CT | |
| Onslow Square | SW7 | p. 30 | CT | |
| Orange Street | WC2 | p. 29 | GM | |
| Orchard Street | W1 | p. 28 | AK | |
| Ordnance Hill | NW8 | p. 21 | GS | |
| Orme Court | W2 | p. 32 | BZ | 328 |
| Ormonde Gate | SW3 | p. 31 | FU | 329 |
| Ornan Road | NW3 | p. 20 | ES | 331 |
| Ossulton Street | NW1 | p. 22 | LT | |
| Outer Circle | NW1 | p. 21 | HT | |
| Oxford Circus | W1 | p. 29 | DJ | |
| Oxford Square | W2 | p. 33 | EZ | 332 |
| Paddington Street | W1 | p. 21 | IU | 333 |
| Page Street | SW1 | p. 26 | LZ | |
| Page's Walk | SE1 | p. 27 | PY | |
| Palace Court | W2 | p. 32 | BZ | |
| Palace Gardens Terrace | W8 | p. 32 | AZ | 335 |
| Palace Gate | W8 | p. 30 | BQ | |
| Palace Street | SW1 | p. 32 | BX | |
| Pall Mall | SW1 | p. 29 | FN | |
| Palmer Street | SW1 | p. 32 | CV | |
| Pancras Road | NW1 | p. 22 | KS | |
| Panton Street | SW1 | p. 29 | FM | 336 |
| Parade (The) | SW11 | p. 25 | HZ | |
| Park Crescent | W1 | p. 21 | IU | 337 |
| Parker Street | WC2 | p. 33 | DV | |
| Parkgate Road | SW11 | p. 25 | HZ | |
| Park Lane | W1 | p. 28 | AM | |
| Park Road | NW1, NW8 | p. 21 | HT | |
| Park Street | W1 | p. 28 | AL | |
| Park Village East | NW1 | p. 21 | JS | |
| Park Walk | SW10 | p. 30 | CU | |
| Parkway | NW1 | p. 21 | JS | |
| Parliament Hill | NW3 | p. 20 | ES | |
| Parliament Street | SW1 | p. 26 | LY | 340 |
| Parry Street | SW8 | p. 26 | LZ | 341 |
| Paul Street | EC2 | p. 23 | PT | |
| Pelham Street | SW7 | p. 31 | DS | |
| Pembridge Gardens | W2 | p. 32 | AZ | |
| Pembridge Road | W11 | p. 32 | AZ | |
| Pembridge Square | W2 | p. 32 | AZ | |
| Pembridge Villas | W11 | p. 32 | AZ | |
| Pembrocke Gardens | W8 | p. 24 | EY | 342 |
| Pembrocke Road | W8 | p. 24 | EZ | |
| Penn Street | N1 | p. 23 | PS | 343 |
| Penton Place | WC1 | p. 27 | OS | |
| Penton Rise | WC1 | p. 22 | MT | 344 |
| Penton Street | N1 | p. 22 | MT | 345 |
| Pentonville Road | N1 | p. 22 | LT | |
| Penywern Road | SW5 | p. 24 | FZ | 347 |
| Percival Street | EC1 | p. 23 | NT | |
| Petty France | SW1 | p. 32 | CV | |
| Philbeach Gardens | SW5 | p. 24 | EZ | 348 |
| Piccadilly Circus | W1 | p. 29 | FM | |
| Pilgrimage Street | SE1 | p. 27 | PY | 349 |
| Pimlico Road | SW1 | p. 25 | IZ | |
| Pitfield Street | N1 | p. 23 | PT | |
| Poland Street | W1 | p. 29 | EJ | |
| Pond Street | NW3 | p. 20 | ES | |
| Pont Street | SW1 | p. 31 | ER | |
| Poole Street | N1 | p. 23 | PS | 350 |
| Porchester Gardens | W2 | p. 32 | BZ | |
| Porchester Road | W2 | p. 20 | FU | 351 |
| Porchester Terrace | W2 | p. 32 | CZ | |
| Portland Place | W1 | p. 21 | JU | |
| Portland Street | SE17 | p. 27 | PZ | |
| Portman Square | W1 | p. 28 | AJ | |
| Potman Street | W1 | p. 28 | AK | |
| Portugal Street | WC2 | p. 33 | EV | |
| Poultry | EC2 | p. 23 | OV | 352 |
| Praed Street | W2 | p. 21 | GV | |
| Pratt Street | NW1 | p. 22 | KS | |
| Primrose Hill Road | NW3 | p. 21 | HS | |
| Prince Albert Road | NW1, NW8 | p. 21 | HS | |
| Prince Consort Road | SW7 | p. 30 | CR | |
| Prince's Gardens | SW7 | p. 30 | CR | 356 |
| Prince's Street | W1 | p. 29 | DK | |
| Princes Street | EC2 | p. 23 | PV | 357 |
| Queen Anne's Gate | SW1 | p. 26 | KY | |
| Queen Anne Street | W1 | p. 28 | BH | |
| Queensberry Place | SW7 | p. 30 | CS | 360 |
| Queensborough Terrace | W2 | p. 32 | CZ | |
| Queen's Circus | SW8 | p. 25 | IZ | 361 |
| Queen's Gardens | W2 | p. 32 | CZ | 362 |
| Queen's Gate | SW7 | p. 30 | BQ | |
| Queen's Gate Gardens | SW7 | p. 30 | BR | |
| Queen's Gate Place | SW7 | p. 30 | BR | 363 |
| Queen's Gate Terrace | SW7 | p. 30 | BR | |
| Queen's Grove | NW8 | p. 21 | GS | |
| Queen Street | EC4 | p. 23 | OV | 365 |
| Queen's Walk | SW1 | p. 29 | DN | |
| Queensway | W2 | p. 32 | BZ | |
| Queen Victoria Street | EC4 | p. 23 | OV | |
| Radnor Place | W2 | p. 33 | DZ | |
| Radnor Walk | SW3 | p. 31 | EU | |
| Randolph Avenue | W9 | p. 20 | FT | |
| Randoplh Street | NW1 | p. 22 | KS | 366 |
| Rawlings Street | SW3 | p. 31 | ES | |
| Redcliffe Gardens | SW10 | p. 30 | AU | |
| Redcliffe Square | SW10 | p. 30 | AU | |
| Redesdale Street | SW3 | p. 31 | EU | 367 |
| Red Lion Street | WC1 | p. 22 | MU | |
| Reeves Mews | W1 | p. 28 | AM | |
| Regency Street | SW1 | p. 26 | KZ | |
| Regent's Park Road | NW1 | p. 21 | HS | |
| Richmond Avenue | N1 | p. 22 | MS | |
| Robert Street | NW1 | p. 22 | JT | |
| Rochester Row | SW1 | p. 32 | CY | |
| Rodney Road | N1 | p. 27 | OZ | |
| Roland Gardens | SW7 | p. 30 | BT | |
| Roman Way | N7 | p. 22 | MS | |
| Romilly Street | W1 | p. 29 | GL | 368 |
| Rosebery Avenue | EC1 | p. 22 | MT | |
| Rosslyn Hill | NW3 | p. 20 | ES | |
| Rossmore Road | NW1 | p. 21 | HT | 369 |
| Royal College Street | NW1 | p. 22 | KS | |
| Royal Crescent | W11 | p. 24 | EX | 371 |
| Royal Hospital Road | SW3 | p. 31 | FU | |
| Rupert Street | W1 | p. 29 | FL | |
| Russell Square | WC1 | p. 22 | LU | |
| Russell Street | WC2 | p. 33 | DX | |
| Rutland Gate | SW7 | p. 31 | DQ | |
| Rylston Road | SW6 | p. 24 | EZ | |
| Sackville Street | W1 | p. 29 | EM | |
| St. Albans Grove | W8 | p. 28 | AR | |
| St. Andrews Street | EC4 | p. 23 | NU | 372 |
| St. Bride Street | EC4 | p. 23 | NV | 376 |
| St. George's Drive | SW1 | p. 26 | KZ | |
| St. George's Road | SE1 | p. 27 | NY | |
| St. George's Square | SW1 | p. 26 | KZ | |
| St. George Street | W1 | p. 29 | DL | |
| St. Giles Circus | W1, WC1, WC2 | p. 29 | GJ | |
| St. Giles High Street | WC2 | p. 33 | DV | 377 |
| St. James's Place | SW1 | p. 29 | EN | |
| St. James's Square | SW1 | p. 29 | FN | |
| St. James's Street | SW1 | p. 29 | EN | |
| St. James Street | E17 | p. 33 | DX | |
| St. John Street | EC1 | p. 23 | NT | |
| St. John's Wood High Street | NW8 | p. 21 | GT | 378 |
| St. John's Wood Park | NW8 | p. 21 | GS | 379 |
| St. John's Wood Road | NW8 | p. 21 | GT | |
| St. Leonard's Terrace | SW3 | p. 31 | FU | |
| St. Martin's Lane | WC2 | p. 33 | DY | |
| St. Martin's-le-Grand | EC1 | p. 23 | OU | 380 |
| St. Pancras Way | NW1 | p. 22 | KS | |
| St. Paul's Road | N1 | p. 23 | OS | |
| St. Petersburgh Place | W2 | p. 32 | BZ | |
| St. Peter's Street | N1 | p. 23 | OS | |
| St. Thomas Street | SE1 | p. 27 | PX | |
| Sardinia Street | WC2 | p. 33 | EV | 381 |
| Savile Row | W1 | p. 29 | DM | |
| Savoy Place | WC2 | p. 33 | DY | |
| Savoy Street | WC2 | p. 33 | EX | |
| Scarsdale Villas | W8 | p. 24 | EY | |
| Seagrave Road | SW6 | p. 24 | EZ | |
| Serle Street | WC2 | p. 33 | EV | |
| Serpentine Road | W2 | p. 28 | AP | |
| Seymour Street | W1, W2 | p. 28 | AK | |
| Shaftesbury Avenue | W1, WC2 | p. 29 | FL | |
| Sheffield Terrace | W8 | p. 24 | EX | |
| Shelton Street | WC2 | p. 33 | DX | |
| Shepherdess Walk | N1 | p. 23 | OT | |
| Shepherd Market | W1 | p. 28 | CN | |

| | | | | |
|---|---|---|---|---|
| Shepherd Street | W1 | p. 28 | BP | |
| Shirland Road | W9 | p. 20 | ET | |
| Shoreditch High Street | E1 | p. 23 | PT | 384 |
| Shorts Gardens | WC2 | p. 33 | DV | |
| Sidmouth Street | WC1 | p. 22 | LT | 385 |
| Sinclair Road | W14 | p. 24 | EY | |
| Sloane Avenue | SW3 | p. 31 | ET | |
| Sloane Square | SW1 | p. 31 | FT | |
| Smith Street | SW3 | p. 31 | EU | |
| Snows Fields | SE1 | p. 27 | PX | 386 |
| Soho Square | W1 | p. 29 | FJ | |
| Southampton Row | WC1 | p. 22 | LU | 387 |
| Southampton Street | WC2 | p. 33 | DX | 388 |
| South Audley Street | W1 | p. 28 | BM | |
| South Eaton Place | SW1 | p. 32 | AY | 389 |
| South End Road | NW3 | p. 20 | ES | |
| South Hill | NW3 | p. 20 | ES | 390 |
| South Lambeth Road | SW8 | p. 26 | LZ | |
| South Molton Street | W1 | p. 28 | BK | |
| South Parade | SW3 | p. 30 | CU | |
| South Place | EC2 | p. 23 | PU | 391 |
| South Street | W1 | p. 28 | BN | |
| South Terrace | SW7 | p. 31 | DS | |
| Southwark Bridge | SE1, EC4 | p. 27 | OV | 395 |
| Southwark Bridge Road | SE1 | p. 27 | OY | |
| Southwark Street | SE1 | p. 27 | OX | |
| Southwick Street | W2 | p. 33 | EZ | |
| Spa road | SE16 | p. 27 | PY | |
| Spencer Street | EC1 | p. 23 | NT | 398 |
| Spital Square | E1 | p. 23 | PU | 399 |
| Spring Street | W2 | p. 33 | DZ | |
| Stamford Street | SE1 | p. 26 | MX | |
| Stanhope Gardens | SW7 | p. 30 | BS | |
| Stanhope Place | W2 | p. 33 | EZ | 400 |
| Stanhope Terrace | W2 | p. 33 | DZ | |
| Star Road | W14 | p. 24 | EZ | |
| Storeys Gate | SW1 | p. 26 | LY | 402 |
| Strand | WC2 | p. 33 | DY | |
| Stratton Street | W1 | p. 29 | DN | |
| Sumner Place | SW7 | p. 30 | CT | |
| Sumner Street | SE1 | p. 27 | OX | |
| Sun Street | EC2 | p. 23 | PU | |
| Surrey Street | WC2 | p. 33 | EX | |
| Sussex Gardens | W2 | p. 33 | DZ | |
| Sussex Place | W2 | p. 33 | DZ | |
| Sussex Square | W2 | p. 33 | DZ | 404 |
| Sutherland Avenue | W9 | p. 20 | FU | |
| Sutherland Street | SW1 | p. 25 | JZ | |
| Swinton Street | WC1 | p. 22 | LT | |
| Sydney Place | SW7 | p. 31 | DT | 405 |
| Sydney Street | SW3 | p. 31 | DT | |
| Symons Street | SW3 | p. 31 | FT | 407 |
| Tabard Street | SE1 | p. 27 | OY | 408 |
| Tachbrook Street | SW1 | p. 26 | KZ | |
| Talgarth Road | W14, W6 | p. 24 | EZ | |
| Tavistock Place | WC1 | p. 22 | LT | |
| Tavistock Square | WC1 | p. 22 | LT | 409 |
| Tavistock Street | WC2 | p. 33 | DX | |
| Tedworth Square | SW3 | p. 31 | EU | |
| Temple Place | WC2 | p. 33 | EX | |
| Templeton Place | SW5 | p. 24 | EZ | 410 |
| Terminus Place | SW1 | p. 32 | BX | 412 |
| Thayer Street | W1 | p. 28 | BJ | 413 |
| Theobald's Road | WC1 | p. 22 | LU | |
| Thirleby Road | SW1 | p. 32 | CX | 416 |
| Thornhill Road | N1 | p. 22 | MS | |
| Threadneedle Street | EC2 | p. 23 | PV | 417 |
| Throgmorton Street | EC2 | p. 23 | PU | 418 |
| Thurloe Place | SW7 | p. 30 | CS | 420 |
| Thurloe Square | SW7 | p. 31 | DS | |
| Thurlow Street | SE17 | p. 27 | PZ | |
| Tilney Street | W1 | p. 28 | BN | 421 |
| Tite Street | SW3 | p. 31 | EU | |
| Tooley Street | SE1 | p. 27 | BX | |
| Tothill Street | SW1 | p. 26 | KY | |
| Tottenham Court Road | W1 | p. 22 | KU | |
| Tower Bridge | E1 | p. 27 | PX | |
| Tower Bridge Road | SE1 | p. 27 | PY | |
| Tower Hill | EC3 | p. 23 | PV | 425 |
| Trafalgar Avenue | SE15 | p. 27 | PZ | |
| Trafalgar Square | WC2, SW1 | p. 33 | DY | |
| Trebovir Road | SW5 | p. 24 | FZ | 426 |
| Tregunter Road | SW10 | p. 30 | BU | |
| Trevor Place | SW7 | p. 31 | EQ | |
| Trevor Square | SW7 | p. 31 | ER | |
| Trinity Church Square | SE1 | p. 27 | OY | |
| Trinity Street | SE1 | p. 27 | OY | |
| Tyers Street | SE11 | p. 26 | MZ | |
| Union Street | SE1 | p. 27 | NX | |
| Upper Belgrave Street | SW1 | p. 32 | AX | |
| Upper Berkeley Street | W1 | p. 33 | EZ | |
| Upper Brook Street | W1 | p. 28 | AM | |
| Upper Grosvenor Street | W1 | p. 28 | AM | |
| Upper Ground | SE1 | p. 27 | NX | 428 |
| Upper St. Martin's Lane | WC2 | p. 33 | DX | 430 |
| Upper Street | N1 | p. 23 | NS | |
| Upper Thames Street | EC4 | p. 23 | OV | 431 |
| Upper Woburn Place | WC1 | p. 22 | LT | 432 |
| Vale (The) | SW3 | p. 30 | CU | |
| Vanston Place | SW6 | p.24 | EZ | |
| Vassal Road | SW9 | p. 27 | NZ | |
| Vauxhall Bridge | SW1, SE1 | p. 26 | LZ | |
| Vauxhall Bridge Road | SW1 | p. 32 | BY | |
| Vauxhall Street | SE11 | p. 26 | MZ | |
| Vauxhall Walk | SE11 | p. 26 | LZ | |
| Vere Street | W1 | p. 28 | BJ | |
| Victoria Embankment | SW1 WC2, EC4 | p. 33 | DY | |
| Victoria Grove | W8 | p. 30 | BR | |
| Victoria Road KENSINGTON | W8 | p. 30 | BQ | |
| Victoria Street | SW1 | p. 32 | BX | |
| Vigo Street | W1 | p. 29 | EM | |
| Villiers Street | WC2 | p. 33 | DY | |
| Vincent Square | SW1 | p. 26 | KZ | |
| Vincent Street | SW1 | p. 26 | LZ | 436 |
| Virginia Road | E2 | p. 23 | PT | |
| Walterton Road | W9 | p. 20 | ET | |
| Walton Street | SW3 | p. 31 | ES | |
| Walworth Road | SE17 | p. 27 | OZ | |
| Wandsworth Road | SW8 | p. 26 | LZ | |
| Wardour Street | W1 | p. 29 | FJ | |
| Warrington Crescent | W9 | p. 20 | FT | |
| Warwick Avenue | W2, W9 | p. 20 | FU | 441 |
| Warwick Road | SW5, W14 | p. 24 | EZ | |
| Warwick Street | W1 | p. 29 | EM | 444 |
| Warwick Way | SW1 | p. 25 | JZ | |
| Waterloo Bridge | WC2, SE1 | p. 33 | EY | |
| Waterloo Place | SW1 | p. 29 | FN | |
| Waterloo Road | SE1 | p. 27 | NY | |
| Waverton Street | W1 | p. 28 | BN | |
| Webber Street | SE1 | p. 27 | NY | |
| Weighhouse Street | W1 | p. 28 | BK | |
| Welbeck Street | W1 | p. 28 | BH | |
| Wellington Road | NW8 | p. 21 | GT | |
| Wellington Street | WC2 | p. 33 | DX | |
| Wells Street | W1 | p. 29 | EJ | |
| Wells Way | SE5 | p. 27 | PZ | |
| Well Walk | NW3 | p. 20 | ES | |
| Westbourne Crescent | W2 | p. 33 | DZ | 448 |
| Westbourne Grove | W2, W11 | p. 32 | AZ | |
| Westbourne Park Road | W2, W11 | p. 20 | EU | |
| Westbourne Park Villas | W2 | p. 20 | FU | 449 |
| Westbourne Street | W2 | p. 33 | DZ | 450 |
| Westbourne Terrace | W2 | p. 33 | DZ | |
| Westbourne Road | N7 | p. 22 | MS | |
| Westbourne Terrace Road | W2 | p. 20 | FU | 452 |
| West Cromwell Road | SW5, W14 | p. 24 | EZ | |
| West Halkin Street | SW1 | p. 31 | FR | |
| Westminster Bridge | SW1, SE1 | p. 26 | LY | |
| Westminster Bridge Road | SE1 | p. 26 | MY | |
| Weston Street | SE1 | p. 27 | PY | |
| West Smithfield | EC1 | p. 23 | NU | 454 |
| Westway | N18 | p. 20 | EU | |
| Wetherby Gardens | SW5 | p. 30 | BT | |
| Wharfdale Road | N1 | p. 22 | LS | 455 |
| Wharf Road | N1 | p. 23 | OT | |
| Whiston Road | E2 | p. 23 | PS | |
| Whitcomb Street | WC2 | p. 29 | GM | |
| Whitechapel High Street | E1 | p. 23 | PU | 456 |
| Whitecross Street | EC1, EC2 | p. 23 | OT | |
| Whitehall | SW1 | p. 26 | LX | |
| Whitehall Court | SW1 | p. 26 | LX | 460 |
| Whitehall Place | SW1 | p. 26 | LX | 462 |
| Whitehead's Grove | SW3 | p. 31 | ET | 463 |
| Whitmore Road | N1 | p. 23 | PS | 464 |
| Wigmore Street | W1 | p. 28 | BJ | |
| Wild Street | WC2 | p. 33 | DV | |
| William IV Street | WC2 | p. 33 | DY | 467 |
| William Street | SW1 | p. 31 | FQ | 468 |
| Willoughby Road | NW3 | p. 20 | ES | 470 |
| Willow Road | NW3 | p. 20 | ES | |
| Willow Walk | SE1 | p. 27 | PY | |
| Wilson Street | EC2 | p. 23 | PU | |
| Wilton Place | SW1 | p. 31 | FQ | |
| Wilton Road | SW1 | p. 32 | BY | |
| Wilton Street | SW1 | p. 32 | AX | |
| Wimpole Street | W1 | p. 28 | BH | |
| Woburn Place | WC1 | p. 22 | LT | |
| Woods Mews | W1 | p. 28 | AL | |
| Wormwood Street | EC2 | p. 23 | PU | 472 |
| Worship Street | EC2 | p. 23 | PU | |
| Wyndham Road | SE5 | p. 27 | OZ | |
| York Road | SE1 | p. 27 | MY | |
| York Way | N1, N7 | p. 22 | LS | |
| Young Street | W8 | p. 30 | AQ | |

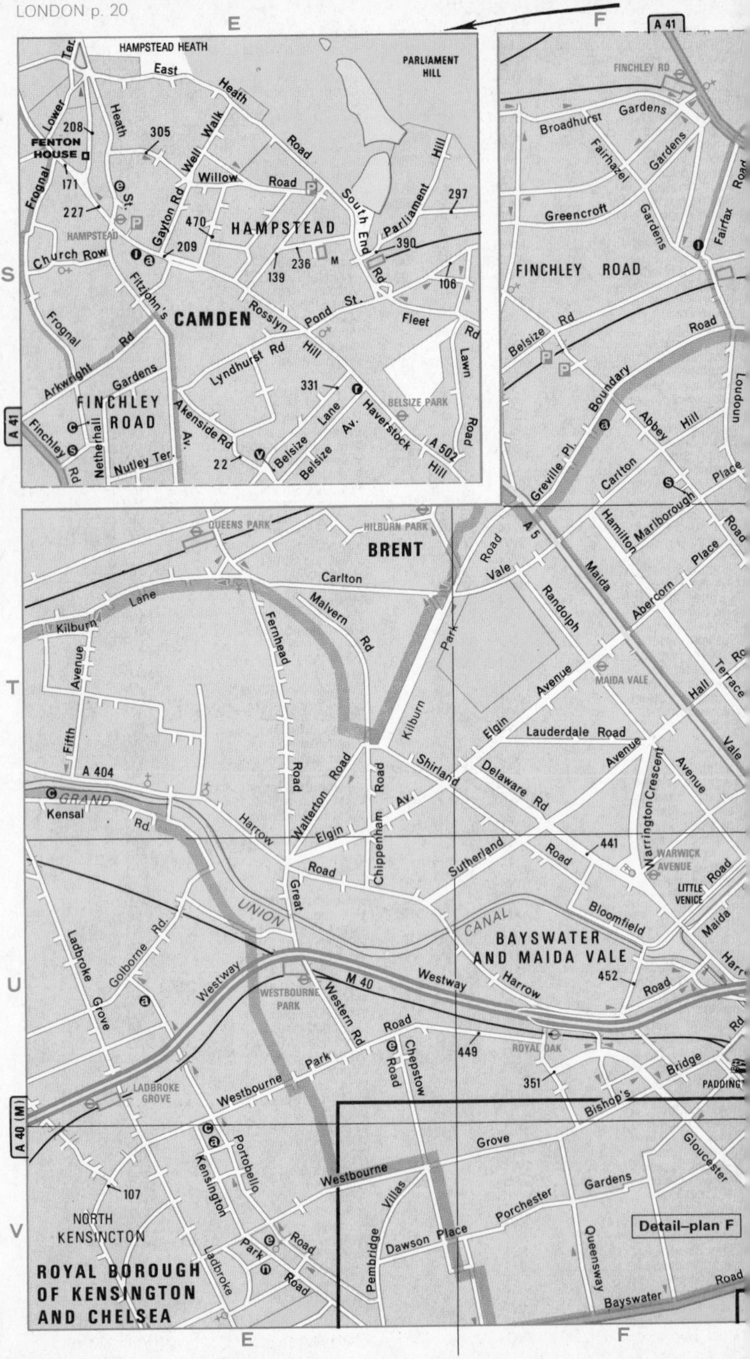
E
F
S
T
U
V
A 41
HAMPSTEAD HEATH
PARLIAMENT HILL
East Heath Road
Lower Ter.
FENTON HOUSE
Frognal
Heath St.
Well Walk
Willow Road
Gayton Rd
South End Rd
Parliament Hill
HAMPSTEAD
Church Row
Fitzjohn's
CAMDEN
Rosslyn Hill
Pond St.
Fleet Rd
Lawn Road
Lyndhurst Rd
Arkwright Rd
Gardens
FINCHLEY ROAD
Netherhall
Nutley Ter.
Akenside Rd
Belsize Lane
Belsize Av.
Haverstock Hill
A 502
BELSIZE PARK
208
305
171
227
470
209
139
236
390
297
106
331
22
FINCHLEY RD
Broadhurst Gardens
Fairhazel Gardens
Greencroft Gardens
Fairfax Road
Belsize Rd
Boundary Road
Abbey Hill
Greville Pl.
Carlton
Loudoun
Marlborough Place
Hamilton
QUEENS PARK
KILBURN PARK
BRENT
A 5
Vale Road
Carlton
Malvern Rd
Kilburn Lane
Fernhead Road
Park
Kilburn
Randolph
Maida
Abercorn Place
MAIDA VALE
Hall Road
Terrace
Vale
Fifth Avenue
A 404
GRAND
Kensal Rd
Harrow Road
Walterton Road
Chippenham Road
Elgin Av.
Elgin Avenue
Lauderdale Road
Shirland Road
Delaware Rd
Sutherland Avenue
Warrington Crescent
WARWICK AVENUE
LITTLE VENICE
441
UNION
CANAL
Great Western Rd
Bloomfield Road
BAYSWATER AND MAIDA VALE
Ladbroke Grove
Golborne Rd.
Westway
M 40
WESTBOURNE PARK
Harrow Road
452
ROYAL OAK
449
Chepstow Road
351
Bishop's Bridge Rd
PADDINGTON
LADBROKE GROVE
Westbourne Park Road
A 40 (M)
Grove
Portobello
Kensington Park Road
Westbourne Grove
Gloucester
Gardens
Porchester
107
Villas
Pembridge
Dawson Place
Queensway
Detail-plan F
NORTH KENSINGTON
ROYAL BOROUGH OF KENSINGTON AND CHELSEA
Ladbroke
Bayswater Road

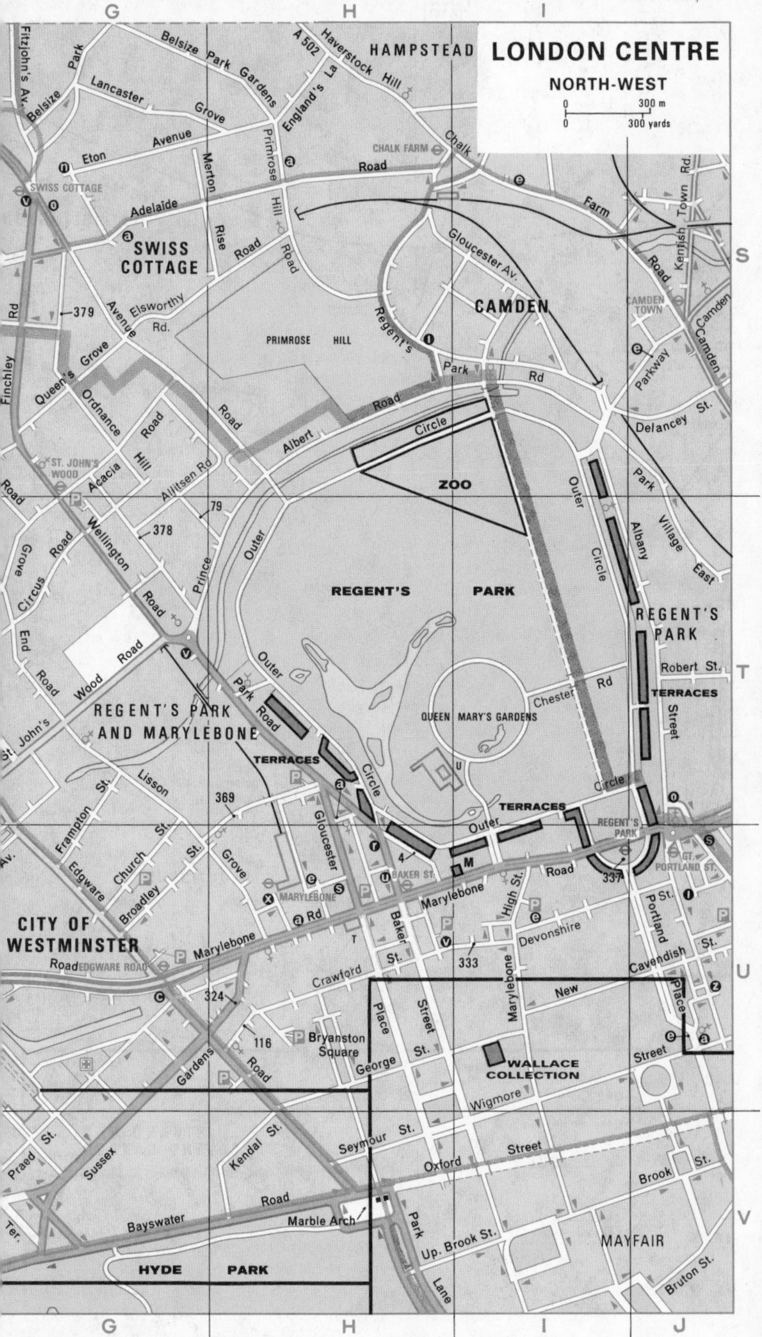
LONDON CENTRE
NORTH-WEST
0 300 m
0 300 yards
HAMPSTEAD
SWISS COTTAGE
CAMDEN
PRIMROSE HILL
ZOO
REGENT'S PARK
QUEEN MARY'S GARDENS
REGENT'S PARK AND MARYLEBONE
TERRACES
CITY OF WESTMINSTER
WALLACE COLLECTION
HYDE PARK
MAYFAIR
Bryanston Square
Marble Arch
CHALK FARM
SWISS COTTAGE
ST. JOHN'S WOOD
CAMDEN TOWN
BAKER ST.
MARYLEBONE
EDGWARE ROAD
REGENT'S PARK
GT. PORTLAND ST.
G
H
I
J
S
T
U
V



3

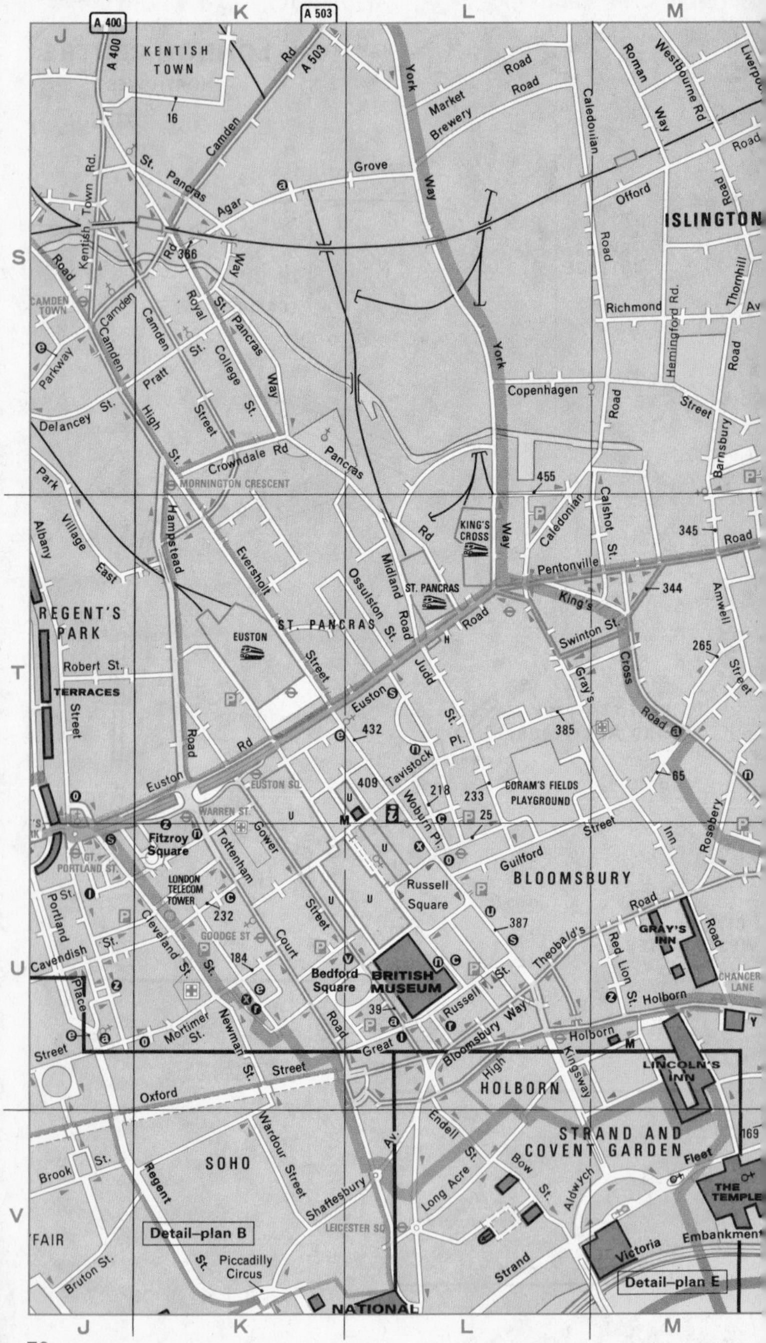
J
K
L
M
A 400
A 503
KENTISH TOWN
16
Camden Rd
York Way
Market Road
Brewery Road
Caledonian Road
Roman Way
Westbourne Rd
Liverpool Road
St. Pancras Way
Grove
Agar
Offord Road
ISLINGTON
Kentish Town Rd.
366
Camden Road
CAMDEN TOWN
Royal College St.
Camden St.
Camden High St.
Pratt St.
Parkway
Delancey St.
Richmond Av
Hemingford Rd.
Thornhill Road
Copenhagen Street
Barnsbury
Crowndale Rd
Pancras Rd
MORNINGTON CRESCENT
455
Park Village East
Albany Street
Hampstead Road
Eversholt Street
Ossulston St.
Midland Road
KING'S CROSS
Caledonian Road
Calshot St.
345
Pentonville Road
344
King's Cross Road
Swinton St.
Amwell Street
ST. PANCRAS
REGENT'S PARK
EUSTON
265
Robert St.
TERRACES
Euston Road
Judd St.
Gray's Inn Road
432
385
Tavistock Pl.
65
EUSTON SQ.
409
218
233
CORAM'S FIELDS PLAYGROUND
25
WARREN ST.
Woburn Pl.
Fitzroy Square
Tottenham Court Road
Gower Street
Guilford Street
Rosebery
GT. PORTLAND ST.
LONDON TELECOM TOWER
232
Russell Square
BLOOMSBURY
Portland Place
387
Theobald's Road
GRAY'S INN
GOODGE ST
Cleveland St.
Red Lion St.
Cavendish Place
184
Bedford Square
BRITISH MUSEUM
CHANCERY LANE
Holborn
39
Russell St.
Bloomsbury Way
Mortimer St.
Newman St.
Great Russell St.
Holborn
Kingsway
Oxford Street
High Holborn
LINCOLN'S INN
HOLBORN
Endell St.
STRAND AND COVENT GARDEN
169
Brook St.
SOHO
Wardour Street
Fleet
Regent St.
Shaftesbury Av.
Long Acre
Bow St.
Aldwych
THE TEMPLE
V
U
T
S
MAYFAIR
Detail–plan B
LEICESTER SQ
Victoria Embankment
Bruton St.
Piccadilly Circus
Strand
Detail–plan E
NATIONAL

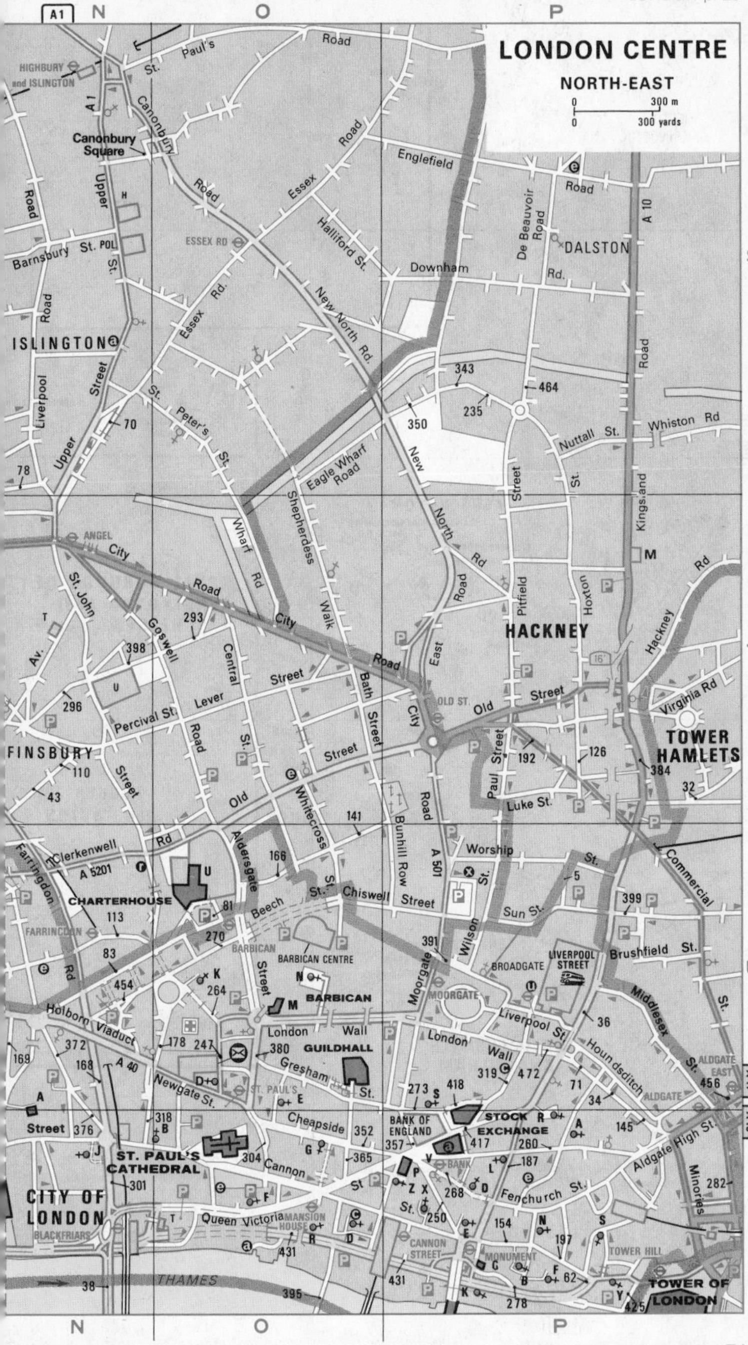
LONDON CENTRE
NORTH-EAST
0 300 m
0 300 yards
N O P
S T U V
A1
HIGHBURY and ISLINGTON
Canonbury Square
Canonbury
St. Paul's Road
Essex Road
Englefield Road
De Beauvoir Road
DALSTON
Halliford St.
Downham Rd.
ESSEX RD
Barnsbury St.
Upper St.
ISLINGTON
Liverpool Road
New North Rd.
Whiston Rd
Nuttall St.
Eagle Wharf Road
Shepherdess Walk
Kingsland Road
A 10
ANGEL
City Road
St. John St.
Goswell Rd
Central St.
Wharf Rd
East Road
Pitfield Street
Hoxton St.
HACKNEY
Hackney Rd
Virginia Rd
TOWER HAMLETS
OLD ST.
Old Street
Lever Street
Bath Street
Percival St.
FINSBURY
Paul Street
Luke St.
Whitecross St.
Bunhill Row
Worship St.
Commercial St.
Clerkenwell Rd
A 5201
Farringdon Rd
CHARTERHOUSE
FARRINGDON
Aldersgate Street
Beech St.
Chiswell Street
Sun St.
Wilson St.
Brushfield St.
BARBICAN
BARBICAN CENTRE
Moorgate
MOORGATE
BROADGATE
LIVERPOOL STREET
Liverpool St.
Middlesex St.
Holborn Viaduct
London Wall
GUILDHALL
Gresham St.
Houndsditch
ALDGATE EAST
ALDGATE
A 40
Newgate St.
ST. PAUL'S
Cheapside
BANK OF ENGLAND
STOCK EXCHANGE
BANK
Aldgate High St.
A 11
A 13
ST. PAUL'S CATHEDRAL
Cannon St.
Fenchurch St.
Minories
CITY OF LONDON
BLACKFRIARS
Queen Victoria St.
MANSION HOUSE
CANNON STREET
MONUMENT
TOWER HILL
TOWER OF LONDON
THAMES
A 501

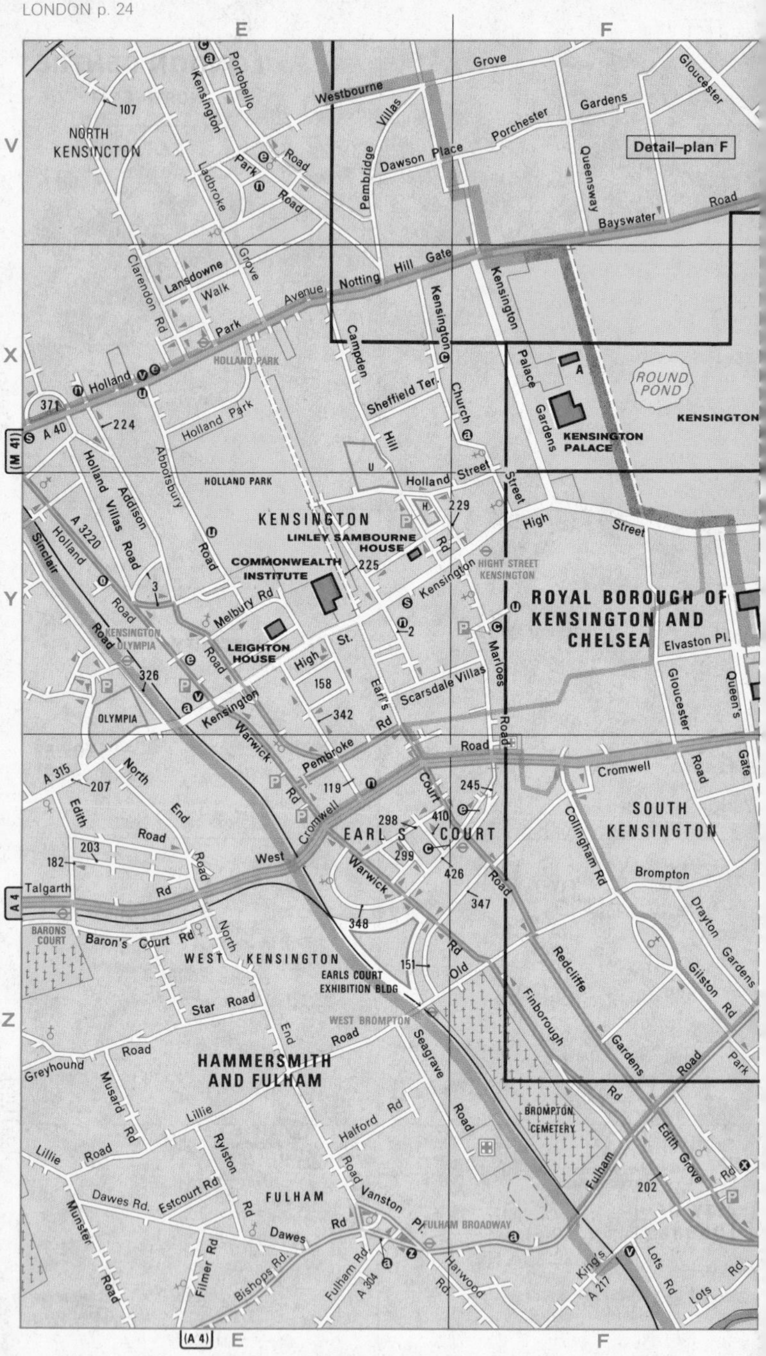

E
F
V
X
Y
Z
Detail–plan F
NORTH KENSINGTON
Westbourne
Grove
Gardens
Porchester
Gloucester
Portobello
Kensington
Park
Road
Ladbroke
Pembridge
Villas
Dawson Place
Queensway
Bayswater
Road
Lansdowne
Walk
Clarendon Rd
Grove
Avenue
Notting
Hill
Gate
Kensington
Campden
Hill
Sheffield Ter.
Church
Palace
Gardens
KENSINGTON PALACE
ROUND POND
KENSINGTON
HOLLAND PARK
Holland
Holland Park
Abbotsbury
Holland Villas
Addison
Road
A 40
M 41
A 3220
Sinclair
Holland Street
Street
High
Street
KENSINGTON
LINLEY SAMBOURNE HOUSE
COMMONWEALTH INSTITUTE
HIGH STREET KENSINGTON
Melbury Rd
Kensington
LEIGHTON HOUSE
High
St.
KENSINGTON OLYMPIA
OLYMPIA
ROYAL BOROUGH OF KENSINGTON AND CHELSEA
Elvaston Pl.
Gloucester
Queen's
Gate
Marloes
Scarsdale Villas
Earl's
Rd
Kensington
Warwick
Pembroke
Road
Cromwell
A 315
North
End
Road
Edith
Rd
EARL'S COURT
Court
Road
SOUTH KENSINGTON
Collingham Rd
Brompton
Drayton
Gardens
Gilston
Rd
West
Cromwell
Talgarth
Rd
A 4
BARONS COURT
Baron's Court Rd
North
WEST KENSINGTON
EARLS COURT EXHIBITION BLDG
Old
Redcliffe
Finborough
Gardens
Road
Park
WEST BROMPTON
Star Road
End
Road
Seagrave
Road
BROMPTON CEMETERY
Greyhound
Road
HAMMERSMITH AND FULHAM
Musard
Rd
Lillie
Lillie
Road
Rylston
Rd
Halford
Rd
Road
Vanston
Pl.
Edith
Grove
Rd
Fulham
Dawes Rd.
Estcourt Rd
FULHAM
FULHAM BROADWAY
Dawes
Munster
Road
Filmer Rd
Bishops Rd.
Fulham Rd.
A 304
Rd
Harwood
King's
A 217
Lots
Rd
Lots
Rd
(A 4)
107
371
224
3
326
225
229
2
158
342
207
203
182
119
245
298
410
299
426
347
348
151
202

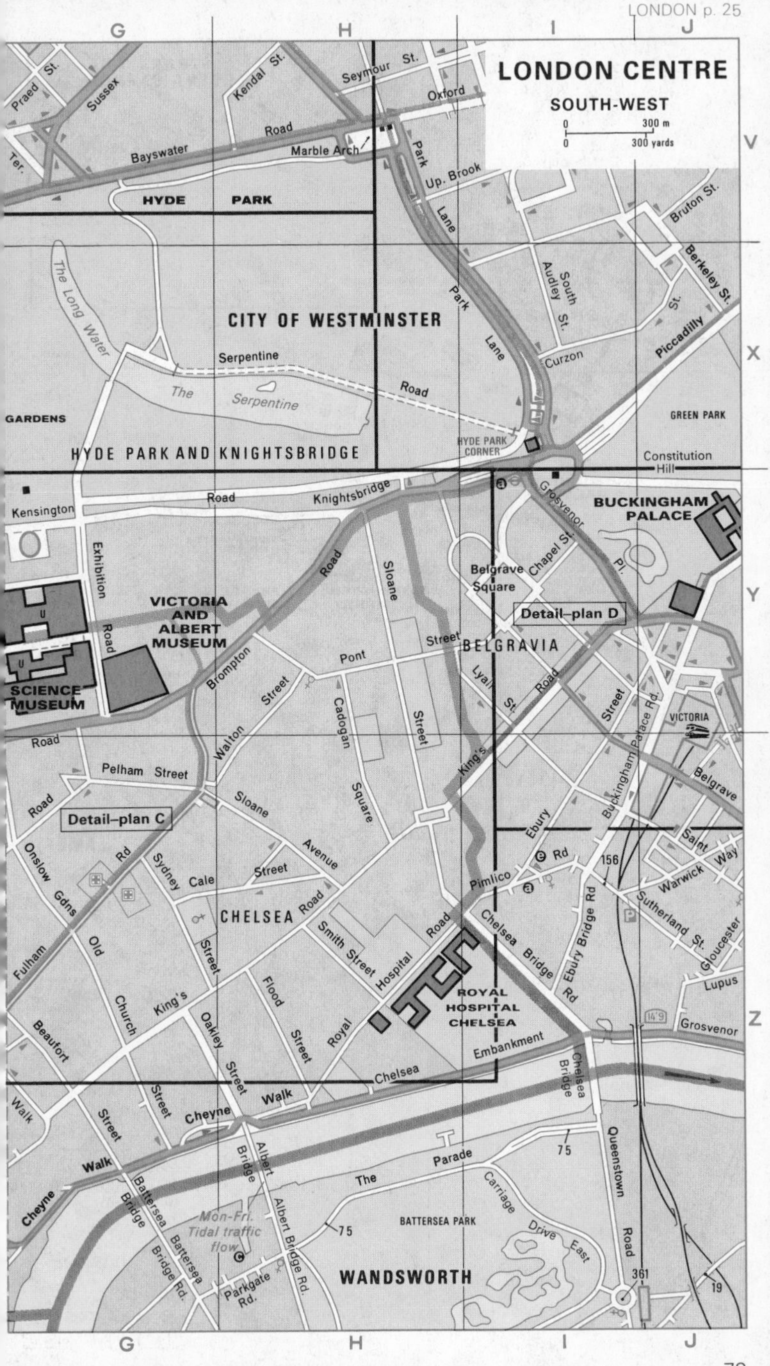
G
H
I
J
LONDON CENTRE
SOUTH-WEST
0 300 m
0 300 yards
V
X
Y
Z
HYDE PARK
CITY OF WESTMINSTER
The Long Water
The Serpentine
Serpentine Road
GARDENS
HYDE PARK AND KNIGHTSBRIDGE
HYDE PARK CORNER
GREEN PARK
Constitution Hill
BUCKINGHAM PALACE
VICTORIA AND ALBERT MUSEUM
SCIENCE MUSEUM
Detail–plan D
Detail–plan C
BELGRAVIA
Belgrave Square
VICTORIA
CHELSEA
ROYAL HOSPITAL CHELSEA
BATTERSEA PARK
WANDSWORTH
Mon-Fri. Tidal traffic flow
Praed St.
Sussex
Ter.
Kendal St.
Seymour St.
Oxford
Bayswater Road
Marble Arch
Park Lane
Up. Brook
Bruton St.
Berkeley St.
South Audley St.
St.
Piccadilly
Curzon
Kensington Road
Knightsbridge
Grosvenor Pl.
Chapel St.
Exhibition Road
Brompton Road
Sloane Street
Pont Street
Lyall St.
Road
Street
Buckingham Palace Rd.
Belgrave
Cadogan Square
Walton Street
Pelham Street
Sloane Avenue
King's Road
Ebury
Rd
Saint Way
Warwick
Sutherland St.
Gloucester
Lupus
Grosvenor
Onslow Gdns
Sydney Street
Cale Street
Pimlico Road
Chelsea Bridge Rd
Ebury Bridge Rd
Fulham Road
Old Church Street
Smith Street
Hospital Road
Royal Hospital Road
Flood Street
Oakley Street
Beaufort Street
Embankment
Chelsea Embankment
Chelsea Bridge
Cheyne Walk
Albert Bridge
Battersea Bridge
Queenstown Road
The Parade
Carriage Drive East
Albert Bridge Rd.
Battersea Bridge Rd.
Parkgate Rd.
156
75
361
19
14'9

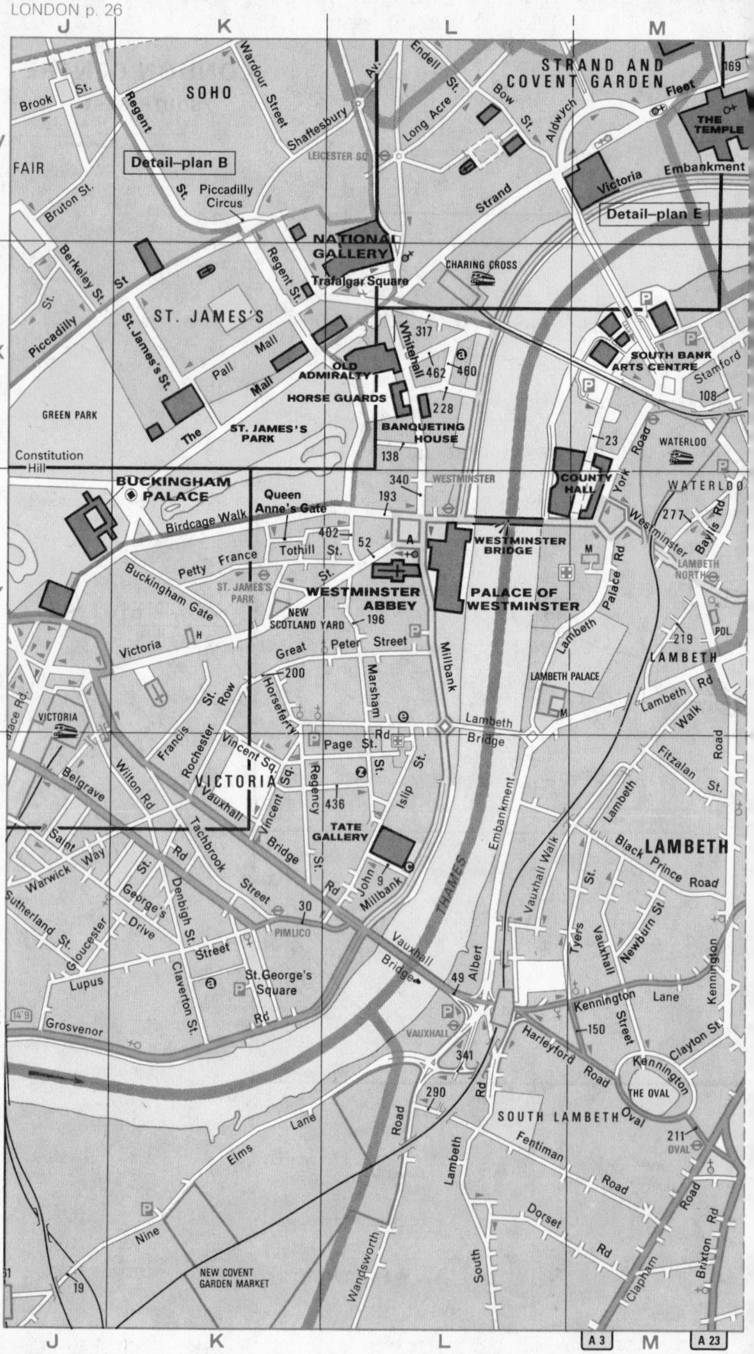
J
K
L
M
V
X
Y
Z
SOHO
STRAND AND COVENT GARDEN
169
Brook St.
Regent St.
Wardour Street
Shaftesbury Av.
Endell St.
Long Acre
Bow St.
Aldwych
Fleet
THE TEMPLE
Detail–plan B
LEICESTER SQ.
Embankment
FAIR
Bruton St.
Piccadilly Circus
Strand
Victoria
Detail–plan E
NATIONAL GALLERY
Berkeley St.
St.
Regent St.
Trafalgar Square
CHARING CROSS
Piccadilly
St. James's St.
ST. JAMES'S
Pall Mall
Mall
OLD ADMIRALTY
Whitehall
317
462
460
SOUTH BANK ARTS CENTRE
Stamford
108
GREEN PARK
The
ST. JAMES'S PARK
HORSE GUARDS
228
BANQUETING HOUSE
23
WATERLOO
Constitution Hill
138
340
WESTMINSTER
York Road
COUNTY HALL
WATERLOO
BUCKINGHAM PALACE
Queen Anne's Gate
193
277
Birdcage Walk
Westminster
Baylis Rd
Petty France
Tothill St.
402
52
WESTMINSTER BRIDGE
LAMBETH NORTH
Buckingham Gate
ST. JAMES'S PARK
WESTMINSTER ABBEY
PALACE OF WESTMINSTER
Lambeth Palace Rd
NEW SCOTLAND YARD
196
POL.
Victoria
Great Peter Street
219
LAMBETH
Horseferry Row
200
Marsham St.
Millbank
LAMBETH PALACE
Lambeth Rd
Francis St.
Rochester Row
Lambeth Bridge
Lambeth Walk
VICTORIA
Page St.
Vincent Sq.
Fitzalan St.
Belgrave
Wilton Rd
Regency St.
436
Islip St.
Embankment
Lambeth
Vauxhall
TATE GALLERY
LAMBETH
Saint
Warwick Way
Tachbrook Street
Vauxhall Bridge Rd
John Islip
9 Millbank
THAMES
Vauxhall Walk
Black Prince Road
Sutherland St.
St. George's Drive
Denbigh St.
30
PIMLICO
Tyers St.
Vauxhall Street
Newburn St.
Gloucester
Street
Claverton St.
St. George's Square
Albert
Kennington Lane
Lupus
49
Grosvenor Rd
150
VAUXHALL
Harleyford Road
Clayton St.
Kennington Oval
THE OVAL
341
290
Lambeth Rd
SOUTH LAMBETH
Fentiman Road
211
OVAL
Lane
Elms
Road
Nine
Dorset Rd
NEW COVENT GARDEN MARKET
Wandsworth Road
South
Clapham Road
Brixton Rd
19
A 3
A 23

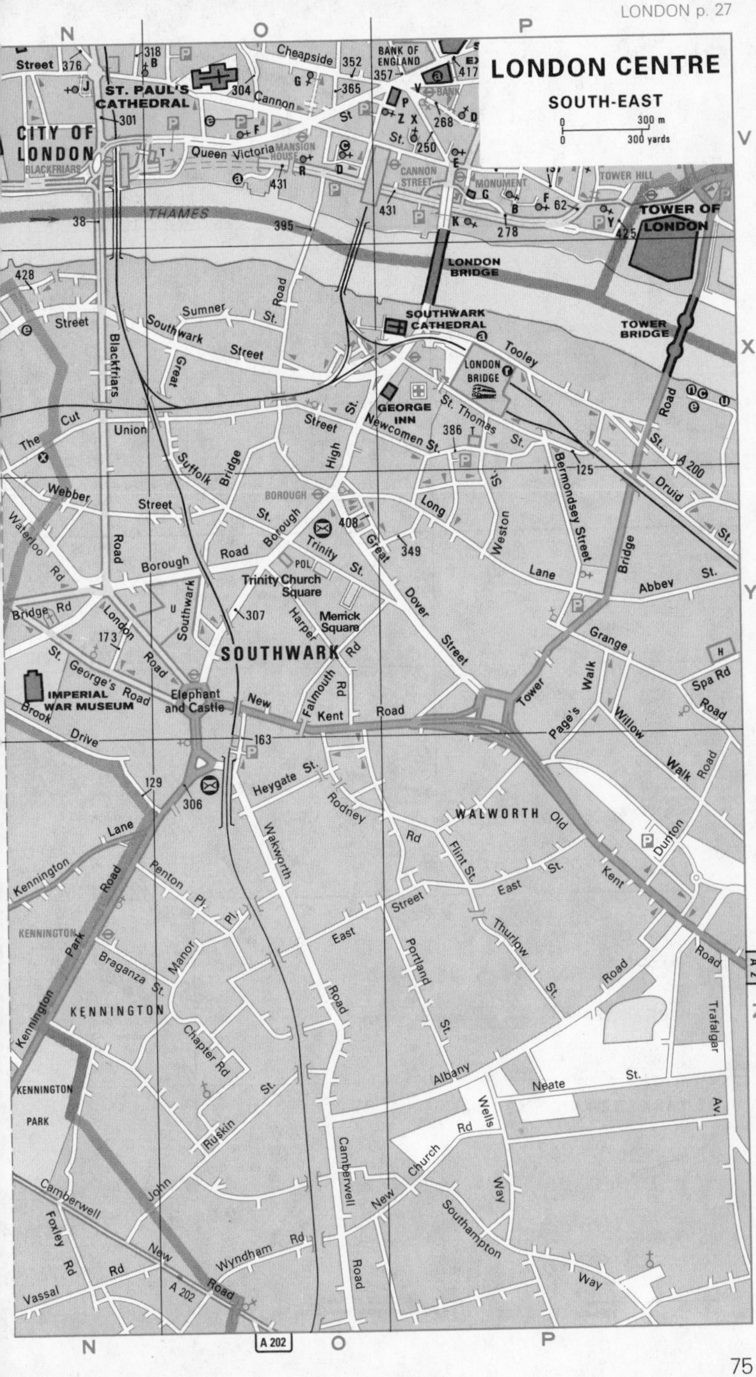
LONDON CENTRE
SOUTH-EAST
0 300 m
0 300 yards
N
O
P
V
X
Y
Z
CITY OF LONDON
ST. PAUL'S CATHEDRAL
BANK OF ENGLAND
Cheapside
Cannon St.
Queen Victoria St.
MANSION HOUSE
CANNON STREET
MONUMENT
TOWER HILL
TOWER OF LONDON
BLACKFRIARS
THAMES
LONDON BRIDGE
SOUTHWARK CATHEDRAL
TOWER BRIDGE
Tooley St.
Southwark Street
Sumner St.
Southwark Bridge Road
Great Guildford St.
Blackfriars Road
The Cut
Union Street
GEORGE INN
St. Thomas St.
Newcomen St.
High St.
Suffolk St.
Bridge St.
Webber Street
Waterloo Rd
BOROUGH
Borough Road
Borough Road
Long Lane
Weston St.
Bermondsey Street
Druid St.
A 200
Trinity St.
Great Dover Street
Trinity Church Square
Merrick Square
Harper Rd
Bridge Rd
London Road
Southwark Bridge Road
St. George's Road
IMPERIAL WAR MUSEUM
Brook Drive
Elephant and Castle
SOUTHWARK
New Kent Road
Falmouth Rd
Tower Bridge Road
Abbey St.
Grange Walk
Page's Walk
Willow Walk
Spa Rd
Road
Heygate St.
Rodney Rd
WALWORTH
Old Kent Road
Dunton Road
Wakworth Road
Flint St.
East St.
Thurlow St.
Kennington Lane
Kennington Park Road
Penton Pl.
KENNINGTON
Manor Pl.
Braganza St.
KENNINGTON
Chapter Rd
East Street
Portland St.
Trafalgar Av.
A 2
KENNINGTON PARK
Albany Road
Neate St.
Wells Way
Ruskin St.
John Ruskin St.
Camberwell Road
New Church Rd
Southampton Way
Camberwell New Road
Foxley Rd
Vassal Rd
Wyndham Rd
A 202
A 202

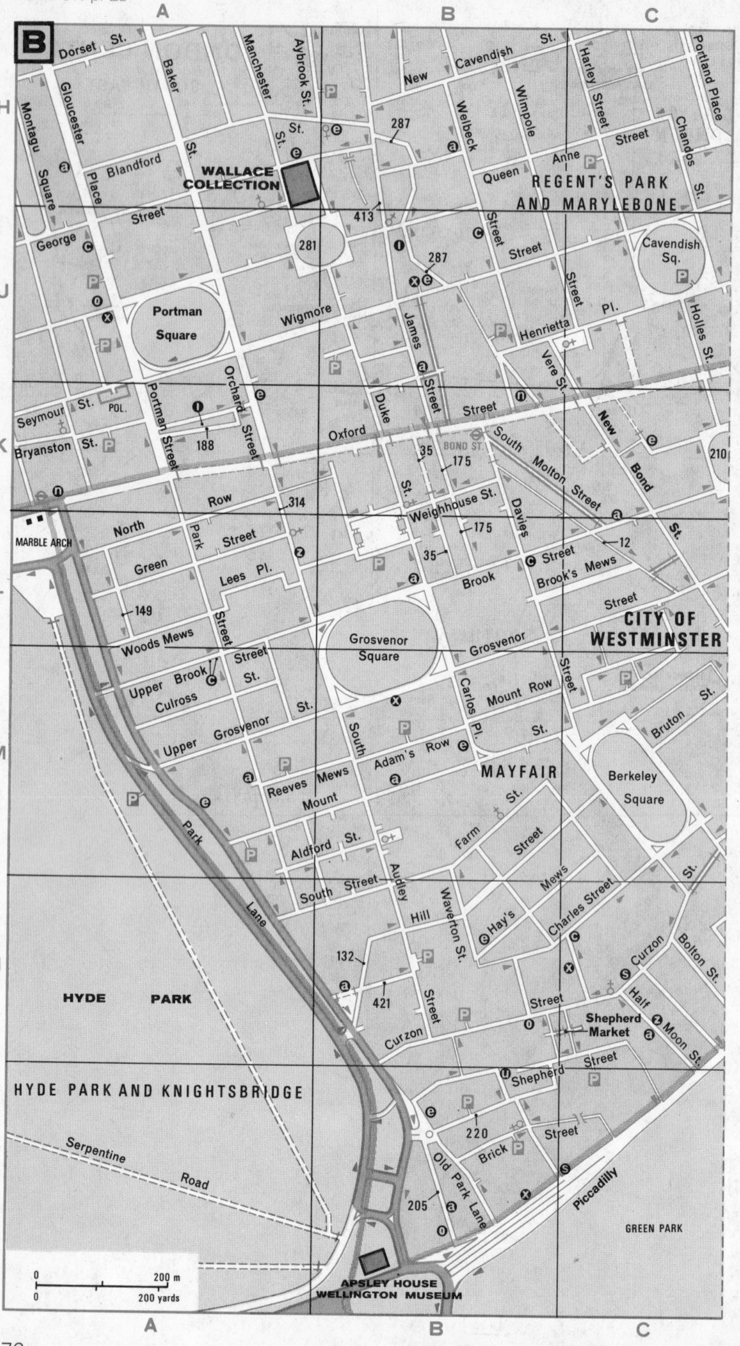
B
WALLACE COLLECTION
REGENT'S PARK AND MARYLEBONE
Portman Square
Cavendish Sq.
MARBLE ARCH
Grosvenor Square
CITY OF WESTMINSTER
MAYFAIR
Berkeley Square
HYDE PARK
HYDE PARK AND KNIGHTSBRIDGE
Serpentine Road
Park Lane
Oxford Street
Piccadilly
GREEN PARK
APSLEY HOUSE WELLINGTON MUSEUM
Shepherd Market
Dorset St.
Baker St.
Manchester St.
Aybrook St.
New Cavendish St.
Harley Street
Portland Place
Montagu Square
Gloucester Place
Blandford Street
George St.
Wigmore Street
Welbeck Street
Wimpole Street
Queen Anne Street
Chandos St.
Henrietta Pl.
Holles St.
Vere St.
James Street
Duke St.
Orchard Street
Portman Street
Seymour St.
Bryanston St.
POL.
BOND ST.
South Molton Street
New Bond St.
Weighhouse St.
Davies Street
North Row
Park Street
Green Street
Lees Pl.
Brook Street
Brook's Mews
Woods Mews
Upper Brook Street
Culross St.
Upper Grosvenor St.
Grosvenor Street
Carlos Pl.
Mount Row
Bruton St.
South Audley St.
Adam's Row
Reeves Mews
Mount St.
Farm Street
Aldford St.
South Street
Hays Mews
Charles Street
Hill St.
Waverton St.
Hay's
Curzon Street
Bolton St.
Half Moon St.
Shepherd Street
Brick Street
Old Park Lane
0 200 m
0 200 yards

| | | | | | |
|---|---|---|---|---|---|
| Arlington Street | DN 6 | Dunraven Street | AL 149 | Manchester Square | AJ 281 |
| Avery Row | CL 12 | Gerrard Street | GL 174 | Market Place | DJ 286 |
| Bateman Street | FK 18 | Gilbert Street | BL 175 | Marylebone Lane | BJ 287 |
| Berwick Street | FK 26 | Glasshouse Street | EM 179 | North Audley Street | AK 314 |
| Binney Street | BL 35 | Granville Place | AK 188 | Old Burlington Street | DM 322 |
| Carlton Gardens | FP 74 | Great Castle Street | DJ 189 | Old Compton Street | GK 323 |
| Deanery Street | BN 132 | Greek Street | GK 198 | Panton Street | FM 336 |
| Denman Street | FM 133 | Hamilton Place | BP 205 | Romilly Street | GL 368 |
| Denmark Street | GJ 134 | Hanover Square | CK 210 | Thayer Street | BJ 413 |
| Duke of York Street | EN 143 | Hertford Street | BP 220 | Tilney Street | BN 421 |
| Duke Street ST. JAMES | EN 146 | Leicester Square | GM 261 | Warwick Street | EM 444 |

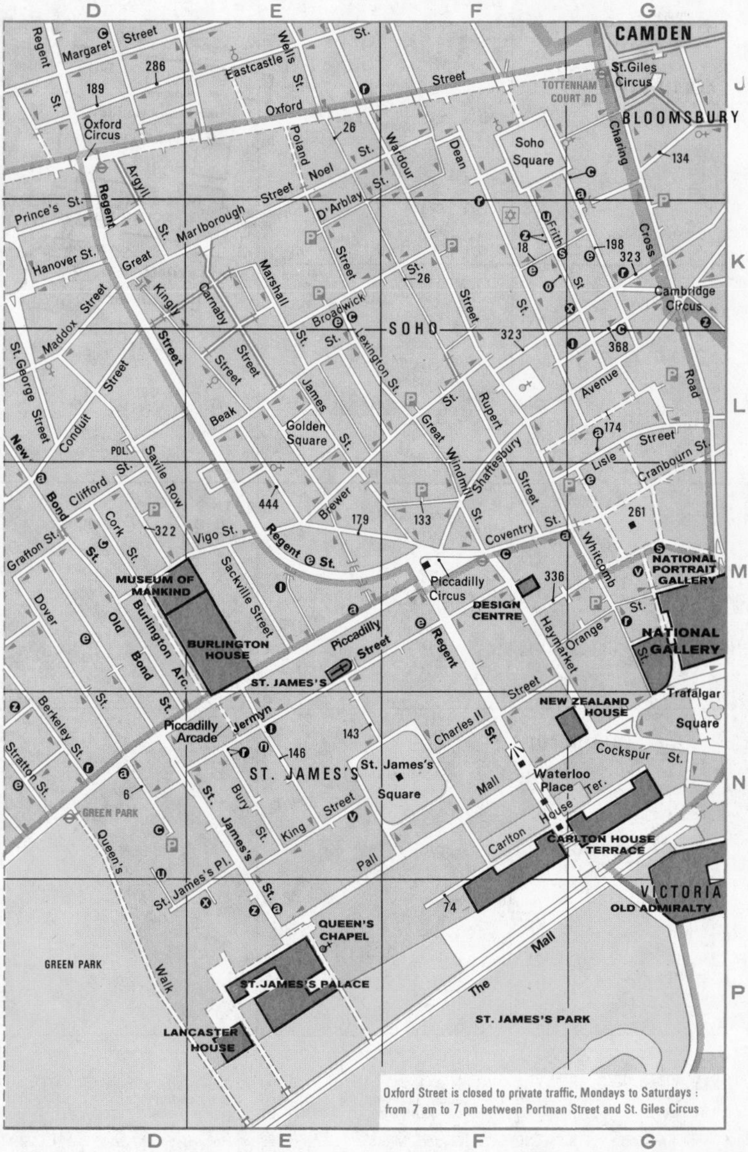

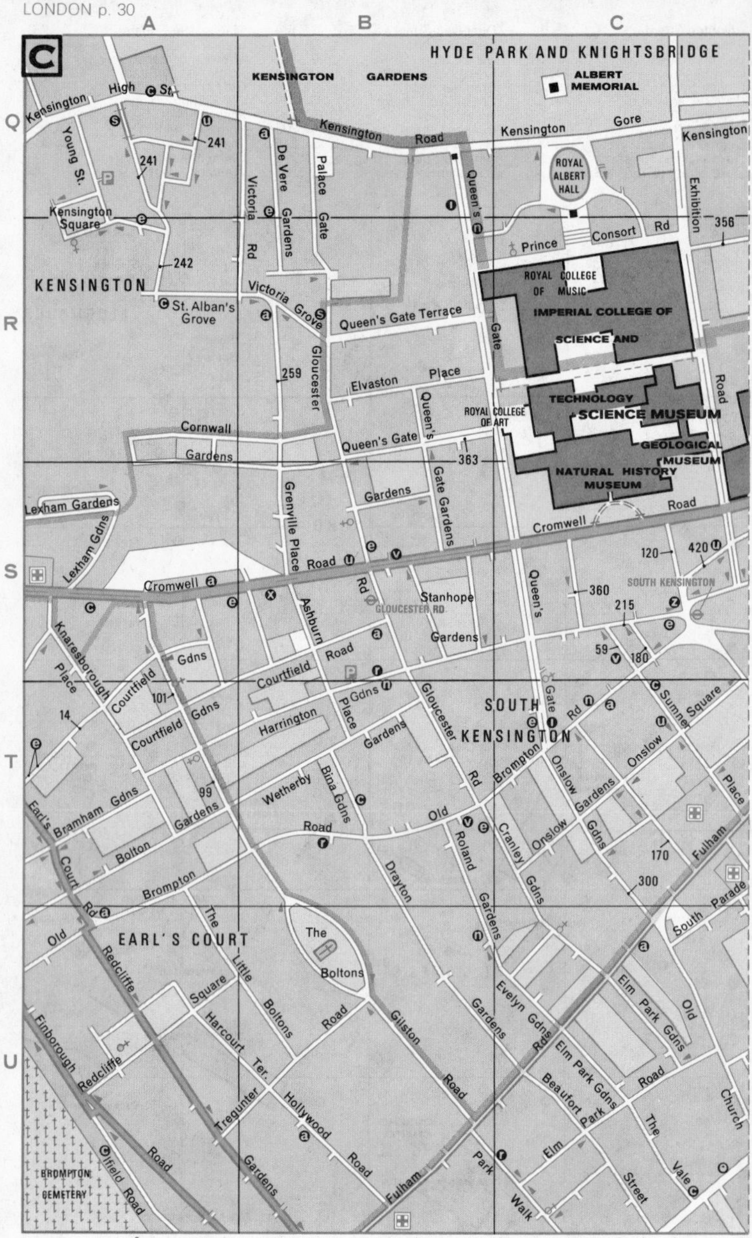
A
B
C
C
HYDE PARK AND KNIGHTSBRIDGE
KENSINGTON GARDENS
ALBERT MEMORIAL
Q
Kensington High St.
Kensington Road
Kensington Gore
Kensington
Young St.
241
De Vere Gardens
Palace Gate
Victoria Rd
Queen's Gate
ROYAL ALBERT HALL
Exhibition Rd
Kensington Square
Prince Consort Rd
356
242
KENSINGTON
ROYAL COLLEGE OF MUSIC
IMPERIAL COLLEGE OF SCIENCE AND TECHNOLOGY
St. Alban's Grove
Victoria Grove
Queen's Gate Terrace
R
Gloucester Rd
259
Elvaston Place
SCIENCE MUSEUM
ROYAL COLLEGE OF ART
Cornwall Gardens
Queen's Gate Gardens
GEOLOGICAL MUSEUM
363
NATURAL HISTORY MUSEUM
Lexham Gardens
Lexham Gdns
Grenville Place
Cromwell Road
120
420
S
Cromwell Road
Stanhope Gardens
360
SOUTH KENSINGTON
GLOUCESTER RD
215
Knaresborough Place
Ashburn Place
Courtfield Road
59
180
Courtfield Gdns
101
Sumner Place
Harrington Gdns
SOUTH KENSINGTON
14
Harrington Gardens
Onslow Square
T
99
Collingham Gardens
Wetherby Gardens
Bina Gdns
Brompton Rd
Onslow Gardens
Bramham Gdns
Old Brompton Road
Cranley Gdns
Earl's Court Rd
Bolton Gardens
Roland Gardens
170
Fulham Road
Brompton
Drayton Gardens
300
The Little Boltons
South Parade
Old
EARL'S COURT
The Boltons
Redcliffe Square
Elm Park Gdns
Old Church Street
Boltons Road
Finborough Road
Harcourt Ter.
Gilston Road
Evelyn Gdns
U
Redcliffe Gardens
Elm Park Road
Beaufort Street
Tregunter Road
Hollywood Road
Park Walk
The Vale
Elm Park Gdns
BROMPTON CEMETERY
Ifield Road
Fulham Road
A
B
C

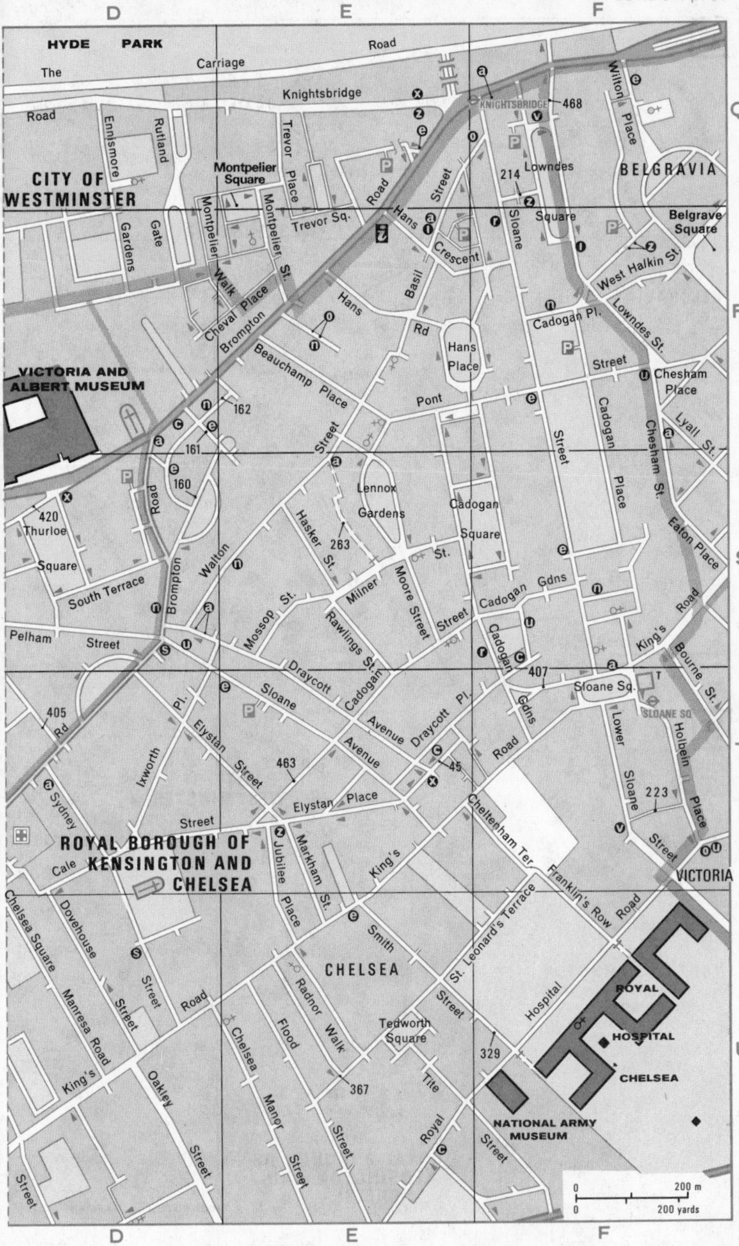
D
E
F
Q
R
S
T
U
HYDE PARK
The Carriage Road
Knightsbridge
KNIGHTSBRIDGE
468
Road
Ennismore Gardens
Rutland Gate
CITY OF WESTMINSTER
Montpelier Square
Montpelier Walk
Montpelier St.
Trevor Place
Trevor Sq.
Road
Hans Crescent
Street
Basil Street
Lowndes Square
214
Sloane Street
BELGRAVIA
Wilton Place
Belgrave Square
West Halkin St.
Cadogan Pl.
Lowndes St.
Cheval Place
Brompton Road
Hans Rd
Hans Place
Beauchamp Place
VICTORIA AND ALBERT MUSEUM
162
161
160
Pont Street
Chesham Place
Lyall St.
Cadogan Place
Chesham St.
Lennox Gardens
Cadogan Square
420
Thurloe Square
Hasker St.
263
Walton Street
Milner St.
Moore Street
Eaton Place
South Terrace
Brompton Road
Mossop St.
Rawlings St.
Cadogan Gdns
Cadogan Street
King's Road
Bourne St.
Pelham Street
Draycott Avenue
Cadogan Gdns
407
Sloane Sq.
SLOANE SQ
Sloane Avenue
Draycott Pl.
405
Sydney Rd
Ixworth Pl.
Elystan Street
463
45
Road
Lower Sloane Street
Holbein Place
223
Elystan Place
Street
Cheltenham Ter.
Franklin's Row
VICTORIA
ROYAL BOROUGH OF KENSINGTON AND CHELSEA
Cale Street
Jubilee Place
Markham St.
King's Road
Road
St. Leonard's Terrace
Chelsea Square
Dovehouse Street
Smith Street
CHELSEA
Radnor Walk
Hospital Road
ROYAL HOSPITAL CHELSEA
Manresa Road
Street
Tedworth Square
329
Chelsea Manor Street
Flood Street
367
Tite Street
King's Road
Oakley Street
Royal
Street
NATIONAL ARMY MUSEUM
0 200 m
0 200 yards
Street
D
E
F

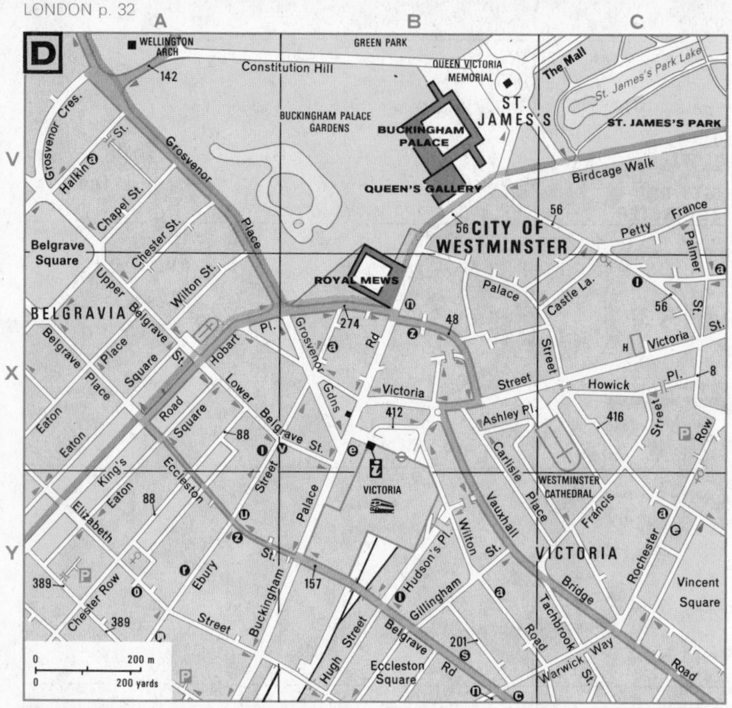
A
B
C
V
X
Y
D
WELLINGTON ARCH
142
GREEN PARK
Constitution Hill
QUEEN VICTORIA MEMORIAL
The Mall
St. James's Park Lake
ST. JAMES'S
ST. JAMES'S PARK
BUCKINGHAM PALACE GARDENS
BUCKINGHAM PALACE
QUEEN'S GALLERY
Birdcage Walk
Grosvenor Cres.
Halkin St.
Chapel St.
Grosvenor Place
Belgrave Square
Chester St.
Wilton St.
Upper Belgrave St.
BELGRAVIA
CITY OF WESTMINSTER
56
Petty France
Palmer St.
ROYAL MEWS
Palace St.
Castle La.
48
274
Grosvenor Pl.
Hobart Pl.
Grosvenor Gdns
Rd
Victoria St.
Victoria Street
H
Howick Pl.
8
Belgrave Place
Eaton Square
Eaton Place
Lower Belgrave St.
412
Ashley Pl.
416
Street
Row
88
Eccleston Street
King's Road
Eaton
Carlisle Place
WESTMINSTER CATHEDRAL
Francis
Rochester
VICTORIA
Vauxhall Bridge Road
Wilton Rd
Palace
Elizabeth
Ebury St.
Buckingham Palace Rd
157
Hudson's Pl.
Gillingham St.
Tachbrook St.
Vincent Square
389
Chester Row
Eccleston Street
Hugh Street
Belgrave Rd
201
Eccleston Square
Warwick Way
0
200 m
200 yards

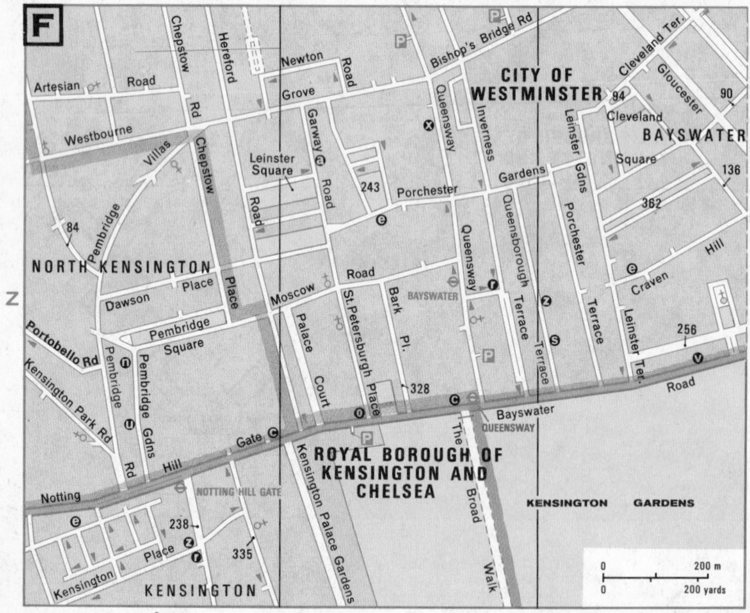
F
Chepstow Rd
Hereford Rd
Newton Road
Bishop's Bridge Rd
Cleveland Ter.
Gloucester Ter.
Artesian Road
Grove
CITY OF WESTMINSTER
94
90
Westbourne Grove
Queensway
Inverness Gardens
Leinster Gdns
Cleveland Square
BAYSWATER
Villas
Chepstow Place
Garway Road
Leinster Square
Road
243
Porchester Gardens
136
362
84
Pembridge Villas
Queensborough Terrace
Porchester Terrace
Hill
NORTH KENSINGTON
Z
Dawson Place
Moscow Road
St.Petersburgh Place
Bark Pl.
BAYSWATER
Craven Hill
Leinster Ter.
256
Portobello Rd
Pembridge Square
Pembridge Rd
Pembridge Gdns
Palace Court
328
Bayswater Road
QUEENSWAY
Kensington Park Rd
Notting Hill Gate
ROYAL BOROUGH OF KENSINGTON AND CHELSEA
The Broad Walk
Kensington Palace Gardens
NOTTING HILL GATE
KENSINGTON GARDENS
238
335
Kensington Place
KENSINGTON
0
200 m
200 yards
A
B
C

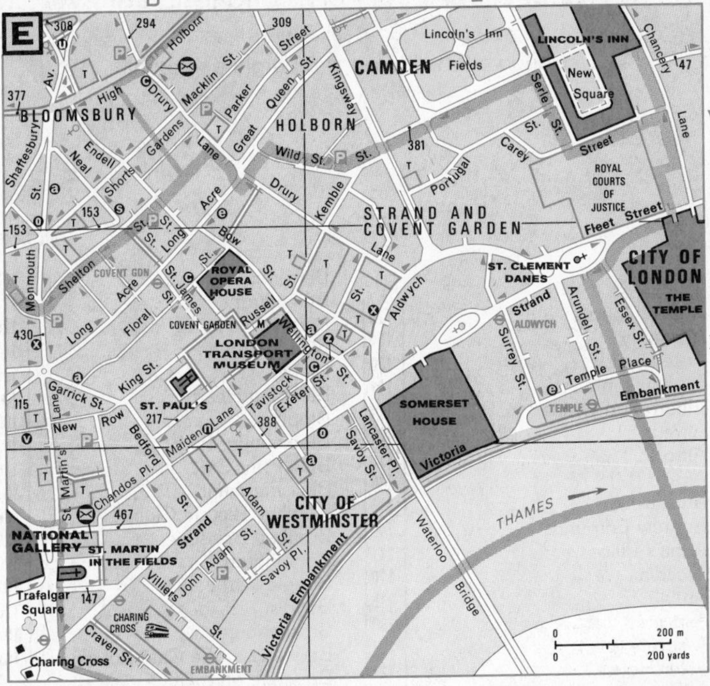


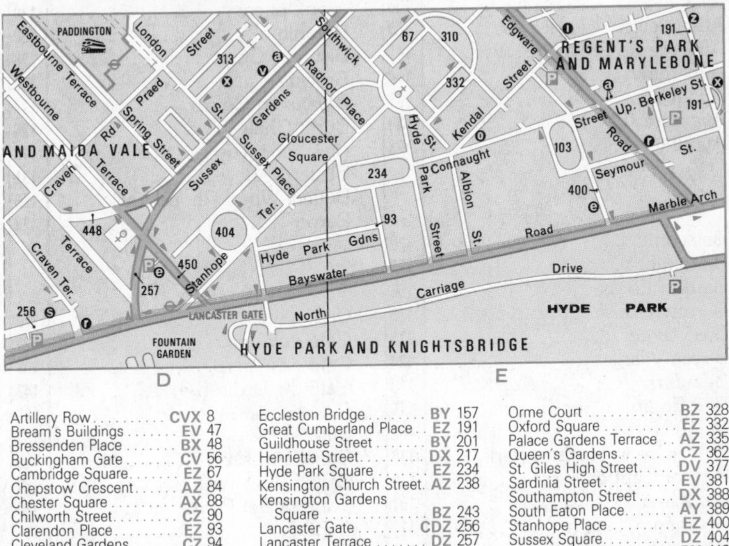


Artillery Row . . . . . . . . . . CVX 8
Bream's Buildings . . . . . . . EV 47
Bressenden Place . . . . . . . BX 48
Buckingham Gate . . . . . . . CV 56
Cambridge Square . . . . . . . EZ 67
Chepstow Crescent . . . . . . AZ 84
Chester Square . . . . . . . . AX 88
Chilworth Street . . . . . . . . CZ 90
Clarendon Place . . . . . . . . EZ 93
Cleveland Gardens . . . . . . CZ 94
Connaught Square . . . . . . . EZ 103
Cranbourn Street . . . . . . . . DX 115
Devonshire Terrace . . . . . . CZ 136
Duke of Wellington Place . AV 142
Duncannon Street . . . . . . . DY 147
Earlham Street . . . . . . . . . . DV 153
Eccleston Bridge . . . . . . . . BY 157
Great Cumberland Place . . EZ 191
Guildhouse Street . . . . . . . BY 201
Henrietta Street . . . . . . . . . DX 217
Hyde Park Square . . . . . . . EZ 234
Kensington Church Street . AZ 238
Kensington Gardens Square . . . . . . . . . . . . . BZ 243
Lancaster Gate . . . . . . . . . CDZ 256
Lancaster Terrace . . . . . . . DZ 257
Lower Grosvenor Place . . . BX 274
Museum Street . . . . . . . . . . DV 294
New Oxford Street . . . . . . . DV 308
Newton Street . . . . . . . . . . DV 309
Norfolk Crescent . . . . . . . . EZ 310
Norfolk Square . . . . . . . . . . DZ 313
Orme Court . . . . . . . . . . . . . BZ 328
Oxford Square . . . . . . . . . . EZ 332
Palace Gardens Terrace . . AZ 335
Queen's Gardens . . . . . . . . CZ 362
St. Giles High Street . . . . . DV 377
Sardinia Street . . . . . . . . . . EV 381
Southampton Street . . . . . DX 388
South Eaton Place . . . . . . . AY 389
Stanhope Place . . . . . . . . . EZ 400
Sussex Square . . . . . . . . . . DZ 404
Terminus Place . . . . . . . . . BX 412
Thirleby Road . . . . . . . . . . CX 416
Upper St. Martin's Lane . . DX 430
Westbourne Crescent . . . . DZ 448
Westbourne Street . . . . . . DZ 450
William IV Street . . . . . . . . DY 467

# Alphabetical list of hotels and restaurants

## Liste alphabétique des hôtels et restaurants

## Elenco alfabetico degli alberghi e ristoranti

## Alphabetisches Hotel- und Restaurantverzeichnis

page
pagina
Seite

# Alphabetical list of areas included

## Liste alphabétique des quartiers cités

## Elenco alfabetico dei quartieri citati

## Liste der erwähnten Bezirke

# Particularly pleasant hotels and restaurants

## Hôtels et restaurants agréables

## Alberghi e ristoranti ameni

## Angenehme Hotels und Restaurants

# Starred establishments in London

## Les établissements à étoiles de Londres

## Gli esercizi con stelle a Londra - Die Stern-Restaurants Londons

### ✿✿✿

| | | |
|---|---|---|
| **Mayfair** | | |
| XXXXX | Chez Nico at Ninety Park Lane (at Grosvenor House H.) | 134 |
| **Chelsea** | | |
| XXXX | La Tante Claire | 114 |
| **Hyde Park & Knightsbridge** | | |
| XXXX | The Restaurant, Marco Pierre White (at Hyde Park H.) | 131 |

### ✿✿

| | | |
|---|---|---|
| **Mayfair** | | |
| XXXX | Le Gavroche | 134 |

### ✿

| | | |
|---|---|---|
| **Mayfair** | | |
| ⌂⌂⌂⌂ | Connaught | 132 |
| **Belgravia** | | |
| ⌂⌂⌂ | Halkin | 130 |
| **Chelsea** | | |
| ⌂⌂⌂ | Capital | 112 |
| **Mayfair** | | |
| XXXXX | Oak Room (at Le Meridien Piccadilly H.) | 134 |
| **Mayfair** | | |
| XXXX | Four Seasons (at Four Season H.) | 134 |
| **Soho** | | |
| XXXX | Grill Room at the Café Royal | 140 |
| **Mayfair** | | |
| XXXX | Oriental (at Dorchester H.) | 134 |
| XXXX | Les Saveurs | 134 |
| **Chelsea** | | |
| XXX | Aubergine | 114 |
| XXX | MPW's, The Canteen | 114 |
| **North Kensington** | | |
| XXX | Leith's | 119 |
| **Bloomsbury** | | |
| XXX | Pied à Terre | 100 |
| **St. James's** | | |
| XXX | The Square | 140 |
| **Chelsea** | | |
| XX | Fulham Road | 115 |

# Further establishments which merit your attention

## Autres tables qui méritent votre attention

## Altre tavole particolarmente interessanti

## Weitere empfehlenswerte Häuser

# Meals

| | | |
|---|---|---|
| **Belgravia** | | |
| XXX | Al Bustan | 131 |
| **Chelsea** | | |
| XXX | Bibendum | 114 |
| XXX | Chutney Mary | 114 |
| XXX | Fifth Floor (at Harvey Nichols) | 114 |
| **Strand and Covent Garden** | | |
| XXX | Ivy | 142 |
| **Southwark** | | |
| XXX | Le Pont de la Tour | 126 |
| **Bayswater and Maida Vale** | | |
| XX | Al San Vincenzo | 130 |
| **St. James's** | | |
| XX | Le Caprice | 140 |
| **Kensington** | | |
| XX | Clarke's | 117 |
| **Mayfair** | | |
| XX | Greenhouse | 135 |
| **South Kensington** | | |
| XX | Hilaire | 122 |
| **Regent's Park and Marylebone** | | |
| XX | Nico Central | 137 |
| **North Harrow** | | |
| XX | Percy's | 108 |
| **Victoria** | | |
| XX | Simply Nico | 145 |
| **Soho** | | |
| X | Alastair Little | 141 |
| X | Bistrot Bruno | 141 |
| **Kensington** | | |
| X | Kensington Place | 118 |
| X | Malabar | 118 |

# Restaurants classified according to type

## Restaurants classés suivant leur genre

## Ristoranti classificati secondo il loro genere

## Restaurants nach Art und Einrichtung geordnet

### Bistro

- X Bangkok (Royal Borough of Kensington & Chelsea - *South Kensington*) .......... 122
- X Bougie (La) (Camden - *Camden Town*) .......... 101
- X Langan's Bistro (City of Westminster - *Regent's Park & Marylebone*) .......... 138
- X Stephen Bull's Bistro (Islington - *Finsbury*) .......... 111

### Seafood

- XXX Overton's (City of Westminster - *St. James's*) .......... 139
- XXX Scotts (City of Westminster - *Mayfair*) .......... 135
- XX Bentleys (City of Westminster - *Mayfair*) .......... 135
- XX Downstairs at One Ninety (Royal Borough of Kensington & Chelsea - *South Kensington*) .......... 122
- XX Gravier (Kingston-upon-Thames - *Kingston*) .......... 123
- XX Park Inn (Royal Borough of Kensington & Chelsea - *North Kensington*) .......... 119
- XX Poissonnerie de l'Avenue (Royal Borough of Kensington & Chelsea - *Chelsea*) .......... 115
- XX Sheekey's (City of Westminster - *Strand & Covent Garden*) .......... 143
- XX Walsh's (City of Westminster - *Regent's Park & Marylebone*) .......... 137

### Chinese

- XXXX ✿ Oriental (City of Westminster - *Mayfair*) .......... 134
- XXX Inn of Happiness (City of Westminster - *Victoria*) .......... 144
- XXX Now and Zen (City of Westminster - *Strand and Covent Garden*) .......... 142
- XXX Pearl of Knightsbridge (City of Westminster - *Hyde Park and Knightsbridge*) .......... 131
- XXX Princess Garden (City of Westminster - *Mayfair*) .......... 134
- XXX Zen Central (City of Westminster - *Mayfair*) .......... 134
- XX Bayee Village (Merton - *Wimbledon*) .......... 124
- XX China Jazz (Camden - *Regent's Park*) .......... 102
- XX Dragon City (Redbridge - *Ilford*) .......... 124
- XX Four Regions (Richmond-Upon-Thames - *Richmond*) .......... 126
- XX Good Earth (Barnet - *Mill Hill*) .......... 97
- XX Good Earth (Royal Borough of Kensington & Chelsea - *Chelsea*) .......... 115
- XX Ho-Ho (Redbridge - *South Woodford*) .......... 124
- XX Hunan (City of Westminster - *Victoria*) .......... 145
- XX Imperial City (City of London) .......... 103
- XX Ken Lo's Memories of China (City of Westminster - *Victoria*) .......... 145
- XX Mao Tai (Hammersmith & Fulham - *Fulham*) .......... 107
- XX Maxim (Ealing - *Ealing*) .......... 105
- XX Ming (City of Westminster - *Soho*) .......... 141
- XX Mr Tang's Mandarin (Harrow - *Stanmore*) .......... 109
- XX Mr Wing (Royal Borough of Kensington & Chelsea - *Earl's Court*) .......... 116

## Chinese



## English



## French

## French

- XX Dordogne (La) (Hounslow - *Chiswick*) ..... 111
- XX Escargot Doré (L') (Kensington - *Kensington*) ..... 118
- XX Estaminet (L') (City of Westminster - *Strand and Covent Garden*) ..... 143
- XX Grafton (The) (Lambeth - *Clapham Common*) ..... 123
- XX Gravier's (Kingston-upon-Thames - *Kingston*) ..... 123
- XX Mon Plaisir (Camden - *Bloomsbury*) ..... 100
- XX Poissonnerie de l'Avenue (Royal Borough of Kensington & Chelsea - *Chelsea*) ..... 115
- XX Pomme d'Amour (La) (Royal Borough of Kensington & Chelsea - *Kensington*) ..... 117
- XX Rive Gauche (La) (Lambeth - *Waterloo*) ..... 123
- XX St. Quentin (Royal Borough of Kensington & Chelsea - *Chelsea*) ..... 115
- XX Truffe Noire (La) (Southwark - *Southwark*) ..... 127
- X Aventure (L') (City of Westminster - *Regent's Park & Marylebone*) ..... 138
- X Magno's Brasserie (City of Westminster - *Strand & Covent Garden*) ..... 143
- X Muscadet (Le) (City of Westminster - *Regent's Park & Marylebone*) ..... 138
- X Poule au Pot (La) (City of Westminster - *Victoria*) ..... 145
- X Soulard (Hackney - *Dalston*) ..... 106

## Hungarian

- XX Gay Hussar (City of Westminster - *Soho*) ..... 141

## Indian & Pakistani

- XXX Bengal Clipper (Southwark - *Bermondsey*) ..... 126
- XXX Bombay Brasserie (Royal Borough of Kensington & Chelsea - *South Kensington*) 121
- XXX Chandni (Bromley - *Bromley*) ..... 98
- XXX Chutney Mary (Anglo-Indian) (Royal Borough of Kensington & Chelsea - *Chelsea*) ..... 114
- XX Cafe Lazeez (Royal Borough of Kensington & Chelsea - *South Kensington*) 122
- XX Delhi Brasserie (Royal Borough of Kensington & Chelsea - *South Kensington*) 122
- XX Gaylord (City of Westminster -*Regent's Park & Marylebone*) ..... 138
- XX Gopal's (City of Westminster -*Soho*) ..... 141
- XX Kanishka (Camden - *Bloomsbury*) ..... 100
- XX Khan's of Kensington (Royal Borough of Kensington & Chelsea - *South Kensington*) 122
- XX Laguna Tandoori (Ealing - *Ealing*) ..... 105
- XX Laksmi (Tower Hamlets - *Stepney*) ..... 127
- XX Memories of India (Royal Borough of Kensington & Chelsea - *South Kensington*) 122
- XX Red Fort (City of Westminster - *Soho*) ..... 141
- XX Spice Merchant (City of Westminster - *Bayswater & Maida Vale*) ..... 130
- XX Tabaq (Wandsworth - *Wandsworth*) ..... 128
- XX Tandoori Nights (Hammersmith & Fulham - *Hammersmith*) ..... 107
- X Bombay Bicycle Club (Wandsworth - *Wandsworth*) 128
- X Jaflong (Harrow - *South Harrow*) ..... 109
- X Jashan (Haringey - *Hornsey*) 108
- X Malabar (Royal Borough of Kensington & Chelsea - *Kensington*) ..... 118
- X Taste of India (Greenwich - *Greenwich*) ..... 106

## Irish

XX Mulligans (City of Westminster - *Mayfair*) .... 135

## Italian

⌂ ✿ Halkin (City of Westminster - *Belgravia*) .... 130

XXX L'Incontro (City of Westminster - *Victoria*) .... 144

XXX Santini (City of Westminster - *Victoria*) .... 144

XX Amico (L') (City of Westminster - *Victoria*) .... 145

XX Caldesi (City of Westminster - *Regent's Park & Marylebone*) .... 137

XX Daphne's (Royal Borough of Kensington & Chelsea - *Chelsea*) .... 115

XX Del Buongustaio (Wandworth - *Putney*) .... 128

XX Fenice (La) (Royal Borough of Kensington & Chelsea - *Kensington*) .... 118

XX Finezza (La) (Royal Borough of Kensington & Chelsea - *Chelsea*) .... 115

XX Formula Veneta (Royal Borough of Kensington & Chelsea - *Earl's Court*) .... 116

XX Giannino's (Bromley - *Keston*) .... 99

XX Gran Paradiso (City of Westminster - *Victoria*) .... 145

XX Loggia (La) (City of Westminster - *Regent's Park & Marylebone*) .... 138

XX Luigi's (Southwark - *Dulwich*) .... 127

XX Mezzaluna (Barnet - *Child's Hill*) .... 97

XX Orchard (Camden - *Hampstead*) .... 102

XX Orso (City of Westminster - *Strand & Covent Garden*) .... 142

XX Primula (La) (Royal Borough of Kensington & Chelsea - *Earl's Court*) .... 116

XX San Vincenzo (Al) (City of Westminster - *Bayswater & Maida Vale*) .... 130

XX Scala (La) (Barking and Dagenham - *Chadwell Heath*) .... 97

XX Toto's (Royal Borough of Kensington & Chelsea - *Chelsea*) .... 115

XX Trattoria Sorrentina (Harrow - *Central Harrow*) .... 108

XX Veranda (La) (Sutton - *Carshalton*) .... 127

X Accento (L') (City of Westminster - *Bayswater and Maida Vale*) .... 130

X Altro (L') (Royal Borough of Kensington & Chelsea - *North Kensington*) .... 119

X Bertorelli's (City of Westminster - *Strand & Covent Garden*) .... 143

X Cantina Del Ponte (Southwark - *Bermondsey*) .... 126

X Castelletto (Il) (Camden - *Bloomsbury*) .... 101

X Cibo (Royal Borough of Kensington & Chelsea - *Kensington*) .... 118

X Florians (Haringey - *Crouch End*) .... 107

X Fontana (La) (City of Westminster - *Victoria*) .... 145

X Issimo ! (City of London) .... 103

X Mario (Croydon - *Croydon*) .... 104

X Mimmo d'Ischia (City of Westminster - *Victoria*) .... 145

X Olivo (City of Westminster - *Victoria*) .... 145

X Paolo's (Ealing - *Ealing*) .... 105

X Pitagora (Richmond-Upon-Thames - *Richmond*) .... 126

X Riva (Richmond-Upon-Thames - *Barnes*) .... 125

X Roberto's (Hillingdon - *Ickenham*) .... 110

X Sambuca (Hillingdon - *Eastcote*) .... 109

X Villa Medici (City of Westminster - *Victoria*) .... 145

## Japanese

XXX Benihana (Camden - *Hampstead*) .......... 101

XXX Benihana (Royal Borough of Kensington & Chelsea - *Chelsea* .......... 114

XXX Suntory (City of Westminster - *St. James's*) .......... 139

XXX Tatsuso (City of London) .......... 103

XX Asuka (City of Westminster - *Regent's Park & Marylebone*) .......... 138

XX Matsuri (City of Westminster - *St. James's*) .......... 140

XX Miyama (City of London) .......... 103

XX Shogun (City of Westminster - *Mayfair*) .......... 135

X Ikeda (City of Westminster - *Mayfair*) .......... 135

X Imari (Camden - *Holborn*) .......... 102

X Nakamura (City of Westminster - *Regent's Park & Marylebone*) .......... 138

## Lebanese

XXX Bustan (Al)(City of Westminster - *Belgravia*) .......... 131

XX Maroush III (City of Westminster - *Regent's Park & Marylebone*) .......... 138

XX Phoenicia (Royal Borough of Kensington & Chelsea - *Kensington*) .......... 118

X Beit Eddine (Royal Borough of Kensington & Chelsea - *Chelsea*) .......... 116

## Polish

X Wódka (Royal Borough of Kensington & Chelsea - *Kensington*) .......... 119

## Spanish

XXX Albero and Grana (Royal Borough of Kensington & Chelsea - *Chelsea*) .......... 114

## Swedish

X Anna's Place (Islington - *Canonbury*) .......... 111

## Thai

XX Blue Elephant (Hammersmith & Fulham - *Fulham*) .......... 107

XX Busabong Too (Royal Borough of Kensington & Chelsea - *Chelsea*) .......... 115

XX Chada (Wandsworth - *Battersea*) .......... 128

XX Lena's (Wandsworth - *Battersea*) .......... 128

XX Tui (Royal Borough of Kensington & Chelsea - *South Kensington*) .......... 122

X Ayudhya (Kingston-upon-Thames - *Kingston*) .......... 123

X Bangkok (Royal Borough of Kensington & Chelsea - *South Kensington*) .......... 122

X Oh Boy (Wandsworth - *Tooting*) .......... 128

X Sri Siam (City of Westminster - *Soho*) .......... 141

X Thai Castle (Harrow - *North Harrow*) .......... 108

X Thai Pepper (Camden - *Swiss Cottage*) .......... 103

## Vietnamese

X Saigon (City of Westminster - *Soho*) .......... 142

# Boroughs and areas

**Greater London** is divided, for administrative purposes, into 32 boroughs plus the City : these sub-divide naturally into minor areas, usually grouped around former villages or quarters, which often maintain a distinctive character.

## BARKING and DAGENHAM p. 7.

### Chadwell Heath – ✉ Essex – ☎ 0181.

XX La Scala JU **e**
19a High Rd RM6 6PU ☎ 983 8818
Ⓟ
**Meals** - Italian.

## BARNET pp. 4 and 5.

### Brent Cross – ✉ NW2 – ☎ 0181.

**Holiday Inn Garden Court** DU **n**
Tilling Rd NW2 3DS ☎ 455 4777, Fax 455 4660
rm TV ☎ Ⓟ – 50. AE VISA JCB.
**Meals** (bar lunch)/dinner 11.95 **st.** and a la carte 4.95 – 8.25 – **153 rm** 69.00 **st.**

### Child's Hill – ✉ NW2 – ☎ 0171.

XX **Mezzaluna** DU **o**
424 Finchley Rd NW2 2HY ☎ 794 3603
AE VISA
*closed Saturday lunch and Monday* – **Meals** - Italian a la carte 16.50/26.50 **t.** 5.50.

X **Quincy's** DU **r**
675 Finchley Rd NW2 2JP ☎ 794 8499
AE VISA
*closed Sunday, Monday and 1 week Christmas* – **Meals** (booking essential) (dinner only) 25.00 **t.** 4.50.

X **Laurent** DU **o**
428 Finchley Rd NW2 2HY ☎ 794 3603
AE VISA
*closed Sunday, first 3 weeks August and Bank Holidays* – **Meals** - Couscous a la carte 13.00 **t.**

### Mill Hill – ✉ NW7 – ☎ 0181.

18 100 Barnet Way, Mill Hill ☎ 959 2282, CT.

XX **Good Earth** CT **a**
143 The Broadway NW7 4RN ☎ 959 7011, Fax 959 7464
AE VISA
*closed 24 to 27 December* – **Meals** - Chinese 17.50/25.50 **t.** and a la carte 4.00.

## BEXLEY pp. 10 and 11.

### Bexley – ✉ Kent – ☎ 01322.

**Forte Posthouse** JX e
Black Prince Interchange, Southwold Rd DA5 1ND, on A 2 ☎ 526900, Fax 526113
lift, ⅔ rm ▤ rest TV ☎ ♿ P – 🏛 70. AE VISA
**Meals** a la carte approx. 15.00 **t.** 🍷 5.50 – **100 rm** 59.50/69.50 **st.**, 2 suites.

### Bexleyheath – ✉ Kent – ☎ 0181.

**Swallow** JX c
1 Broadway DA6 7JZ ☎ 298 1000, Fax 298 1234
Fitness, ▢ – lift ⅔ rm ▤ TV ☎ ♿ P – 🏛 200. AE VISA
***Galleria* : Meals** (dinner only and Sunday lunch) 25.00
***Copper* : Meals** 12.50/19.00 – **142 rm** ☕ 88.00/120.00 **st.** – SB.

*Dans le guide Vert Michelin* ***"Londres"*** *(édition en français) vous trouverez :*
- *des descriptions détaillées des principales curiosités*
- *de nombreux renseignements pratiques*
- *des itinéraires de visite dans les secteurs sélectionnés*
- *des plans de quartiers et de monuments.*

## BRENT pp. 4 and 5.

### Wembley – ✉ Middx – ☎ 0181.

**Hilton National Wembley** CU z
Empire Way HA9 8DS ☎ 902 8839, Fax 900 2201
Fitness, sauna, ▢ – lift ⅔ rm ▤ rest TV ☎ P – 🏛 300. AE VISA JCB
***Celebrities* : Meals** (carving rest.) 15.95/19.95
***Terracotta* : Meals** - Italian (dinner only) 15.95/19.95 – ☕ 10.25 – **306 rm** 119.00/146.00 **st.** – SB.

## BROMLEY pp. 10 and 11.

Golf 18, Golf 9 Cray Valley, Sandy Lane, St. Paul's Cray ☎ (01689) 831927, JY.

### Bromley – ✉ Kent – ☎ 0181.

Golf 9 Magpie Hall Lane ☎ 462 7014, HY.

**Bromley Court** HY z
Bromley Hill BR1 4JD ☎ 464 5011, Fax 460 0899
garden – lift ⅔ rm TV ☎ P – 🏛 150. AE VISA
**Meals** *(closed Saturday lunch)* 9.95/14.95 **st.** and a la carte 🍷 4.65 – **118 rm** ☕ 79.00/89.00 **st.**

XXX **Chandni** HY e
123-125 Mason's Hill BR2 9HT ☎ 290 4447, Fax 313 1477
▤. AE VISA
*closed 25 and 26 December* – **Meals** - Indian 5.95/17.50 **t.** and a la carte 🍷 3.25.

XX **Peking Diner** HX u
71 Burnt Ash Lane BR1 5AA ☎ 464 7911
▤. AE VISA
*closed Sunday and 25-26 December* – **Meals** - Chinese (Peking) 10.00/25.00 and a la carte 🍷 3.75.

### Keston - ✉ Kent - ☎ 01689.

XX **Giannino's** HZ **x**
6 Commonside BR2 6BP ✆ 856410
AE VISA
*closed Sunday, Monday, first 2 weeks August and 24 December-10 January* – **Meals** - Italian 15.75 **t.** and a la carte 4.75.

### Orpington - ✉ Kent - ☎ 01689.

18 High Elms, High Elms Rd, Downe, Orpington ✆ 858175 – 9, 18 Hewitts Golf Centre, Court Rd ✆ 896266.

XX **Xian** JY **a**
324 High St. BR6 0NG ✆ 871881
AE VISA
*closed Sunday lunch and second week August* – **Meals** - Chinese (Peking, Szechuan) 7.50/12.60 **t.** and a la carte 5.20.

## CAMDEN Except where otherwise stated see pp. 20-23.

### Bloomsbury - ✉ NW1/W1/WC1 - ☎ 0171.

34-37 Woburn Pl., WC1H 0JR ✆ 580 4599.

**Holiday Inn Kings Cross** MT **a**
1 Kings Cross Rd WC1X 9HX ✆ 833 3900, Fax 917 6163
squash – rm – 240
**397 rm**, 8 suites.

**Russell** (Forte) LU **o**
Russell Sq. WC1B 5BE ✆ 837 6470, Telex 24615, Fax 837 2857
rm rest – 450
**325 rm**, 3 suites.

**Marlborough** (Radisson Edwardian) LU **i**
9-14 Bloomsbury St. WC1B 3QD ✆ 636 5601, Fax 636 0532
rm rest – 200. AE VISA JCB.
**Meals** 16.95 **st.** and a la carte – 10.95 – **167 rm** 85.00/197.00, 2 suites – SB.

**Mountbatten** (Radisson Edwardian) p.33 DV **o**
20 Monmouth St. WC2H 9HD ✆ 836 4300, Fax 240 3540
rm rest – 75. AE VISA JCB.
**Meals** *(closed lunch Saturday and Sunday)* 18.00/35.00 **st.** and a la carte – 12.00 – **121 rm** 153.00/181.00 **st.**, 6 suites – SB.

**Grafton** (Radisson Edwardian) KU **n**
130 Tottenham Court Rd W1P 9HP ✆ 388 4131, Telex 297234, Fax 387 7394
– 100. AE VISA JCB.
**Meals** *(closed Saturday lunch)* 18.50 **st.** and a la carte – 10.00 – **320 rm** 111.00/140.00 **st.**, 4 suites – SB.

**Kenilworth** (Radisson Edwardian) LU **a**
97 Great Russell St. WC1B 3LB ✆ 637 3477, Fax 631 3133
rm rest – 100. AE VISA JCB.
**Meals** (carving rest.) 16.95 – 10.00 – **187 rm** 79.00/134.00 **st.**

**Forte Crest Bloomsbury** LT **c**
Coram St. WC1N 1HT ✆ 837 1200, Telex 22113, Fax 837 5374
rm rest – 700
**282 rm**, 2 suites.

**Montague Park** LU **c**
12-20 Montague St. WC1B 5BJ ✆ 637 1001, Telex 23307, Fax 637 2506
rest – 80. AE VISA JCB.
**Meals** (bar lunch)/dinner 12.50 **t.** and a la carte 5.75 – **109 rm** 95.00/170.00 **st.**

**Blooms** LU **n**
7 Montague St. WC1B 5BP ✆ 323 1717, Fax 636 6498
**Meals** (room service only) 5.00/23.00 **st.** and dinner a la carte – **26 rm** 100.00/250.00 **st.** – SB.

**Bonnington** LU **s**
92 Southampton Row WC1B 4BH ✆ 242 2828, Telex 261591, Fax 831 9170
rm – rest – 250.
**Meals** *(closed lunch Saturday, Sunday and Bank Holidays)* 9.50/16.75 **st.** and a la carte 10.00 – **215 rm** 79.00/100.00 **st.**

**Bloomsbury Park** (Mt. Charlotte Thistle) LU **u**
126 Southampton Row WC1B 5AD ✆ 430 0434, Telex 25757, Fax 242 0665
rm – 30
**95 rm.**

**Academy** KLU **v**
17-21 Gower St. WC1E 6HG ✆ 631 4115, Fax 636 3442
– rest
**Meals** *(closed lunch Saturday and Sunday)* 10.00/16.95 **st.** and a la carte 6.95 – 8.95 – **33 rm** 74.00/145.00 **s.** – SB.

**Harlingford** LT **n**
61-63 Cartwright Gdns WC1H 9EL ✆ 387 1551, Fax 387 4616
without rest., – **44 rm.**

**Mabledon Court** LT **s**
10-11 Mabledon Pl. WC1H 9BA ✆ 388 3866, Fax 387 5686
without rest. –
**33 rm.**

**Pied à Terre** (Neat) KU **e**
34 Charlotte St. W1P 1HJ ✆ 636 1178, Fax 916 1178
*closed Saturday lunch, Sunday, last 2 weeks August, 2 weeks December-January and Bank Holidays* – **Meals** 19.50/39.50 **st.** 7.00
**Spec.** Snails with morilles and asparagus, garlic purée, Roasted pigeon with a neck confit, fondant celeriac and liver sauce, Fillet of sea bass with a sardine purée and a bouillabaisse sauce.

**Neal Street** p. 33 DV **s**
26 Neal St. WC2H 9PS ✆ 836 8368, Fax 497 1361
*closed Sunday, Christmas-New Year and Bank Holidays* – **Meals** a la carte 29.90/45.45 **t.** 8.00.

**Mon Plaisir** p. 33 DV **a**
21 Monmouth St. WC2H 9DD ✆ 836 7243, Fax 379 0121
*closed Saturday lunch, Sunday and Bank Holidays* – **Meals** - French 13.95 **st.** and a la carte 5.80.

**Poons of Russell Square** LU **x**
50 Woburn Pl. WC1H 0JE ✆ 580 1188
*closed 24 to 28 December* – **Meals** - Chinese 10.00/25.00 **t.** and a la carte.

**Bleeding Heart** NU **e**
Bleeding Heart Yard EC1N 8SJ, off Greville St., Hatton Garden ✆ 242 2056, Fax 831 1402
*closed Saturday, Sunday and 2 weeks Christmas* – **Meals** 13.95 **t.** and a la carte 17.20/22.65 **t.** 3.95.

**Kanishka** KTU **z**
161 Whitfield St. W1P 5RY ✆ 388 0860
*closed lunch Saturday and Bank Holidays, Sunday and 25 to 26 December* – **Meals** - Indian 6.95/25.00 **t.** and a la carte.

**Auntie's** JU **s**
126 Cleveland St. W1P 5DN ✆ 387 1548, Fax 387 3226
AE VISA
*closed dinner Saturday and Sunday, 25 to 26 December and 1 January* – **Meals** - English a la carte 13.30/20.50 **st.** 4.00.

**Il Castelletto** LU **r**
17 Bury Pl. WC1A 2IB ✆ 405 2232
AE VISA
*closed Saturday lunch, Sunday and Bank Holidays* – **Meals** - Italian 14.00 **t.** (lunch) and a la carte 16.50/21.60 **t.** 4.75.

**Alfred** p. 33 DV **u**
245 Shaftesbury Av. WC2H 8EH ✆ 240 2566, Fax 497 0672
AE VISA
*closed Sunday dinner and 24 to 31 December* – **Meals** - English a la carte 18.45/25.45 **t.** 6.00.

## Camden Town – ✉ NW1 – 0171.

**La Bougie** KS **a**
7 Murray St. NW1 9RE ✆ 485 6400
**Meals** - Bistro a la carte 13.25/16.00 4.00.

## Euston – ✉ WC1 – 0171.

**Euston Plaza** KLT **e**
17/18 Upper Woburn Pl. WC1H 0HT ✆ 383 4105, Fax 383 4106
– rm – 110. AE VISA JCB.
**Meals** 12.00/26.00 **st.** and dinner a la carte – 9.50 – **149 rm** 112.00/129.00 **st.**, 1 suite.

## Hampstead – ✉ NW3 – 0171.

Winnington Rd, Hampstead ✆ 455 0203.

**Swiss Cottage** GS **n**
4 Adamson Rd NW3 3HP ✆ 722 2281, Fax 483 4588
« Antique furniture collection » – – 60. AE VISA.
**Meals** (bar lunch)/dinner 22.50 **t.** and a la carte 5.95 – **74 rm** 75.00/95.00 **t.**, 6 suites – SB.

**Forte Posthouse** ES **r**
215 Haverstock Hill NW3 4RB ✆ 794 8121, Fax 435 5586
rm – 30. AE VISA JCB
**Meals** a la carte approx. 15.00 **t.** 5.50 – **140 rm** 59.50/69.50 **st.**

**Clive** (Hilton) HS **a**
Primrose Hill Rd NW3 3NA ✆ 586 2233, Fax 586 1659
– 200. AE VISA.
**Meals** 15.00 **t.** and a la carte – **93 rm** 60.00/70.00 **t.**, 3 suites – SB.

**Charles Bernard** ES **s**
5-7 Frognal NW3 6AL ✆ 794 0101, Fax 794 0100
. AE VISA.
**Meals** (bar lunch)/dinner 15.00 **st.** and a la carte – **57 rm** 55.00/65.00 **st.**

**Langdorf** ES **c**
20 Frognal NW3 6AG ✆ 794 4483, Fax 435 9055
without rest. – . AE VISA.
5.50 – **31 rm** 61.00/115.00 **st.**

**Benihana** GS **o**
100 Avenue Rd NW3 3HF ✆ 586 9508, Fax 586 6740
AE VISA JCB
*closed Monday lunch and 25 December* – **Meals** - Japanese (Teppan-Yaki) 8.45/13.95 **t.** and a la carte.

XX **Carapace** ES **e**
118 Heath St. NW3 1DR ☎ 435 8000, Fax 935 9582
AE VISA
**Meals** (dinner only and Sunday lunch)/dinner 13.80 **t.** and a la carte 4.60.

XX **Zen W3** ES **a**
83-84 Hampstead High St. NW3 1RE ☎ 794 7863, Fax 794 6956
AE VISA
**Meals** - Chinese a la carte 15.20/21.40 **t.**

XX **Orchard** ES **v**
12a Belsize Terr. NW3 4AX ☎ 794 4288
AE VISA
*closed Bank Holidays* – **Meals** - Italian 14.50 **t.** (lunch) and a la carte 20.50/24.00 **t.** 5.50.

X **Café des Arts** ES **i**
82 Hampstead High St. NW3 1RE ☎ 435 3608
AE VISA
*closed 25 and 26 December* – **Meals** a la carte 14.00/21.20 **t.** 5.50.

## Holborn – ✉ WC2 – ☎ 0171.

**Drury Lane Moat House** (Q.M.H.) p. 33 DV **c**
10 Drury Lane, High Holborn WC2B 5RE ☎ 836 6666, Telex 8811395, Fax 831 1548
rm – 100. AE VISA.
**Meals** *(closed lunch Saturday and Sunday)* 12.00/19.00 **t.** and a la carte 7.00 – 10.25 – **151 rm** 120.00/180.00 **st.**, 2 suites – SB.

X **Imari** MU **z**
71 Red Lion St. WC1R 4NA ☎ 405 0486, Fax 405 0473
AE VISA JCB
*closed Saturday lunch, Sunday and Bank Holidays* – **Meals** - Japanese 9.00/25.00 **st.** and a la carte.

## Regent's Park – ✉ NW1 – ☎ 0171.

**White House** JT **o**
Albany St. NW1 3UP ☎ 387 1200, Telex 24111, Fax 388 0091
rm rest – 120. AE VISA JCB.
**Meals** *(closed Saturday lunch, Sunday and Bank Holidays)* (bar lunch Saturday and Sunday) 18.75/22.75 **t.** and a la carte 8.00 – 10.75 – **561 rm** 105.00/150.00 **st.**, 15 suites.

XX **Odette's** HS **i**
130 Regent's Park Rd NW1 8XL ☎ 586 5486
AE VISA
*closed Saturday lunch, Sunday dinner, 1 week Christmas and Bank Holidays*
**Meals** 10.00 **t.** (lunch) and a la carte 19.00/25.50 **t.** 5.50.

XX **China Jazz** JS **e**
29-31 Parkway NW1 7PN ☎ 482 3940
AE VISA
*closed Saturday lunch and 25 to 26 December* – **Meals** - Chinese 10.00/24.00 **t.** and a la carte.

X **Belgo** IS **e**
72 Chalk Farm Rd NW1 8AN ☎ 267 0718, Fax 267 7508
AE VISA
**Meals** 10.00/35.00 **t.** and a la carte.

## Swiss Cottage – ✉ NW3 – ☎ 0171.

**Regents Park Marriott** GS **a**
128 King Henry's Rd NW3 3ST ☎ 722 7711, Telex 267396, Fax 586 5822
rm – 400. AE VISA
**Meals** 14.95/18.50 **st.** and a la carte 7.25 – 11.85 – **298 rm** 145.00/158.00 **st.**, 5 suites.

XX **Peter's** FS **i**
65 Fairfax Rd NW6 4EE ✆ 624 5804
AE VISA
*closed Saturday lunch* – **Meals** 11.95 **t.** and a la carte 4.00.

X **Thai Pepper** GS **v**
115 Finchley Rd NW3 6HY ✆ 722 0026
AE VISA
*closed lunch Saturday and Sunday and Bank Holidays* – **Meals** - Thai 17.00/20.00 **t.** and a la carte 3.90.

**CITY OF LONDON** – 0171 Except where otherwise stated see p. 23.

XXX **Tatsuso** PU **u**
32 Broadgate Circle EC2M 2QS ✆ 638 5863, Fax 638 5864
AE VISA JCB
*closed Saturday, Sunday, and Bank Holidays* – **Meals** - Japanese (booking essential) 19.00/70.00 **st.** and a la carte.

XX **Le Quai** OV **a**
Riverside Walkway, 1 Broken Wharf EC4V 3QQ, off High Timber St. ✆ 236 6480, Fax 236 6479
AE VISA JCB
*closed Saturday, Sunday and Bank Holidays* – **Meals** (dinner booking essential) 32.50 and lunch a la carte.

XX **Corney and Barrow** PU **c**
109 Old Broad St. EC2N 1AP ✆ 638 9308
AE VISA JCB
*closed Saturday, Sunday and Bank Holidays* – **Meals** (lunch only) 20.95 **t.** and a la carte 4.50.

XX **Miyama** OV **e**
17 Godliman St. EC4V 5BD ✆ 489 1937
AE VISA JCB
*closed Saturday dinner, Sunday and Bank Holidays* – **Meals** - Japanese 15.00/20.00 **t.** and a la carte 5.00.

XX **Imperial City** PV **a**
Royal Exchange, Cornhill EC3V 3LL ✆ 626 3437, Fax 338 0125
AE VISA
*closed Saturday, Sunday and Bank Holidays* – **Meals** 13.80/24.80 **t.** and a la carte.

X **Whittington's** OV **c**
21 College Hill EC4R 2RP ✆ 248 5855
AE VISA JCB
*closed Saturday, Sunday and Bank Holidays* – **Meals** (lunch only) a la carte 22.70/26.70 **t.** 4.75.

X **Issimo !** (Forte) PV **e**
8-11 Lime St. EC3 7AA ✆ 623 3616
AE VISA JCB
*closed Saturday, Sunday and Bank Holidays* – **Meals** - Italian (lunch only) (booking essential) a la carte 18.65/22.95 **t.** 4.95.

**CROYDON** pp. 10 and 11.

**Addington** – Surrey – 0181.

18, 18, 9 Addington Court, Featherbed Lane ✆ 657 0281/2/3, GZ
18 The Addington, Shirley Church Rd ✆ 777 1055, GZ.

XX **Willow** GZ **x**
88 Selsdon Park Rd CR2 8JT ✆ 657 4656
P. AE VISA
*closed 25 to 27 December* – **Meals** - Chinese (Peking, Szechuan) 13.50/16.50 **t.** and a la carte 4.50.

## Coulsdon – Surrey – 0181.

Coulsdon Court, Coulsdon Rd 660 6083.

**Coulsdon Manor** EZ **e**
Coulsdon Court Rd, via Stoats Nest Rd CR5 2LL 668 0414, Fax 668 3118
, squash – rest – 180. VISA
**Meals** *(closed Saturday lunch)* 14.95/17.50 **t.** and a la carte 5.95 – **35 rm** 76.00/86.00 **st.** – SB.

## Croydon – Surrey – 0181.

Katherine St., CR9 1ET 760 5630.

**Hilton National** FZ **e**
Waddon Way CR9 4HH 680 3000, Fax 681 6171
– – 400. VISA JCB.
***Latitudes :* Meals** 12.95/18.00
***Ike's American Diner :* Meals** a la carte 19.40/23.65 – 9.95 – **168 rm** 87.00 **t.** – SB.

**Croydon Park** FZ **u**
7 Altyre Rd CR9 5AA 680 9200, Fax 760 0426
, squash – rm – 300. VISA JCB
***Oscars :* Meals** 13.95/14.95 – **203 rm** 87.00/97.00 **st.**, 2 suite – SB.

**Forte Posthouse** FZ **o**
Purley Way CR9 4LT 688 5185, Fax 681 6438
– rm – 170. VISA
**Meals** a la carte approx. 15.00 **t.** 5.50 – **83 rm** 59.50/69.50 **st.**

**Windsor Castle Toby** FZ **a**
415 Brighton Rd, South Croydon CR2 6EJ 680 4559, Fax 680 5121
– rm . VISA.
**Meals** (grill rest.) 7.95 **st.** and a la carte 4.75 – **29 rm** 60.00/70.00 **st.** – SB.

**Travel Inn** GZ **s**
Coombe Rd CR0 5RB, on A 212 686 2030, Fax 686 6435
– rm . VISA.
**Meals** (Beefeater grill) a la carte approx. 16.00 **t.** – 4.95 – **39 rm** 33.50 **t.**

**Mario** FZ **s**
299 High St. CR0 1QL 686 5624
VISA
*closed Saturday lunch, Monday dinner, Sunday, last 2 weeks August and Bank Holidays* – **Meals** - Italian 12.50 **t.** and a la carte.

## Sanderstead – Surrey – 0181.

Selsdon Park Hotel, Addington Rd, Sanderstead 657 8811, GZ.

**Selsdon Park** GZ **n**
Addington Rd CR2 8YA 657 8811, Fax 651 6171
, park, , squash – rm – 150. VISA JCB
**Meals** (dancing Saturday) 15.50/25.00 **t.** and a la carte – 9.50 – **163 rm** 85.00/140.00 **t.**, 7 suites – SB.

# EALING pp. 4 and 5.

## Ealing – W5 – 0181.

West Middlesex, Greenford Rd 574 3450, BV – Horsenden Hill, Woodland Rise 902 4555, BU.

**Carnarvon** CV **v**
Ealing Common W5 3HN 992 5399, Fax 992 7082
rm – 220. VISA JCB.
**Meals** a la carte 13.65/20.65 **st.** 5.50 – 9.95 – **145 rm** 85.00/105.00 **st.**

XX **Maxim** BV **a**
153-155 Northfield Av. W13 9QT ✆ 567 1719
**Meals** - Chinese (Peking).

XX **Laguna Tandoori** BV **i**
1-4 Culmington Par., Uxbridge Rd W13 9BD ✆ 579 9992
*closed 25 December* – **Meals** - Indian 15.00 **t.** and a la carte 3.70.

X **Noughts 'n' Crosses** BV **u**
77 The Grove W5 5LL ✆ 840 7568, Fax 840 1905
AE VISA
*closed Sunday dinner, Monday, August and 26 December-5 January* – **Meals** (dinner only and Sunday lunch)/dinner 19.90 **t.** 4.45.

X **Paolo's** CV **r**
7 Hanger Green W5 3EL ✆ 997 8560
AE VISA
*closed Saturday lunch, Sunday and Bank Holidays* – **Meals** - Italian 21.00/25.00 **t.** and a la carte 4.00.

**Hanwell** – ✉ W7 – ☎ 0181.

Brent Valley, Church Rd, ✆ 567 1287, BV.

**Wellmeadow Lodge** BV **r**
24 Wellmeadow Rd W7 2AL ✆ 567 7294, Fax 566 3468
AE VISA
**Meals** (by arrangement) 15.00 – **6 rm** 45.00/72.00.

X **New Happiness Garden** BV **c**
22 Boston Par., Boston Rd W7 2DG ✆ 567 9314
AE VISA
*closed Sunday, 25-26 December and 1 January* – **Meals** - Chinese 12.00/23.00 **t.** and a la carte 4.25.

## ENFIELD pp. 6 and 7.

Lee Valley, Picketts Lock Lane, Edmonton ✆ 803 3611, GT.

**Enfield** – ✉ Middx – ☎ 0181.

Whitewebbs, Beggars Hollow, Clay Hill ✆ 363 4454, N : 1 m. FT.

**Royal Chace** ET **a**
The Ridgeway EN2 8AR ✆ 366 6500, Fax 367 7191
270. AE VISA
*closed 24 to 29 December* – **Meals** *(closed Saturday lunch, Sunday dinner and Bank Holidays)* (bar lunch Monday to Saturday)/dinner 16.95 **st.** and a la carte 5.45 – **92 rm** 71.50/130.00 **st.**

**Oak Lodge** FT **e**
80 Village Rd, Bush Hill Park EN1 2EU ✆ 360 7082
AE VISA JCB
**Meals** (by arrangement) 17.50 **t.** 6.00 **5 rm** 55.00/80.00 **st.** – SB.

**Hadley Wood** – ✉ Herts – ☎ 0181.

**West Lodge Park** ET **i**
off Cockfosters Rd, ✉ Barnet EN4 0PY ✆ 440 8311, Fax 449 3698
park – rest – 80. AE VISA
**Meals** 18.95/22.50 **st.** – 8.75 – **45 rm** 64.50/170.00 **st.** – SB.

*Pleasant hotels and restaurants are shown in the Guide by a red sign.*
*Please send us the names of any where you have enjoyed your stay.*
*Your Michelin Guide will be even better.*

## GREENWICH pp. 10 and 11.

### Blackheath – ✉ SE3 – 0181.

**Bardon Lodge** HV **a**
15 Stratheden Rd SE3 7TH ✆ 853 4051, Fax 858 7387
– 40.
***Lamplight* : Meals** *(closed Sunday dinner)* (bar lunch Monday to Saturday)/ dinner 13.95 **t.** and a la carte 5.25 – 4.95 – **30 rm** 53.50/85.00 **t.**

**Vanbrugh** HV **e**
21 St. John's Park SE3 7TD ✆ 853 5505 (Reservations : 853 4051), Fax 858 7387
**Meals** (see ***Bardon Lodge*** above) – 4.95 – **30 rm** 53.50/74.00 **t.**

### Greenwich – ✉ SE10 – 0181.

46 Greenwich Church St., SE10 9BL ✆ 858 6376.

**Hamilton** GX **a**
14 West Grove SE10 8QT ✆ 694 9899, Fax 694 2370
**11 rm.**

**Treasure of China** GV **e**
10-11 Nelson Rd SE10 9JB ✆ 858 9884, Fax 293 5327
*closed 25-26 December* – **Meals** - Chinese (Peking, Szechuan) a la carte 14.60/19.50 **t.** 3.50.

**Spread Eagle** GV **c**
1-2 Stockwell St. SE10 9JN ✆ 853 2333
*closed Sunday dinner, 25 to 30 December and Bank Holiday Mondays* – **Meals** 13.50 **t.** (lunch) and dinner a la carte 19.00/26.00 **t.**

**Taste of India** GV **n**
57 Greenwich Church St. SE10 9BL ✆ 858 2668
**Meals** - Indian 12.00/15.00 **t.** and a la carte 3.50.

*This Guide is not a comprehensive list of all hotels and restaurants, nor even of all good hotels and restaurants in London. Since our aim is to be of service to all motorists, we must show establishments in all categories and so we have made a selection of some in each.*

## HACKNEY p. 23.

### Dalston – ✉ N 1 – 0171.

**Soulard** PS **e**
113 Mortimer Rd N1 4JY ✆ 254 1314
*closed Sunday, Monday, 2 weeks August and 1 week Christmas* – **Meals** - French (dinner only) 15.00 **t.** and a la carte 9.50.

## HAMMERSMITH and FULHAM Except where otherwise stated see pp. 24-25.

### Fulham – ✉ SW6 – 0171.

**La Reserve** FZ **a**
422-428 Fulham Rd SW6 1DU ✆ 385 8561, Fax 385 7662
« Contemporary decor » – rm
**Meals** *(closed Sunday dinner)* a la carte 13.50/21.00 **t.** 5.50 – **37 rm** 75.00/90.00 **t.** – SB.

XX **Blue Elephant** EZ **z**
4-6 Fulham Broadway SW6 1AA ☎ 385 6595, Fax 386 7665
▤. AE VISA
*closed Saturday lunch and 24 to 27 December* – **Meals** - Thai (booking essential) 25.00/28.00 **t.** and a la carte 5.95.

XX **Mao Tai** p. 12 BQ **e**
58 New Kings Rd., Parsons Green SW6 4LS ☎ 731 2520
▤. AE VISA
*closed 25 to 27 December* – **Meals** - Chinese (Szechuan) 7.00/15.00 **t.** and a la carte 5.00.

XX **Fleurie** BQ **n**
755 Fulham Rd SW6 5UU ☎ 371 0695
AE VISA
*closed Saturday lunch and Bank Holidays* – **Meals** 12.50/15.00 **t.** and a la carte.

X **Le Midi** EZ **a**
488 Fulham Rd SW6 5NH ☎ 386 0657
AE VISA
**Meals** 7.95/10.95 **t.** and a la carte 3.90.

### Hammersmith – ✉ W6/W12/W14 – ☎ 0181.

XX **Tandoori Nights** p. 9 CV **u**
319-321 King St. W6 9NH ☎ 741 4328
▤. AE VISA JCB
*closed 25 and 26 December* – **Meals** - Indian 9.95/18.00 **t.** and a la carte 5.95.

X **Snows on the Green** p. 9 CV **x**
166 Shepherd's Bush Rd, Brook Green W6 7PB ☎ (0171) 603 2142, Fax 602 7553
VISA
*closed Saturday lunch, Sunday dinner, New Year and Bank Holidays* – **Meals** 12.50 **t.** (lunch) and a la carte 16.95/23.70 **t.**

X **Brackenbury** p. 9 CV **a**
129-131 Brackenbury Rd W6 0BQ ☎ 748 0107, Fax 741 0905
AE VISA
*closed lunch Monday and Saturday, Sunday dinner and 10 days Christmas-New Year* – **Meals** a la carte 12.25/18.25 **t.** 4.25.

### Shepherd's Bush – ✉ W12/W14 – ☎ 0171.

X **Wilsons** p. 9 DV **a**
236 Blythe Rd W14 0HJ ☎ 603 7267
AE VISA
**Meals** 7.50/12.00 **t.** and a la carte.

## HARINGEY pp. 6 and 7.

### Crouch End – ✉ N 8 – ☎ 0181.

XX **Les Associés** EU **e**
172 Park Rd N8 8JY ☎ 348 8944
VISA
*closed lunch Tuesday and Saturday, Sunday, Monday and August* – **Meals** - French 15.95/35.00 **st.** and a la carte.

X **Florians** EU **c**
4 Topsfield Par., Middle Lane N8 8RP ☎ 348 8348
VISA
*closed 25-26 December and Bank Holidays* – **Meals** - Italian a la carte 18.50/21.75 **t.** 5.90.

### Hornsey – ✉ N8 – ☎ 0181.

X **Jashan** EU **z**
19a Turnpike Lane N8 0EP ✆ 340 9880, Fax 347 8770
▤. AE VISA
*closed 25-26 December and Mondays except Bank Holidays* – **Meals** - Indian (dinner only) 12.50 **t.** and a la carte.

*When visiting Scotland,*
*use the Michelin Green Guide* **"Scotland".**
– *Detailed descriptions of places of interest*
– *Touring programmes*
– *Maps and street plans*
– *The history of the country*
– *Photographs and drawings of monuments, beauty spots, houses...*

## HARROW pp. 4 and 5.

### Central Harrow – ✉ Middx – ☎ 0181.

ℹ Civic Centre, Station Rd, HA1 2XF ✆ 424 1103/424 1100, BU.

**Cumberland** BU **x**
1 St. John's Rd HA1 2EF ✆ 863 4111, Fax 861 5668
– rm TV ☎ P – 50. AE VISA.
**Meals** 9.95/15.50 **st.** and a la carte 4.95 – **80 rm** 62.00/67.00 **st.**

XX **Trattoria Sorrentina** BU **x**
6 Manor Par., Sheepcote Rd HA1 2JA ✆ 427 9411
▤. VISA
*closed Saturday lunch and Sunday* – **Meals** - Italian 10.00/25.00 **t.** and a la carte 4.50.

XX Taste of China BU **u**
174 Station Rd HA1 2RH ✆ 863 2080
▤
**Meals** - Chinese.

### Hatch End – ✉ Middx – ☎ 0181.

XX **Swan** BT **n**
322-326 Uxbridge Rd HA5 4HR ✆ 428 8821, Fax 420 1505
▤. AE VISA JCB
*closed 25 and 26 December* – **Meals** - Chinese (Peking) 12.00/19.50 **st.** and a la carte.

### Kenton – ✉ Middx. – ☎ 0181.

**Travel Inn** BU **e**
Kenton Rd HA3 8AT ✆ 907 1671, Fax 909 1604
rm TV ♿ P. AE VISA.
**Meals** (Beefeater grill) a la carte approx. 16.00 **t.** – 4.95 – **44 rm** 33.50 **st.**

### North Harrow – ✉ Middx. – ☎ 0181.

XX **Percy's** BU **n**
66-68 Station Rd HA2 7SJ ✆ 427 2021, Fax 427 8134
. AE VISA
*closed Sunday and Monday* – **Meals** (booking essential) a la carte 19.00/26.00 **t.** 4.90.

X **Thai Castle** BU **c**
28 The Broadwalk, Pinner Rd HA2 6ED ✆ 427 4732
VISA
*closed lunch Saturday and Sunday and 25-26 December* – **Meals** - Thai 9.00/39.00 **t.** and a la carte 3.35.

### Pinner – Middx. – 0181.

**Friends** BU **a**
11 High St. HA5 5PJ 866 0286
*closed Sunday dinner and Bank Holidays* – **Meals** 13.50/17.50 **t.** and a la carte 4.50.

**Olde Village Bakery** BU **a**
33 High St. HA5 5PS 868 4704
**Meals** 10.00 **t.** and a la carte 4.50.

### South Harrow – Middx. – 0181.

**Jaflong** BU **r**
299 Northolt Rd HA2 8JA 864 7345
**Meals** - Indian 9.50/14.90 **t.** and a la carte.

### Stanmore – Middx – 0181.

**Mr Tang's Mandarin** BT **i**
28 The Broadway HA7 4DW 954 0339
**Meals** - Chinese (Peking) 15.00/17.00 **t.** and a la carte 4.00.

## HAVERING pp. 6 and 7.

### Hornchurch by A 12 – JT – on A 127 – Essex – 01708.

**Palms**
Southend Arterial Rd (A 127) RM11 3UJ 346789, Fax 341719
rm – 270.
**Meals** *(closed Saturday lunch)* 17.00 **st.** and a la carte 5.75 – 7.95 – **137 rm** 56.00 **t.**

### Romford by A 118 – JU – Essex – 01708.

18, 9 Havering, Risebridge Chase, Lower Bedfords Rd 41429, JT.

**Coach House**
48 Main Rd RM1 3DB, on A 118 751901, Fax 730290
without rest., – rest.
**32 rm** 29.50/49.50 **st.**

## HILLINGDON pp. 4 and 8.

18 Haste Hill, The Drive (01927) 422877, AU – 18 Harefield Pl., The Drive (01895) 231169, by B 467, AU.

### Eastcote – Middx – 0181.

18 Ruislip, Ickenham Rd (01895) 638835, AU.

Central Library, 14 High St., Uxbridge, UB8 1HD (01895) 250706.

**Sambuca** AU **s**
113 Field End Rd HA5 1QG 866 7500
*closed Sunday dinner, Monday and Bank Holidays* – **Meals** - Italian (dinner only and Sunday lunch)/dinner a la carte 12.90/20.00 **t.** 3.80.

### Hayes – Middx. – 0181.

**Travel Inn** AV **a**
362 Uxbridge Rd UB4 0HF 573 7479, Fax 569 1204
rm.
**Meals** (Beefeater grill) a la carte approx. 16.00 **t.** – 4.95 – **40 rm** 33.50 **t.**

## Heathrow Airport – ✉ Middx – ☎ 0181.

Heathrow Terminals 1,2,3, Underground Station Concourse, TW6 2JA ✆ (0171) 730 3488/824 8000, AX.

**Radisson Edwardian** AX **e**
140 Bath Rd, Hayes UB3 5AW ✆ 759 6311, Fax 759 4559
– rm – 500.
***Henleys* : Meals** 18.00/28.00 **st.** and a la carte
***Brasserie* : Meals** a la carte approx. 20.50 – 12.00 – **442 rm** 153.00/224.00 **st.**, 17 suites – SB.

**Holiday Inn Crowne Plaza Heathrow London** AV **v**
Stockley Rd, West Drayton UB7 9NA ✆ (01895) 445555, Fax 445122
– rm – 200.
***Marlowe* : Meals** *(closed Sunday)* (dinner only)
***Cafe Galleria* : Meals** – 10.95 – **373 rm** 120.00 **st.**, 2 suites.

**Sheraton Skyline** AX **u**
Bath Rd, Hayes UB3 5BP ✆ 759 2535, Telex 934254, Fax 750 9150
« Exotic indoor garden », – rm – 500
**349 rm**, 5 suites.

**London Heathrow Hilton** AX **n**
Terminal 4 TW6 3AF ✆ 759 7755, Telex 925094, Fax 759 7579
– rm – 240.
***Brasserie* : Meals** a la carte 16.75/26.50
***Zen Oriental* : Meals** a la carte approx. 19.30 – 11.95 – **397 rm** 145.00/155.00 **st.**, 4 suites – SB.

**Excelsior Heathrow** (Forte) AX **x**
Bath Rd, West Drayton UB7 0DU ✆ 759 6611, Telex 24525, Fax 759 3421
– rm – 700
**823 rm**, 16 suites.

**Forte Crest** AV **c**
Sipson Rd, West Drayton UB7 0JU ✆ 759 2323, Telex 934280, Fax 897 8659
rm – 200
**570 rm**, 2 suites.

**Sheraton Heathrow** AVX **a**
Colnbrook by-pass, West Drayton UB7 0HJ ✆ 759 2424, Telex 934331, Fax 759 2091
rm – 70.
**Meals** 15.00/20.00 **t.** and a la carte 6.00 – 12.00 – **424 rm** 150.00/170.00, 1 suite – SB.

**Novotel** AV **n**
Cherry Lane, West Drayton UB7 9HB ✆ (01895) 431431, Fax 431221
– rm rest – 200.
**Meals** 12.50/20.00 **st.** and a la carte 4.95 – **175 rm** 69.50 **st.**, 3 suites.

**Forte Posthouse** AX **i**
Bath Rd, Hayes UB3 5AJ ✆ 759 2552, Fax 564 9265
rm rest .
**Meals** a la carte approx. 15.00 **t.** 5.50 – **186 rm** 59.50/69.50 **st.**

**Heathrow Park** (Mt. Charlotte Thistle) off A 4 AX
Bath Rd, Longford, West Drayton UB7 0EQ ✆ 759 2400, Telex 934093, Fax 759 5278
rm – 700.
**Meals** (carving lunch) 12.00/14.75 **st.** and a la carte 5.50 – 8.25 – **306 rm** 75.00/160.00 **st.** – SB.

## Ickenham – ✉ Middx. – ☎ 01895.

**Roberto's** AU **i**
15 Long Lane UB10 8TB ✆ 632519
.
*closed Sunday* – **Meals** - Italian 12.95/16.00 **t.** and a la carte 6.95.

**Yiewsley** – ✉ Middx. – ☎ 0181.

XXX **Waterfront Brasserie** AV **r**
The Arena, Stockley Park UB11 1AA ✆ 899 1733, Fax 899 1711
▤ Ⓟ. AE VISA
*closed dinner Monday to Wednesday and Sunday* – **Meals** (dancing Friday) 16.70 **t.** and a la carte.

## HOUNSLOW pp. 8 and 9.

18 Wyke Green, Syon Lane, Isleworth ✆ (0181) 560 8777, BV – 18 Airlinks, Southall Lane ✆ 561 1418, ABV – 18 Hounslow Heath, Staines Rd ✆ 570 5271, BX.

24 The Treaty Centre, Hounslow High St., TW3 1ES ✆ 572 8279.

**Chiswick** – ✉ W4 – ☎ 0181.

XX **La Dordogne** CV **o**
5 Devonshire Rd W4 2EU ✆ 747 1836, Fax 994 9144
AE VISA
*closed lunch Saturday and Sunday and Bank Holidays* – **Meals** - French a la carte 17.90/26.70 **t.** 4.60.

**Cranford** – ✉ Middx. – ☎ 0181.

**Jarvis International Heathrow** AX **r**
Bath Rd TW5 9QE ✆ 897 2121, Fax 897 7014
– rm TV Ⓟ – 120. AE VISA JCB.
**Meals** *(closed Saturday lunch)* 9.95/15.95 **st.** and a la carte 6.95 – 6.95 – **60 rm** 69.00/79.00 **st.** – SB.

**Heston Service Area** – ✉ Middx. – ☎ 0181.

**Granada Lodge** ABV **e**
TW5 9NA, on M 4 (between junctions 2 and 3 westbound carriageway) ✆ 574 5875, Fax 574 1891
without rest., Reservations (Freephone) 0800 555300 – TV Ⓟ. AE VISA
4.00 – **71 rm** 39.95 **st.**

## ISLINGTON Except where otherwise stated see pp. 20-23.

**Canonbury** – ✉ N1 – ☎ 0171.

X **Anna's Place** p. 6 FU **a**
90 Mildmay Park N1 4PR ✆ 249 9379
*closed Sunday and Monday* – **Meals** - Swedish (booking essential) a la carte 19.00/23.00 **t.**

**Finsbury** – ✉ WC1/EC1/EC2 – ☎ 0171.

X **Stephen Bull's Bistro** NU **r**
71 St. John St. EC1M 4AN ✆ 490 1750, Fax 490 3128
▤. AE VISA
*closed Saturday lunch, Sunday, 1 week Christmas and Bank Holidays* – **Meals** a la carte 15.25/22.00 **t.** 5.00.

X **Le Mesurier** OT **e**
113 Old St. EC1V 9JR ✆ 251 8117, Fax 608 3504
AE VISA JCB
*closed Saturday, Sunday, 3 weeks August, 2 weeks Christmas-New Year and Bank Holidays* – **Meals** (lunch only) (booking essential) a la carte 17.00/23.00 **t.** 4.50.

X **Rouxl Britannia**                                                   PU **x**
Triton Court, 14 Finsbury Sq. EC2A 1BR ℰ 256 6997
🔃 ⓞ 𝘝𝘐𝘚𝘈
*Le Restaurant* : **Meals** *(closed Saturday, Sunday and Bank Holidays)* (lunch only) 21.75
*Le Café* : **Meals** *(closed Saturday, Sunday and* Bank Holidays) (lunch only) a la carte 11.30/16.45.

X **Quality Chop House**                                              MT **n**
94 Farringdon Rd EC1R 3EA ℰ 837 5093
*closed Saturday lunch and Christmas-New Year* – **Meals** a la carte 13.75/19.50 **t.**

**Islington** – ✉ N1 – ☏ 0171.

X **Granita**                                                          NS **a**
127 Upper St. N1 1PQ ℰ 226 3222
✖ ▤ 🔃 𝘝𝘐𝘚𝘈
*closed Tuesday lunch, Monday, 5 days Easter, 2 weeks August and 10 days Christmas* – **Meals** 13.50 **t.** (lunch) and dinner a la carte 18.65/21.65 **t.**

## KENSINGTON and CHELSEA (Royal Borough of).

**Chelsea** – ✉ SW1/SW3/SW10 – ☏ 0171 – Except where otherwise stated see pp. 30 and 31.

🏨 **Hyatt Carlton Tower**                                            FR **n**
2 Cadogan Pl. SW1X 9PY ℰ 235 1234, Telex 21944, Fax 245 6570
≼, ℔, ☞, 🍴, ✗ – 📶 ✖ rm ▤ 📺 ☎ 🚗 – 🔬 260. 🔃 🅰🅴 ⓞ 𝘝𝘐𝘚𝘈 🅹🅲🅱. ✖
*Chelsea Room* : **Meals** 22.50/29.50
*Rib Room* : **Meals** *(closed 1 to 3 January)* 22.50/29.50 – ☑ 14.50 – **194 rm** 250.00 **s.**, 30 suites.

🏨 **Sheraton Park Tower**                                            FQ **v**
101 Knightsbridge SW1X 7RN ℰ 235 8050, Telex 917222, Fax 235 8231
≼ – 📶 ✗ rm ▤ 📺 ☎ ♿ Ⓟ – 🔬 60. 🔃 🅰🅴 ⓞ 𝘝𝘐𝘚𝘈 🅹🅲🅱. ✖
**Meals** a la carte 18.80/34.30 **t.** 🍷 8.00 – ☑ 14.75 – **267 rm** 205.00/235.00 **s.**, 22 suites.

🏨 **Conrad London**                                            p. 13 CQ **i**
Chelsea Harbour SW10 0XG ℰ 823 3000, Fax 351 6525
≼, ℔, ☞, 📓 – 📶 ✗ rm ▤ 📺 ☎ ♿ 🚗 – 🔬 180. 🔃 🅰🅴 ⓞ 𝘝𝘐𝘚𝘈 🅹🅲🅱
**Meals** 13.00/25.00 **t.** and a la carte – ☑ 17.00, **159 suites** 195.00/215.00 – SB.

🏨 **Durley House**                                                   FS **e**
115 Sloane St. SW1X 9PJ ℰ 235 5537, Fax 259 6977
« Tastefully furnished Georgian town house », ☞, ✗ – 📶 ✗ rm 📺 ☎. 🔃 🅰🅴 𝘝𝘐𝘚𝘈. ✖
**Meals** (room service only) a la carte 17.50/21.50 **t.** – ☑ 12.50 –, **11 suites** 195.00/300.00 **t..**

🏨 **Capital**                                                        ER **a**
22-24 Basil St. SW3 1AT ℰ 589 5171, Fax 225 0011
📶 ▤ 📺 ☎ 🚗 – 🔬 25. 🔃 🅰🅴 ⓞ 𝘝𝘐𝘚𝘈. ✖
**Meals** 25.00/40.00 **st.** and a la carte 34.50/44.50 **st.** – ☑ 12.50 – **48 rm** 184.50/340.75 **st.**
**Spec.** Langoustine risotto with pearls of caviar, tarragon and chives, Grilled beef fillet with sage, red onions and horseradish, sauce Sauternes, Assiette vanille.

🏨 **Draycott**                                                       FS **c**
24-26 Cadogan Gdns SW3 2RP ℰ 730 6466, Fax 730 0236
℔, ☞, ☞, ✗ – 📶 ✗ rm 📺 ☎. 🔃 🅰🅴 ⓞ 𝘝𝘐𝘚𝘈 🅹🅲🅱. ✖
**Meals** (room service only) – ☑ 12.95 – **25 rm** 100.00/250.00 **t.**

🏨 **Cadogan**                                                        FR **e**
75 Sloane St. SW1X 9SG ℰ 235 7141, Fax 245 0994
☞, ✗ – 📶 ✗ rm ▤ rest 📺 ☎ – 🔬 30. 🔃 🅰🅴 ⓞ 𝘝𝘐𝘚𝘈. ✖
**Meals** *(closed Saturday lunch)* 16.90/21.90 **t.** and dinner a la carte 🍷 6.25 – ☑ 12.50 – **60 rm** 135.00/175.00 **st.**, 5 suites – SB.

**Franklin** DS **e**
28 Egerton Gdns. SW3 2DB ℘ 584 5533, Fax 584 5449
AE VISA
**Meals** (room service only) – 12.50 – **36 rm** 110.00/210.00 **s.**, 1 suite.

**Basil Street** FQ **o**
8 Basil St. SW3 1AH ℘ 581 3311, Fax 581 3693
– 55. AE VISA JCB
**Meals** (carving lunch Saturday) 14.95/19.75 **t.** 5.00 – 10.90 – **91 rm** 115.00/170.00 **st.**, 1 suite – SB.

**Chelsea** FR **r**
17-25 Sloane St. SW1X 9NU ℘ 235 4377, Telex 919111, Fax 235 3705
rm – 100. AE VISA JCB
**Meals** 15.00 **st.** and a la carte 7.00 – 11.95 – **219 rm** 150.00/165.00 **st.**, 7 suites.

**Sydney House** DT **a**
9-11 Sydney St. SW3 6PU ℘ 376 7711, Fax 376 4233
« Tastefully furnished Victorian town house » – AE VISA
**Meals** (room service only) – 11.00 – **21 rm** 110.00/175.00.

**Egerton House** DR **e**
17-19 Egerton Terr. SW3 2BX ℘ 589 2412, Fax 584 6540
AE VISA
**Meals** (room service only) 7.00 – 12.50 – **27 rm** 100.00/180.00, 1 suite.

**Sloane** ET **c**
29 Draycott Pl. SW3 2SH ℘ 581 5757, Fax 584 1348
« Victorian town house, antiques » – AE VISA
**Meals** (room service only) – 9.00 – **12 rm** 120.00/190.00 **s.**

**Fenja** FS **r**
69 Cadogan Gdns SW3 2RB ℘ 589 7333, Fax 581 4958
without rest., – AE VISA
11.75 – **12 rm** 130.00/195.00 **t.**

**Beaufort** ER **n**
33 Beaufort Gdns SW3 1PP ℘ 584 5252, Telex 929200, Fax 589 2834
without rest., « English floral watercolour collection » – AE VISA
*closed 23 to 27 December* – **28 rm** 110.00/240.00 **s.**

**Eleven Cadogan Gardens** FS **u**
11 Cadogan Gdns SW3 2RJ ℘ 730 3426, Fax 730 5217
AE VISA
**Meals** (room service only) 17.00/22.00 **t.** 5.50 – 10.00 – **55 rm** 98.00/188.00 **st.**, 5 suites.

**Claverley** ER **o**
13-14 Beaufort Gdns SW3 1PS ℘ 589 8541, Fax 584 3410
without rest. – AE VISA
**33 rm** 65.00/175.00 **t.**

**L'Hotel** ER **i**
28 Basil St. SW3 1AT ℘ 589 6286, Telex 919042, Fax 225 0011
AE VISA
***Le Metro* : Meals** (closed Sunday and Bank Holidays) a la carte 14.95/19.20 – 6.50 – **12 rm** 125.00/145.00 **st.**

**Royal Court** FST **a**
Sloane Sq. SW1W 8EG ℘ 730 9191, Telex 296818, Fax 824 8381
rm rest – 40. AE VISA
**Meals** 11.00/21.50 **st.** and a la carte 6.45 – 9.50 – **102 rm** 105.00/160.00 **st.** – SB.

🏨 **Knightsbridge** ER **o**
12 Beaufort Gdns. SW3 1PT ☎ 589 9271, Fax 823 9692
without rest. – |♦| 📺 ☎ – **22 rm.**

🏨 **Wilbraham** FS **n**
1-5 Wilbraham Pl., Sloane St. SW1X 9AE ☎ 730 8296, Fax 730 6815
|♦| ☎. ✗
**Meals** *(closed Saturday lunch, Sunday and Bank Holidays)* (restricted menu) a la carte 8.70/17.45 **t.** 🍷 3.50 – ☕ 5.50 – **53 rm** 39.00/86.00.

XXXX ✿✿✿ **La Tante Claire** (Koffmann) EU **c**
68-69 Royal Hospital Rd SW3 4HP ☎ 352 6045, Fax 352 3257
▤. AE ⓓ VISA
*closed Saturday, Sunday, 3 weeks Summer and 1 week Christmas* – **Meals** - French (booking essential) 25.00/45.00 **st.** and a la carte 53.00 **st.**
Spec. Pied de cochon aux morilles, Coquilles St. Jacques, sauce encre, Chevreuil au chocolat amer et vinaigre de framboises.

XXX **Waltons** DS **a**
121 Walton St. SW3 2HP ☎ 584 0204
▤. AE ⓓ VISA JCB
**Meals** 14.75/21.00 **t.** and a la carte 🍷 4.50.

XXX **Bibendum** DS **s**
Michelin House, 81 Fulham Rd SW3 6RD ☎ 581 5817, Fax 823 7925
▤. AE VISA
*closed 24 to 29 December* – **Meals** 27.00 **t.** (lunch) and dinner a la carte 37.00/50.75 **t.** 🍷 5.75.

XXX ✿ **MPW's, The Canteen** p. 13 CQ **i**
Harbour Yard, Chelsea Harbour SW10 0XL ☎ 351 7330, Fax 351 6189
▤. VISA
**Meals** a la carte 21.95/24.00 **t.**
Spec. Roast sea scallops 'gros sel', sauce vierge, Fillet of cod Viennoise with a grain mustard sabayon, Crème vanille with poached fruits.

XXX **Fifth Floor** (at Harvey Nichols) FQ **a**
Knightsbridge SW1X 7RJ ☎ 235 5250, Fax 235 5020
▤. AE ⓓ VISA JCB
*closed Sunday and 25 to 26 December* – **Meals** 21.50 **t.** and dinner a la carte 20.25/35.50 **t.** 🍷 4.75.

XXX ✿ **Aubergine** (Ramsay) CU **r**
11 Park Walk SW10 0AJ ☎ 352 3449
▤. AE ⓓ VISA
*closed Saturday lunch, Sunday, first 2 weeks August, 24 December-2 January and Bank Holidays* – **Meals** (booking essential) 18.00/36.00 **t.** and a la carte
Spec. Cappuccino of haricots blancs with truffle oil, Fillet of sea bass roasted with braised salsify, jus vanille, Bitter tarte au chocolat.

XXX **Turner's** ES **n**
87-89 Walton St. SW3 2HP ☎ 584 6711, Fax 584 4441
▤. AE ⓓ VISA
*closed Saturday lunch, 25 to 30 December and Bank Holidays* – **Meals** 13.50/26.50 **st.** and a la carte 🍷 9.50.

XXX **Chutney Mary** p. 24 FZ **v**
535 King's Rd SW10 0SZ ☎ 351 3113, Fax 351 7694
▤. AE ⓓ VISA JCB
**Meals** - Anglo-Indian 12.95 **t.** and a la carte 23.00/28.00 **t.** 🍷 4.50.

XXX **Albero & Grana** ET **e**
Chelsea Cloisters, Sloane Av. SW3 3DX ☎ 225 1048, Fax 581 3259
▤. AE ⓓ VISA
**Meals** - Spanish (dinner only) a la carte 26.00/37.00 **st.** 🍷 5.00.

XXX **Benihana** EU **e**
77 King's Rd SW3 4NX ☎ 376 7799, Fax 376 7377
▤. AE ⓓ VISA JCB
**Meals** - Japanese (Teppan-Yaki) 8.75/60.00 **t.** and a la carte.

XX ✿ **Fulham Road** CU **a**
257-259 Fulham Rd SW3 6HY ✆ 351 7823, Fax 490 3128
AE VISA
*closed Bank Holidays* – **Meals** 19.50 **t.** (lunch) and a la carte 22.00/32.50 **t.** 6.00
**Spec.** Ravioli of suckling pig with wild mushroom consommé, Rare roast rump of lamb with aubergine and pepper stew, rosemary cream, Pecan pie with maple ice cream.

XX **Argyll** CU **e**
316 King's Rd SW3 5UH ✆ 352 0025, Fax 352 1652
AE VISA
*closed Monday lunch, Sunday and Bank Holidays* – **Meals** 15.00 **t.** (lunch) and dinner a la carte 17.00/23.75 **t.** 7.00.

XX **English Garden** ET **x**
10 Lincoln St. SW3 2TS ✆ 584 7272
AE VISA JCB
*closed 25 and 26 December* – **Meals** - English 14.75 **t.** (lunch) and a la carte 22.75/31.50 **t.**

XX **St. Quentin** DR **a**
243 Brompton Rd SW3 2EP ✆ 589 8005, Fax 584 6064
AE VISA JCB
**Meals** - French 10.00 **t.** and a la carte 5.60.

XX **Poissonnerie de l'Avenue** DS **u**
82 Sloane Av. SW3 3DZ ✆ 589 2457, Fax 581 3360
AE VISA JCB
*closed Sunday, 10 days at Christmas and Bank Holidays* – **Meals** - French Seafood 16.50 **t.** (lunch) and a la carte 19.00/29.50 **t.** 5.50.

XX **Daphne's** DS **a**
112 Draycott Av. SW3 3AE ✆ 589 4257, Fax 581 2232
AE VISA
**Meals** - Italian a la carte 17.50/31.50 **t.** 6.50.

XX **La Finezza** FT **v**
62-64 Lower Sloane St. SW1N 8BP ✆ 730 8639
AE VISA
*closed Sunday and Bank Holidays* – **Meals** - Italian a la carte approx. 32.50 **t.** 7.50.

XX **Busabong Too** p. 24 FZ **x**
1a Langton St. SW10 0JL ✆ 352 7517
AE VISA
*closed Christmas* – **Meals** - Thai (dinner only) 24.95 **t.** and a la carte.

XX **Toto's** ES **a**
Walton House, Walton St. SW3 2JH ✆ 589 0075
AE VISA JCB
*closed 25 and 26 December* – **Meals** - Italian 14.00 **st.** (lunch) and a la carte approx. 35.00 **st.**

XX **Good Earth** DR **c**
233 Brompton Rd SW3 2EP ✆ 584 3658, Fax 823 8769
AE VISA JCB
*closed 24 to 27 December* – **Meals** - Chinese 7.95/25.00 **t.** and a la carte 8.00.

XX **Dan's** DU **s**
119 Sydney St. SW3 6NR ✆ 352 2718, Fax 352 3265
AE VISA
*closed Saturday lunch, Sunday dinner, 24 December-2 January and Bank Holidays* – **Meals** 16.50 **t.** and a la carte 5.00.

XX **Red** DR **n**
8 Egerton Garden Mews SW3 2EH ✆ 584 7007, Fax 584 0972
AE VISA
**Meals** - Chinese 6.00/30.00 **t.** and a la carte 4.50.

X **Thierry's** CU **c**
342 King's Rd SW3 5UR ✆ 352 3365, Fax 352 3365
▤. AE VISA
*closed Christmas* – **Meals** 9.90/13.50 **t.** and a la carte 5.50.

X **Monkey's** ET **z**
1 Cale St., Chelsea Green SW3 3QT ✆ 352 4711
▤. VISA
*closed Saturday, Sunday, 2 weeks Easter, 3 weeks August and Bank Holidays* – **Meals** 17.50/22.50 **t.** and a la carte 5.50.

X **Beit Eddine** FQ **z**
8 Harriet St. SW1 9JW ✆ 235 3969
AE VISA
**Meals** - Lebanese a la carte 20.75/29.75 **t.** 5.50.

**Earl's Court** – ✉ SW5/SW10 – ☎ 0171 – Except where otherwise stated see pp. 30 and 31.

**Comfort Inn** p. 24 EZ **n**
22-32 West Cromwell Rd SW5 9QJ ✆ 373 3300, Fax 835 2040
without rest. – ▤ TV ☎ – 100. AE VISA JCB
☕ 8.50 – **125 rm** 68.00/86.00 **st.**

**Periquito** AT **e**
34-44 Barkston Gdns. SW5 0EW ✆ 373 7851, Fax 370 6570
rm TV ☎ – 70. AE VISA JCB.
**Meals** 9.50/15.00 **t.** and a la carte – ☕ 7.00 – **75 rm** 64.00 **st.**

**Henley House** AT **e**
30 Barkston Gdns. SE5 0EN ✆ 370 4111, Fax 370 0026
without rest., – rest TV ☎. AE VISA JCB.
**Meals** (by arrangement) (dinner only) (unlicensed) – ☕ 3.40 – **20 rm** 55.00/79.00 **st.**

**Rushmore** p. 24 EZ **c**
11 Trebovir Rd SW5 9LS ✆ 370 3839, Fax 370 0274
without rest. – TV ☎. AE VISA JCB
☕ 6.50 – **22 rm** 59.00/90.00 **st.**

**Amsterdam** p. 24 EZ **c**
7 Trebovir Rd SW5 9LS ✆ 370 2814, Fax 244 7608
without rest. – TV ☎. AE VISA JCB.
☕ 2.75 – **20 rm** 49.00/62.00 **t.**

XX **Formula Veneta** BU **a**
14 Hollywood Rd SW10 9HY ✆ 352 7612
▤. AE VISA
*closed Sunday dinner and Bank Holidays* – **Meals** - Italian a la carte 13.50/19.00 4.00.

XX **Mr Wing** AU **a**
242-244 Old Brompton Rd SW5 0DE ✆ 370 4450, Fax 370 2624
AE VISA
**Meals** - Chinese a la carte 20.50/30.00 **t.**

XX **La Primula** p. 24 FZ **e**
12 Kenway Rd SW5 ORR ✆ 370 5958
▤. AE VISA JCB
*closed lunch Saturday and Sunday, Easter and Christmas* – **Meals** - Italian 8.50/14.50 **t.**

X **Chez Max** AU **c**
168 Ifield Rd SW10 9AF ✆ 835 0874
VISA
*closed lunch Saturday and Monday, Sunday and Bank Holidays* – **Meals** 15.50/23.50 **t.** 9.00.

**Kensington** – SW7/W8/W11/W14 – 0171 – Except where otherwise stated see pp. 24-27.

**The Milestone** p. 30 AQ **u**
1-2 Kensington Court W8 5DL 917 1000, Fax 917 1010
– rm TV. AE VISA.
***Chenestons* : Meals** 13.00 **st.** (lunch)and a la carte 18.00/34.50 – 15.00 – **50 rm** 180.00/210.00 **st.**, 6 suites.

**Halcyon** EX **u**
81 Holland Park W11 3RZ 727 7288, Telex 266721, Fax 229 8516
TV. AE VISA JCB.
***The Room* : Meals** *(closed Saturday lunch)* 18.00 **t.** (lunch) and dinner a la carte 22.95/33.00 – 12.00 – **40 rm** 165.00/250.00 **st.**, 3 suites – SB.

**Copthorne Tara** FY **u**
Scarsdale Pl. W8 5SR 937 7211, Telex 918834, Fax 937 7100
rm TV – 500. AE VISA JCB.
***Brasserie* : Meals** 17.00 **st.** and a la carte
***Jerome K. Jerome* : Meals** *(closed Sunday)* (dinner only) 24.00 and a la carte – 11.30 – **817 rm** 110.00/145.00 **st.**, 8 suites.

**Kensington Park** (Mt. Charlotte Thistle) p. 30 BQ **e**
16-32 De Vere Gdns W8 5AG 937 8080, Telex 929643, Fax 937 7616
rm rest TV – 120. AE VISA.
***Moniques Brasserie* : Meals** 13.95/14.75 **st.** and a la carte
***Cairngorm Grill* : Meals** a la carte 17.30/27.70 – 10.75 – **325 rm** 120.00/175.00 **st.**, 7 suites – SB.

**London Kensington Hilton** EX **s**
179-199 Holland Park Av. W11 4UL 603 3355, Telex 919763, Fax 602 9397
rm TV – 300. AE VISA JCB
***Market* : Meals** *(closed Saturday lunch)*
***Hiroko* : Meals** - Japanese – 12.50 – **596 rm** 99.00/155.00 **st.**, 7 suites.

**Hilton National London Olympia** EY **a**
380 Kensington High St. W14 8NL 603 3333, Telex 22229, Fax 603 4846
rm rest TV – 400. AE VISA JCB.
**Meals** (bar lunch Saturday)/dinner a la carte 17.00/26.50 **t.** 7.00 – 12.50 – **394 rm** 115.00/160.00 **t.**, 11 suites – SB.

**Kensington Palace Thistle** (Mt. Charlotte Thistle) p. 30 BQ **a**
8 De Vere Gdns W8 5AF 937 8121, Telex 262422, Fax 937 2816
rm rest TV – 180. AE VISA JCB.
**Meals** 13.95/15.95 **st.** and a la carte 6.25 – 10.75 – **297 rm** 95.00/135.00 **st.**, 1 suite – SB.

Kensington Close (Forte) FY **c**
Wrights Lane W8 5SP 937 8170, Fax 937 8289
, squash – rm rest TV – 180 – **530 rm.**

**Holland Court** EY **c**
31 Holland Rd W14 8HJ 371 1133, Fax 602 9114
without rest., – TV. AE VISA.
**22 rm** 65.00/100.00 **st.**

**Russell Court** EY **v**
9 Russell Rd W14 8JA 603 1222, Fax 371 2286
without rest. – TV. AE VISA.
**18 rm** 39.50/49.50 **st.**

**Clarke's** EX **c**
124 Kensington Church St. W8 4BH 221 9225, Fax 229 4564
VISA
*closed Saturday, Sunday, 4 days Easter, 2 weeks August, 10 days Christmas and Bank Holidays* – **Meals** 26.00/37.00 **st.** 8.00.

**La Pomme d'Amour** EX **e**
128 Holland Park Av. W11 4UE 229 8532
AE VISA
*closed Saturday lunch, Sunday and Bank Holidays* – **Meals** - French 13.25/20.50 **t.** and a la carte 4.50.

XX **L'Escargot Doré** p. 30 AQR **e**
2-4 Thackeray St. W8 5ET ✆ 937 8508, Fax 937 8508
▤. AE ① VISA
*closed Saturday lunch, Sunday, last 2 weeks August and Bank Holidays* – **Meals** - French 15.50 **t.** and a la carte.

XX **Belvedere in Holland Park** EY **u**
Holland House, off Abbotsbury Rd W8 6LU ✆ 602 1238
« 19C orangery in park » – ▤. AE ① VISA
*closed Sunday dinner, 25 December and lunch 1 January* – **Meals** a la carte 16.00/25.00 **t.**

XX **La Fenice** EX **v**
148 Holland Park Av. W11 4UE ✆ 221 6090, Fax 221 4096
▤. AE ① VISA
*closed Saturday lunch, Monday and Bank Holidays* – **Meals** - Italian 8.50/12.50 **t.** and a la carte 4.75.

XX **Launceston Place** p. 30 BR **a**
1a Launceston Pl. W8 5RL ✆ 937 6912, Fax 938 2412
▤. AE VISA
*closed Saturday lunch, Sunday dinner and Bank Holidays* – **Meals** 16.50 **t.** and a la carte 4.50.

XX **Arcadia** p. 30 AQ **s**
Kensington Court, 35 Kensington High St. W8 5BA ✆ 937 4294, Fax 937 4393
▤. AE VISA
*closed Saturday and Sunday lunch, 3 days Christmas and 28 August* – **Meals** 16.00 **t.** (lunch) and a la carte 20.20/23.75 **t.**

XX **Boyd's** p. 32 AZ **r**
135 Kensington Church St. W8 7LP ✆ 727 5452, Fax 221 0615
▤. AE ① VISA
*closed Sunday, 2 weeks Christmas and Bank Holidays* – **Meals** 14.00 **t.** (lunch) and a la carte 19.95/33.75 **t.**

XX **Phoenicia** EY **n**
11-13 Abingdon Rd W8 6AH ✆ 937 0120, Fax 937 7668
▤. AE ① VISA
*closed 24 and 25 December* – **Meals** - Lebanese 15.30/22.80 **st.** and a la carte 4.75.

XX **Shanghai** FX **a**
38c-d Kensington Church St. W8 4BX ✆ 938 2501
▤. AE ① VISA
*closed Saturday lunch and Sunday* – **Meals** - Chinese 12.50/24.50 **t.** and a la carte 4.20.

X **Kensington Place** p. 32 AZ **z**
201 Kensington Church St. W8 7LX ✆ 727 3184, Fax 229 2025
▤. VISA
*closed 4 days Christmas* – **Meals** 13.50 **t.** (lunch) and a la carte 15.50/29.50 **t.**

X **Cibo** EY **o**
3 Russell Gdns W14 8EZ ✆ 371 6271
AE ① VISA
*closed Saturday lunch* – **Meals** - Italian a la carte 22.00/25.25 **t.** 5.90.

X **Malabar** p. 32 AZ **e**
27 Uxbridge St. W8 7TQ ✆ 727 8800
VISA
*closed last week August and 4 days at Christmas* – **Meals** - Indian (booking essential) (buffet lunch Sunday) a la carte 14.15/26.80 **st.** 4.60.

X **Wódka** p. 30 AR **c**
12 St. Albans Grove W8 5PN ✆ 937 6513, Fax 937 8621
AE VISA
*closed lunch Saturday and Sunday and Bank Holidays* – **Meals** - Polish a la carte 16.70/22.30 **t.** 4.50.

X **Mandarin** EY **s**
197c Kensington High St. W8 6BA ✆ 937 1551
AE VISA
*closed 24 to 26 December* – **Meals** - Chinese a la carte 15.00/20.00 **st.** 4.75.

**North Kensington** – ✉ W2/W10/W11 – 0171 – Except where otherwise stated see pp. 20-23.

**Abbey Court** p. 32 AZ **u**
20 Pembridge Gdns W2 4DU ✆ 221 7518, Telex 262167, Fax 792 0858
without rest., « Tastefully furnished Victorian town house » – TV. AE VISA.
**22 rm** 80.00/160.00 **t.**

**Pembridge Court** p. 32 AZ **n**
34 Pembridge Gdns W2 4DX ✆ 229 9977, Fax 727 4982
« Collection of antique clothing » – rest TV. AE VISA.
**Meals** *(closed Sunday and Bank Holidays)* (dinner only) 9.95 **st.** and a la carte 4.95 – **20 rm** 90.00/150.00 **st.**

**Portobello** EV **n**
22 Stanley Gdns W11 2NG ✆ 727 2777, Fax 792 9641
« Attractive town house in Victorian terrace » – TV. AE VISA
*closed 23 December-2 January* – **Meals** 15.00 **st.** and a la carte 4.75 – **25 rm** 70.00/180.00 **st.**

XXX **Leith's** EV **e**
92 Kensington Park Rd W11 2PN ✆ 229 4481
AE VISA
*closed 27-28 August and 4 days at Christmas* – **Meals** (dinner only) 32.00 **t.** and a la carte 28.50/39.75 **t.** 7.25
Spec. Hors d'oeuvre trolley, Roast fillet of sea bass with scallops and a tomato and caper vinaigrette, Pot roasted guinea fowl with leek mousseline and sherry vinegar dressing.

XX **Chez Moi** p. 24 EX **n**
1 Addison Av., Holland Park W11 4QS ✆ 603 8267
AE VISA
*closed Saturday lunch, Sunday and Bank Holidays* – **Meals** - French 14.00 **t.** (lunch) and a la carte 17.50/26.25 **t.** 4.50.

XX **Park Inn** AZ **c**
6 Wellington Terr., Bayswater Rd W2 4LW ✆ 229 3553, Fax 229 3553
AE VISA
**Meals** - Chinese Seafood (Peking) 5.00/12.00 **t.** and a la carte 4.50.

X **L'Altro** EUV **c**
210 Kensington Park Rd W11 1NR ✆ 792 1066
AE VISA
*closed Sunday dinner, 4 days Christmas and Bank Holidays* – **Meals** - Italian a la carte 19.40/31.75 **t.** 5.95.

X **192** EV **a**
192 Kensington Park Rd W11 2JF ✆ 229 0482
AE VISA
*closed 25 to 26 December and Bank Holidays* – **Meals** 10.50 **t.** (lunch) and a la carte 17.00/24.50 **t.**

X **Canal Brasserie** ET **c**
Canalot Studios, 222 Kensal Rd W10 5BN ✆ (0181) 960 2732
VISA
*closed lunch Saturday and Sunday and dinner Monday and Tuesday* – **Meals** a la carte 13.40/16.50 **t.**

**Brasserie du Marché aux Puces** EU **a**
349 Portobello Rd W10 5SA (0181) 968 5828
*closed Sunday dinner and Bank Holidays* – **Meals** a la carte 16.45/19.45 **t.** 5.50.

**Surinder's** EU **e**
109 Westbourne Park Rd W2 5QL 229 8968
AE VISA
*closed Sunday and Monday* – **Meals** (dinner only) 14.95 **st.**

**South Kensington** – SW5/SW7/W8 – 0171 – Except where otherwise stated see pp. 30 and 31.

**Harrington Hall** BT **n**
5-25 Harrington Gdns SW7 4JW 396 9696, Fax 396 9090
– rm – 250. AE VISA JCB.
***Wetherby's* : Meals** 18.50/38.20 – 10.00 – **200 rm** 99.00/145.00 **st.** – SB.

**Gloucester** BS **r**
4-18 Harrington Gdns SW7 4LH 373 6030, Telex 917505, Fax 373 0409
rm – 400. AE VISA JCB
**Meals** a la carte 15.15/23.70 **t.** 10.00 – 13.50 – **542 rm** 150.00/185.00 **t.**, 6 suites.

**Pelham** CS **z**
15 Cromwell Pl. SW7 2LA 589 8288, Fax 584 8444
« Tastefully furnished Victorian town house » – . AE VISA.
**Meals** *(closed Sunday lunch and Saturday)* 16.00/22.00 **t.** – 11.50 – **34 rm** 120.00/170.00 **t.**, 3 suites – SB.

**Blakes** BU **n**
33 Roland Gdns SW7 3PF 370 6701, Telex 8813500, Fax 373 0442
« Antique oriental furnishings » – rest . AE VISA.
**Meals** 32.00 (lunch) and a la carte 44.50/64.75 **t.** 8.00 – 16.50 – **46 rm** 125.00/300.00 **st.**, 6 suites – SB.

**Rembrandt** DS **x**
11 Thurloe Pl. SW7 2RS 589 8100, Telex 295828, Fax 225 3363
– rm rest – 250. AE VISA JCB.
**Meals** 12.50/15.95 **st.** and a la carte 5.00 – 9.25 – **195 rm** 105.00/125.00 **st.** – SB.

**Swallow International** AS **c**
Cromwell Rd SW5 0TH 973 1000, Telex 27260, Fax 244 8194
– rm rest – 200. AE VISA
**Meals** (carving lunch) 14.50/15.95 **st.** and a la carte – 10.25 – **414 rm** 105.00/135.00 **st.**, 1 suite – SB.

**Holiday Inn** BS **u**
100 Cromwell Rd SW7 4ER 373 2222, Telex 911311, Fax 373 0559
– rm – 150. AE VISA JCB.
**Meals** 9.95 **st.** and a la carte 6.50 – 10.95 – **143 rm** 140.00/165.00 **st.**, 19 suites – SB.

**Regency** CT **e**
100 Queen's Gate SW7 5AG 370 4595, Telex 267594, Fax 370 5555
– rm rest – 100. AE VISA JCB.
**Meals** *(closed lunch Saturday and Sunday)* 16.50/18.50 **st.** and a la carte 6.00 – 13.50 – **192 rm** 85.00/120.00 **s.**, 6 suites – SB.

**Vanderbilt** (Radisson Edwardian) BS **v**
68-86 Cromwell Rd SW7 5BT 589 2424, Fax 225 2293
rest – 120. AE VISA JCB.
**Meals** 13.50/15.50 – **223 rm.**

**Jury's Kensington** CT **i**
109-113 Queen's Gate SW7 5LR ✆ 589 6300, Telex 262180, Fax 581 1492
rest TV – 80. AE VISA.
**Meals** (bar lunch Monday to Saturday)/dinner 15.00/11.95 **st.** and a la carte – 7.25 – **171 rm** 65.00/175.00 **st.** – SB.

**Forum** (Inter-Con) BS **x**
97 Cromwell Rd SW7 4DN ✆ 370 5757, Fax 373 1448
rm rest TV P – 400. AE VISA JCB
**Meals** 10.50/22.50 **st.** and a la carte 6.50 – 11.50 – **906 rm** 135.00/155.00 **st.**, 4 suites.

**Gore** BR **n**
189 Queen's Gate SW7 5EX ✆ 584 6601, Fax 589 8127
« Attractive decor » – rm TV. AE VISA JCB
*closed 24 and 25 December* – ***Bistrot 190 :*** **Meals** (only members and residents may book) a la carte 14.50/21.50
(see also ***Downstairs at One Ninety*** below) – 9.50 – **54 rm** 99.00/146.00 **st.**

Cranley BT **c**
10-12 Bina Gardens SW5 0LA ✆ 373 0123, Fax 373 9497
without rest., « Tasteful decor, antiques » – TV
**32 rm**, 4 suites.

John Howard BQ **i**
4 Queen's Gate SW7 5EH ✆ 581 3011, Telex 8813397, Fax 589 8403
TV
**43 rm**, 9 suites.

Park International AS **e**
117-125 Cromwell Rd SW7 4DS ✆ 370 5711, Telex 296822, Fax 244 9211
TV – 40
**117 rm.**

**Kensington Plaza** BS **e**
61 Gloucester Rd SW7 4PE ✆ 584 8100, Telex 8950993, Fax 823 9175
rest TV – 100. AE VISA
***Mongolian Brasserie :*** **Meals** (dinner only) 14.95 – 4.75 – **88 rm** 69.00/85.00 **st.**

**Number Sixteen** CT **c**
14-17 Sumner Pl. SW7 3EG ✆ 589 5232, Fax 584 8615
without rest., « Attractively furnished Victorian town houses », – TV.
AE VISA.
**36 rm** 99.00/170.00 **t.**

**Five Sumner Place** DR **a**
5 Sumner Pl. SW7 3EE ✆ 584 7586, Fax 823 9962
without rest. – TV. AE VISA JCB.
**13 rm** 62.00/95.00 **s.**

**Aster House** CT **u**
3 Sumner Pl. SW7 3EE ✆ 581 5888, Fax 584 4925
without rest., – TV. AE.
**12 rm** 61.00/99.00.

**Cranley Gardens** BT **e**
8 Cranley Gdns SW7 3DB ✆ 373 3232, Telex 894489, Fax 373 7944
without rest. – TV. AE VISA
**85 rm** 63.00/89.00 **st.**

**Hotel 167** BT **r**
167 Old Brompton Rd SW5 0AN ✆ 373 3221, Fax 373 3360
without rest. – TV. AE VISA JCB.
**19 rm** 59.00/82.50 **st.**

XXX **Bombay Brasserie** BS **a**
Courtfield Close, 140 Gloucester Rd SW7 4UH ✆ 370 4040
« Raj-style decor, conservatory garden » – . VISA
*closed 25 and 26 December* – **Meals** - Indian (buffet lunch) 14.95 **t.** and dinner a la carte 20.95/27.95 **t.** 4.95.

XX **Hilaire** CT **n**
68 Old Brompton Rd SW7 3LQ ✆ 584 8993
*closed Saturday lunch and Sunday* – **Meals** (booking essential) 17.00/21.50 **t.** and dinner a la carte 23.00/32.00 **t.** 6.75.

XX **Shaw's** BT **v**
119 Old Brompton Rd SW7 3RN ✆ 373 7774
*closed Saturday lunch, Sunday dinner, 2 weeks August and 2 weeks Christmas-New Year* – **Meals** 13.00/28.50 **t.** 9.50.

XX **Downstairs at One Ninety** BR **n**
190 Queen's Gate SW7 5EU ✆ 581 5666, Fax 581 8172
*closed Sunday and Christmas* – **Meals** - Seafood (booking essential) (dinner only) a la carte 18.15/26.40 **t.** 12.00.

XX **Khan's of Kensington** CS **e**
3 Harrington Rd SW7 3ES ✆ 581 2900, Fax 581 2900
**Meals** - Indian 7.50/14.50 **t.** and a la carte 4.95.

XX **Tui** CS **u**
19 Exhibition Rd SW7 2HE ✆ 584 8359, Fax 352 8343
*closed 5 days at Christmas and Bank Holiday Mondays* – **Meals** - Thai 10.00 **st.** (lunch) and a la carte 13.50/20.20 **t.** 4.10.

XX **Delhi Brasserie** AS **a**
134 Cromwell Rd SW7 4HA ✆ 370 7617
*closed 25 and 26 December* – **Meals** - Indian 7.50/14.95 **t.** and a la carte.

XX **Cafe Lazeez** CT **a**
93-95 Old Brompton Rd SW7 3LD ✆ 581 9993, Fax 581 8200
North Indian – **Meals** a la carte 11.65/22.75 **t.** - ***Restaurant* : Meals** (dinner only) a la carte 11.65/22.75.
X ***Cafe*** – **Meals** and a la carte 11.65/22.75 **t.**

XX **Memories of India** BR **s**
18 Gloucester Rd SW7 4RB ✆ 589 6450
**Meals** - Indian 14.50/20.00 and a la carte.

X **Bangkok** CS **v**
9 Bute St. SW7 3EY ✆ 584 8529
*closed Sunday, one week Christmas to New Year and Bank Holidays* – **Meals** - Thai Bistro a la carte 13.40/20.25 **t.**

## KINGSTON UPON THAMES pp. 8 and 9.

Home Park, Hampton Wick ✆ **(0181) 977 6645**, BY.

### Chessington – Surrey – 01372.

**Travel Inn** BZ **c**
Leatherhead Rd KT9 2NE, on A 243 ✆ 744060, Fax 720889
rm
**Meals** (Beefeater grill) a la carte approx. 16.00 **t.** – 4.95 – **42 rm** 33.50 **t.**

### Kingston – Surrey – 0181 – Garrison Lane ✆ 391 0948, CZ.

**Kingston Lodge** (Forte) CY **u**
Kingston Hill KT2 7NP ✆ 541 4481, Fax 547 1013
rest – 60.
**Meals** (bar lunch Monday to Saturday)/dinner 18.95 **st.** and a la carte 5.95 – 7.50 – **62 rm** 95.00/127.50 **st.** – SB.

XX **Gravier's** CY **x**
9 Station Rd, Norbiton KT2 7AA ✆ 549 5557
AE VISA
*closed Saturday lunch, Sunday, 1 week Easter, 1 week August, 1 week Christmas and Bank Holidays* – **Meals** - French Seafood 16.50 **t.** (lunch) and a la carte 20.35/28.35 **t.** 4.50.

X **Ayudhya** CY **z**
14 Kingston Hill KT2 7NH ✆ 549 5984
AE VISA
*closed Monday lunch, Easter Sunday, 25 December and 1 January* – **Meals** - Thai 15.50/18.50 **t.** and a la carte 3.60.

**Surbiton** – ✉ Surrey – 0181.

XX **Chez Max** BY **o**
85 Maple Rd KT6 4AW ✆ 399 2365
AE VISA
*closed Saturday lunch, Sunday, Monday, 24 to 30 December and Good Friday* – **Meals** (booking essential) 15.95/19.45 **t.** and dinner a la carte 18.50/23.10 **t.** 7.00.

## LAMBETH Except where otherwise stated see pp.10 and 11.

**Brixton** – ✉ SW9 – 0171.

X **Twenty Trinity Gardens** EX **n**
20 Trinity Gdns SW9 8DP ✆ 733 8838
VISA
*closed 25 and 26 December* – **Meals** (dinner only and Sunday lunch)/dinner 16.75 **t.** and a la carte 5.00.

**Clapham Common** – ✉ SW4 – 0171.

**Windmill on the Common** DQ **e**
Clapham Common South Side SW4 9DE ✆ 673 4578, Fax 675 1486
– rm rest . AE VISA.
**Meals** (bar lunch Monday to Saturday)/dinner 18.50 **st.** and a la carte – **29 rm** 75.00/85.00 **st.**

XX **The Grafton** p. 13 DQ **a**
45 Old Town SW4 OJL ✆ 627 1048
AE VISA
*closed Saturday lunch, Sunday, last 3 weeks August, 1 week Christmas and Bank Holidays* – **Meals** - French 12.50/32.00 **t.** and a la carte 4.50.

**Streatham** – ✉ SW16 – 0181.

**Barrow House** EY **s**
45 Barrow Rd SW16 5PE ✆ 677 1925, Fax 677 1925
without rest., « Victoriana », – .
**5 rm** 20.00/45.00 **st.**

**Waterloo** – ✉ SE1 – 0171.

XX **RSJ** p. 27 NX **e**
13a Coin St. SE1 8YQ ✆ 928 4554
. AE VISA
*closed Saturday lunch, Sunday, 25-26 December and Bank Holidays* – **Meals** 15.95 **t.** and a la carte 5.25.

XX **La Rive Gauche** p. 27 NX **x**
61 The Cut SE1 8LL ✆ 928 8645
AE VISA
*closed Saturday lunch and Sunday* – **Meals** - French 12.00/16.85 **st.** and a la carte 5.50.

## LONDON HEATHROW AIRPORT – see Hillingdon, London p. 56.

## MERTON pp. 8 and 9.

### Morden – ✉ Morden – ☎ 0181.

Forte Travelodge — DY **c**
Epsom Rd SM4 5PH, SW : on A 24 ☎ 640 8227
Reservations (Freephone) 0800 850950 – TV, P. AE VISA.
**Meals** (Harvester grill) a la carte approx. 16.00 **t.** – 5.50 – **32 rm** 33.50 **t.**

### Wimbledon – ✉ SW19 – ☎ 0181.

Cannizaro House (Mt. Charlotte Thistle) — DXY **x**
West Side, Wimbledon Common SW19 4UF ☎ 879 1464, Fax 879 7338
« 18C country house overlooking Cannizaro Park », – rm TV
P – 45. AE VISA JCB.
**Meals** 16.95/25.75 **t.** and a la carte – 9.75 – **44 rm** 105.00/175.00 **t.**, 2 suites – SB.

Bayee Village — DX **i**
24 High St. SW19 5DX ☎ 947 3533, Fax 944 8392
AE VISA JCB
**Meals** - Chinese (Peking, Szechuan) 8.00/23.00 **st.** and a la carte 5.00.

## REDBRIDGE pp. 6 and 7.

Town Hall, High Rd, IG1 1DD ☎ (0181) 478 3020 ext 2126.

### Ilford – ✉ Essex – ☎ 0181.

Wanstead Park Rd ☎ 554 5174, HU – Fairlop Waters, Forest Rd, Barkingside ☎ 500 9911, JT.

Travel Inn — HU **i**
Redbridge Lane East IG4 5BG ☎ 550 6451
rm TV P. AE VISA.
**Meals** (Beefeater grill) a la carte approx. 16.00 **t.** – 4.95 – **40 rm** 33.50 **t.**

Forte Travelodge — HU **e**
Beehive Lane RG4 5DR ☎ 550 4248
Reservations (Freephone) 0800 850950 – TV P. AE VISA.
**Meals** (Harvester grill) a la carte approx. 16.00 **t.** – **32 rm** 33.50 **t.**

Dragon City — HJU **a**
97 Cranbrook Rd IG1 4PG ☎ 553 0312
**Meals** - Chinese (Canton, Peking).

### South Woodford – ✉ Essex – ☎ 0181.

Ho-Ho — HU **c**
20 High Rd E18 2QL ☎ 989 1041
AE VISA
*closed Saturday lunch* – **Meals** - Chinese (Peking, Szechuan) 16.50/27.50 **st.** and a la carte.

### Woodford – ✉ Essex – ☎ 0181.

Hainault Forest, Chigwell Row ☎ 500 2097, JT – Chingford, 158 Station Rd ☎ 529 2107, HT.

Prince Regent — HT **a**
Manor Rd, Woodford Bridge IG8 8AE ☎ 505 9966, Fax 506 0807
– rest TV P – 350. AE VISA
**Meals** 12.75/14.75 **st.** and a la carte – **51 rm** 72.50/130.00 **t.** – SB.

Woodford Moat House (Q.M.H.) — HT **c**
30 Oak Hill, Woodford Green IG8 9NY ☎ 505 4511, Fax 506 0941
– TV P – 150. AE VISA.
*closed 3 days Christmas* – **Meals** 15.00/17.50 **st.** and a la carte – 9.50 – **99 rm** 58.00/70.00 **st.** – SB.

## RICHMOND-UPON-THAMES pp. 8 and 9.

### Barnes – ✉ SW13 – ☎ 0181.

XX **Sonny's** CX **x**
94 Church Rd SW13 0DQ ☎ 748 0393, Fax 748 2698
▤. AE VISA
*closed Sunday dinner and lunch Bank Holidays* – **Meals** 12.75 **t.** and a la carte
🌢 3.50.

X **Riva** CX **a**
169 Church Rd SW13 9HR ☎ 748 0434
AE VISA
*closed Saturday lunch, Easter, last 2 weeks August, Christmas and Bank Holidays* – **Meals** - Italian a la carte 14.50/25.00 **t.** 🌢 6.00.

### East Sheen – ✉ SW14 – ☎ 0181.

XX **Crowther's** CX **n**
481 Upper Richmond Rd West SW14 7PU ☎ 876 6372
▤. VISA
*closed Saturday lunch, Sunday, Monday, 2 weeks August and 1 week Christmas* – **Meals** (booking essential) 12.75/21.00 **t.** 🌢 4.75.

### Hampton Court – ✉ Surrey – ☎ 0181.

**Mitre** BY **v**
Hampton Court Rd KT8 9BN ☎ 979 9988, Fax 979 9777
≤ – |♦| ⇔ rm TV ☎ P – 25. AE ⓪ VISA. ✻
**Meals** 14.50/18.50 **t.** and a la carte 🌢 8.00 – ☕ 8.50 – **35 rm** 89.00/115.00 **t.**, 1 suite – SB.

### Hampton Wick – ✉ Surrey – ☎ 0181.

**Chase Lodge** BY **e**
10 Park Rd KT1 4AS ☎ 943 1862, Fax 943 9363
TV ☎ P. AE ⓪ VISA
**Meals** (lunch by arrangement Monday to Saturday)/dinner a la carte approx. 17.00 **t.** 🌢 3.50 – **9 rm** ☕ 48.00/80.00 **t.** – SB.

### Richmond – ✉ Surrey – ☎ 0181.

**18, 18 Richmond Park, Roehampton Gate ☎ 876 3205/1795,** CX – **18 Sudbrook Park ☎ 940 1463,** CX.

**Old Town Hall, Whittaker Av., TW9 1TP ☎ 940 9125.**

**Petersham** CX **c**
Nightingale Lane, Richmond Hill TW10 6UZ ☎ 940 7471, Telex 928556, Fax 940 9998
≤, – |♦| TV ☎ P – 50. AE ⓪ VISA. ✻
**Meals** - (see ***Nightingales*** below) – **54 rm** ☕ 100.00/155.00 **st.**

**Richmond Gate** CX **c**
158 Richmond Hill TW10 6RP ☎ 940 0061, Fax 332 0354
– ⇔ rm TV ☎ P – 50. AE ⓪ VISA. ✻
**Meals** *(closed Saturday lunch)* 14.50/18.50 **t.** and a la carte – ☕ 7.00 – **64 rm** 89.00/155.00 **t.** – SB.

**Bingham** CX **z**
61-63 Petersham Rd TW10 6UT ☎ 940 0902, Fax 948 8737
– TV ☎ – 30. AE ⓪ VISA. ✻
**Meals** *(closed Sunday and Bank Holidays)* (dinner only) 11.75 **t.** and a la carte 🌢 4.25 – **35 rm** ☕ 67.50/95.00 **t.**

XXX **Nightingales** (at Petersham H.) CX **c**
Nightingale Lane, Richmond Hill TW10 6UZ ☎ 940 7471, Telex 928556, Fax 940 9998
≤, – P. AE ⓪ VISA
**Meals** 18.50/28.50 **t.** and a la carte 🌢 8.50.

XX **Four Regions** CX **e**
102-104 Kew Rd TW9 2PQ ✆ 940 9044, Fax 332 6130
▤. ⊡ AE VISA
**Meals** - Chinese 10.00/30.00 **t.** and a la carte.

X **Burnt Chair** BX **e**
5 Duke St. TW9 1HP ✆ 940 9488
⊡ VISA
*closed Sunday, 2 weeks August, 24 to 29 December and Bank Holidays* – **Meals** (dinner only) 15.00 **t.** and a la carte.

X **Chez Lindsay** BX **c**
11 Hill Rise TW9 1JS ✆ 948 7473
⊡ VISA
*closed Saturday lunch, Sunday, 25 to 28 December and Bank Holiday Monday lunch* – **Meals** - French Bistro a la carte 18.50/24.75 **t.** 5.75.

X **Pitagora** CX **e**
106 Kew Rd TW9 5PQ ✆ 948 2443
**Meals** - Italian.

## Twickenham – ✉ Middx. – ☎ 0181.

Twickenham Park, Staines Rd ✆ 783 1698, BX.

44 York St., TW1 3BZ ✆ 891 1411.

XX **McClements** BX **s**
12 The Green TW2 5AA ✆ 755 0176, Fax 890 1372
. ⊡ VISA
*closed Sunday and Monday* – **Meals** 15.00/25.00 **t.** and a la carte 6.00.

THE CHANNEL TUNNEL Map Guide

260 *French edition with tourist sights in England*

261 *English edition with tourist sights on the Continent*

## SOUTHWARK Except where otherwise stated see pp. 10 and 11.

## Bermondsey – ✉ SE1 – ☎ 0171.

XXX **Le Pont de la Tour** p. 27 PX **c**
36d Shad Thames, Butlers Wharf SE1 2YE ✆ 403 8403, Fax 403 0267
<, « Riverside setting » – ▤. ⊡ AE ⓓ VISA
*closed Saturday lunch and 4 days Christmas* – **Meals** 25.00 **t.** (lunch) and dinner a la carte 26.50/37.75 **t.** 6.50.

XXX **Bengal Clipper** PX **e**
Cardamom Building, Shad Thames, Butlers Wharf SE1 2YE ✆ 357 9001, Fax 357 9002
▤. ⊡ AE ⓓ VISA
**Meals** - Indian a la carte 11.65/17.20 4.95.

X **Blue Print Café** p. 27 PX **u**
Design Museum, Shad Thames, Butlers Wharf SE1 2YD ✆ 378 7031, Fax 378 6540
<, « Riverside setting », – ⊡ AE ⓓ VISA
*closed Sunday dinner and 4 days at Christmas* – **Meals** a la carte 16.00/24.75 **t.**

X **Cantina Del Ponte** p. 27 PX **c**
36c Shad Thames, Butlers Wharf SE1 2YE ✆ 403 5403, Fax 403 0267
<, « Riverside setting » – ⊡ AE ⓓ VISA
*closed Sunday dinner and 4 days at Christmas* – **Meals** - Italian-Mediterranean a la carte 16.15/24.25 **t.** 8.95.

X **Butlers Wharf Chop House** PX **n**
36e Shad Thames, Butlers Wharf SE1 2YE ✆ 403 3403, Fax 403 3414
« Riverside setting, <Tower Bridge » – ⊡ AE ⓓ VISA
*closed Sunday dinner* – **Meals** 19.50 **t.** (lunch) and dinner a la carte 22.00/27.50 **t.** 5.50.

### Dulwich – ✉ SE19 – ☎ 0181.

XX **Luigi's** FX **a**
129 Gipsy Hill SE19 1QS ✆ 670 1843
▤. AE VISA
*closed Saturday lunch, Sunday and Bank Holidays* – **Meals** - Italian a la carte approx. 16.00 **t.**

### Rotherhithe – ✉ SE16 – ☎ 0171.

**Scandic Crown** GV **r**
265 Rotherhithe St., Nelson Dock SE16 1EJ ✆ 231 1001, Fax 231 0599
<, Ls, ≘s, ▢, % – |‡| ⇔ rm ▤ rest TV ☎ & P – 350. AE VISA JCB.
**Meals** 18.95 **st.** and dinner a la carte 9.50 – ☐ 9.50 – **384 rm** 85.00/105.00 **st.**, 2 suites – SB.

### Southwark – ✉ SE1 – ☎ 0171.

XX **La Truffe Noire** p. 27 PX **a**
29 Tooley St. SE1 2QF ✆ 378 0621, Fax 403 0689
▤. AE VISA JCB
*closed Saturday lunch, Sunday, 24 December-2 January and Bank Holidays* – **Meals** - French 10.00 **st.** and a la carte 6.00.

X **Café dell'Ugo** PX **r**
56-58 Tooley St. SE1 2SZ ✆ 407 6001
▤. AE VISA
**Meals** 10.00 **t.** (dinner) and a la carte 14.85/24.35 **t.**

## SUTTON pp. 8 and 9.

### Carshalton – ✉ Surrey – ☎ 0181.

XX **La Veranda** EZ **a**
18-19 Beynon Rd SM5 3RL ✆ 647 4370
▤. AE VISA
**Meals** *(closed Sunday and Bank Holidays)* a la carte 18.60/26.90 **t.** 7.80.

### Sutton – ✉ Surrey – ☎ 0181.

18, 9 Oak Sports Centre, Woodmansterne Rd, Carshalton ✆ 643 8363.

**Holiday Inn** EZ **a**
Gibson Rd SM1 2RF ✆ 770 1311, Fax 770 1539
Ls, ≘s, ▢ – |‡| ⇔ rm ▤ rest TV ☎ & P – 220. AE VISA JCB
**Meals** *(closed Saturday lunch)* 12.95/22.50 **st.** and a la carte 4.95 – ☐ 9.50 – **115 rm** 99.50/115.00 **st.**, 1 suite – SB.

**Thatched House** DZ **e**
135-141 Cheam Rd SM1 2BN ✆ 642 3131, Fax 770 0684
– TV ☎ P – 50. VISA.
**Meals** *(closed Sunday)* (dinner only) 15.50 **t.** 3.95 – **28 rm** ☐ 39.50/59.50 **st.** – SB.

XX **Partners Brasserie** DY **v**
23 Stonecot Hill SM3 9HB ✆ 644 7743
▤. AE VISA
*closed Saturday lunch, Sunday, Monday and 1 week Christmas* – **Meals** 9.95 **t.** and a la carte 4.00.

## TOWER HAMLETS pp. 6 and 7.

Bethnal Green Library, Cambridge Heath Rd, E2 0HL ✆ (0171) 980 4831.

### Stepney – ✉ E1 – ☎ 0171.

XX Laksmi GV **a**
116 Mile End Rd E1 4UN ✆ 265 9403
▤ – **Meals** - Indian.

## WANDSWORTH Except where otherwise stated see pp. 12 and 13.

### Battersea – ✉ SW8/SW11 – ☎ 0171.

XX **Ransome's Dock** p. 25 HZ **c**
35-37 Parkgate Rd SW11 4NP ☎ 223 1611, Fax 924 2614
AE VISA
*closed Sunday dinner and Christmas* – **Meals** 11.50 **t.** (lunch) and a la carte 17.50/23.75 **t.** 4.50.

XX **Chada** CQ **x**
208-210 Battersea Park Rd SW11 4ND ☎ 622 2209
AE VISA
*closed Saturday lunch and Bank Holidays* – **Meals** - Thai a la carte 16.05/25.65 **st.**

XX Lena's CQ **z**
196 Lavender Hill SW11 1JA ☎ 228 3735
**Meals** - Thai.

### Clapham – ✉ SW11 – ☎ 0171.

X **Jasmin** CQ **u**
50/52 Battersea Rise SW11 1EG ☎ 228 0336
AE VISA
**Meals** - Chinese (Canton, Peking) 5.50/12.80 **t.** and a la carte.

### Putney – ✉ SW15 – ☎ 0181.

XX **Royal China** AQ **a**
3 Chelverton Rd SW15 1RN ☎ 788 0907, Fax 785 2305
AE VISA
**Meals** - Chinese a la carte 20.00/26.00 **t.**

XX **Del Buongustaio** AQ **e**
283 Putney Bridge Rd SW15 2PT ☎ 780 9361, Fax 789 9659
AE VISA
*closed Saturday lunch, 29 August, Christmas-New Year and Bank Holidays* – **Meals** - Italian 19.50 **st.** and a la carte 5.80.

### Tooting – ✉ SW17 – ☎ 0181.

X **Oh Boy** CR **c**
843 Garratt Lane SW17 0PG ☎ 947 9760
AE VISA
**Meals** - Thai (dinner only) a la carte 9.50/11.45 **st.** 3.60.

### Wandsworth – ✉ SW12/SW17/SW18 – ☎ 0181.

XX **Harvey's** CR **e**
2 Bellevue Rd SW17 7EG ☎ 672 0114
AE VISA
*closed lunch Saturday and Monday, Sunday, Christmas-New Year and Easter* – **Meals** 13.50/21.50 **t.** 6.00.

XX **Tabaq** DR **v**
47 Balham Hill SW12 9DR ☎ 673 7820
AE VISA
**Meals** - Indian (dinner only) a la carte 11.20/23.75 **t.** 4.25.

X **Bombay Bicycle Club** DR **o**
95 Nightingale Lane SW12 8NX ☎ 673 6217
AE VISA
*closed Christmas* – **Meals** - Indian (dinner only) a la carte approx. 17.75 **t.**

**Bayswater and Maida Vale** – ✉ W2/W9 – ☎ 0171 – Except where otherwise stated see pp. 32 and 33.

**Royal Lancaster** DZ **e**
Lancaster Terr. W2 2TY ☎ 262 6737, Fax 724 3191
← – rm – 1400. AE VISA JCB.
**Meals** 22.50/27.50 **t.** and a la carte 8.00 – 14.50 – **398 rm** 147.00/176.00 **st.**, 20 suites – SB.

**London Metropole** p. 21 GU **c**
Edgware Rd W2 1JU ☎ 402 4141, Telex 23711, Fax 724 8866
←, – rm – 1200. AE VISA JCB.
**Meals** - (see ***Aspects*** below) – 14.40 – **716 rm** 135.00/200.00 **t.**, 26 suites.

**Whites** (Mt. Charlotte Thistle) CZ **v**
Bayswater Rd, 90-92 Lancaster Gate W2 3NR ☎ 262 2711, Telex 24771, Fax 262 2147
rm. AE VISA JCB.
**Meals** *(closed Saturday lunch)* 17.50/21.50 **t.** and a la carte 7.15 – 10.25 – **52 rm** 145.00/225.00 **t.**, 2 suites – SB.

**Plaza on Hyde Park** (Hilton) DZ **r**
1-7 Lancaster Gate W2 3NA ☎ 262 5022, Telex 8954372, Fax 724 8666
rm. AE VISA JCB.
**Meals** 9.90/15.00 **st.** and a la carte – 9.80 – **402 rm** 81.00/150.00 **st.** – SB.

**Stakis London Coburg** BZ **c**
129 Bayswater Rd W2 4RJ ☎ 221 2217, Fax 229 0557
rm – 80. AE VISA JCB
**Meals** - (see ***Spice Merchant*** below) – 7.50 – **131 rm** 75.00/85.00 **t.**, 1 suite – SB.

**London Embassy** (Jarvis) BZ **o**
150 Bayswater Rd W2 4RT ☎ 229 1212, Telex 27727, Fax 229 2623
rm rest – 60. AE VISA.
**Meals** (carving rest.) 15.95 **t.** and a la carte 6.75 – 9.50 – **192 rm** 100.00/140.00 **st.**, 1 suite.

**Hyde Park Towers** BZ **r**
41-51 Inverness Terr. W2 3JN ☎ 221 8484, Fax 792 3201
rest – 40. AE VISA JCB.
**Meals** (buffet lunch) 13.50 **st.** and a la carte 4.50 – 7.50 – **115 rm** 86.00/96.00 **st.**

**Queen's Park** CZ **s**
48 Queensborough Terr. W2 3SS ☎ 229 8080, Telex 21723, Fax 792 1330
rest – 60. AE VISA JCB.
**Meals** *(closed Friday and Saturday)* (dinner only) a la carte 10.75/17.50 **t.** 5.70 – 7.50 – **86 rm** 86.00/106.00 **st.**

**Mornington** DZ **s**
12 Lancaster Gate W2 3LG ☎ 262 7361, Fax 706 1028
without rest. – . AE VISA
**68 rm** 79.00/109.00 **st.**

**Phoenix** BZ **e**
1 Kensington Garden Sq. W2 4BH ☎ 229 2494, Telex 298854, Fax 727 1419
without rest. – . AE VISA JCB.
**125 rm** 69.00/140.00 **st.**

**Byron** CZ **z**
36-38 Queensborough Terr. W2 3SH ☎ 243 0987, Telex 263431, Fax 792 1957
without rest. – . AE VISA.
**41 rm** 75.50/89.00 **t.**, 1 suite.

**Comfort Inn** CZ **e**
18-19 Craven Hill Gdns W2 3EE ☎ 262 6644, Fax 262 0673
AE VISA.
**Meals** 15.00/25.00 **st.** and a la carte 4.00 – **60 rm** 57.00/86.00 **st.**

**Delmere** DZ **v**
130 Sussex Gdns W2 1UB ✆ 706 3344, Fax 262 1863
**Meals** *(closed Sunday)* 16.00 **st.** and a la carte 6.50 – 6.00 – **38 rm** 58.40/72.80 **st.**

**Gresham** DZ **a**
116 Sussex Gdns W2 1UA ✆ 402 2920, Fax 402 3137
without rest. – AE VISA.
**38 rm** 50.00/75.00 **st.**

**Norfolk Plaza** DZ **x**
29-33 Norfolk Sq. W2 1RX ✆ 723 0792, Telex 266977, Fax 224 8770
without rest. – AE VISA JCB.
**81 rm** 69.00/98.00 **st.**, 6 suites.

**Parkwood** EZ **e**
4 Stanhope Pl. W2 2HB ✆ 402 2241, Fax 402 1574
without rest. – VISA.
**18 rm** 39.75/67.50 **st.**

**Aspects** (at London Metropole H.) p. 64 GU **c**
Edgware Rd W2 1JU ✆ 402 4141, Telex 23711, Fax 724 8866
< London – AE VISA JCB
**Meals** 18.50/29.50 **st.** and a la carte 8.50.

**Spice Merchant** (at Stakis London Coburg H.) BZ **c**
130 Bayswater Rd W2 4RJ ✆ 221 2442, Fax 229 0557
AE VISA
**Meals** - Indian a la carte 11.45/16.15 **st.** 5.00.

**Poons** BZ **x**
Whiteleys, Queensway W2 4YN ✆ 792 2884
AE VISA
*closed 3 days at Christmas* – **Meals** - Chinese a la carte 9.50/14.70 **t.** 5.50.

**Al San Vincenzo** EZ **o**
30 Connaught St. W2 2AE ✆ 262 9623
VISA
*closed Saturday lunch, Sunday and 2 weeks Christmas* – **Meals** - Italian a la carte 21.95/30.50 **t.** 7.50.

**L'Accento** BZ **a**
16 Garway Rd W2 4NH ✆ 243 2201, Fax 243 2201
VISA
*closed Bank Holidays* – **Meals** - Italian 10.50 **st.** and a la carte.

## Belgravia – ✉ SW1 – 0171 – Except where otherwise stated see pp. 30 and 31.

**Berkeley** FQ **e**
Wilton Pl. SW1X 7RL ✆ 235 6000, Telex 919252, Fax 235 4330
– 220. AE VISA JCB.
***Restaurant* : Meals** *(closed Saturday)* 19.50/21.00 **st.** and a la carte 5.75.
***The Perroquet* : Meals** *(closed Sunday)* 16.00/21.00 **st.** and dinner a la carte 5.75 – 16.00 – **133 rm** 180.00/260.00 **s.**, 27 suites.

**Lanesborough** p. 25 IY **a**
1 Lanesborough Pl. SW1X 7TA ✆ 259 5599, Telex 911866, Fax 259 5606
rm – 90. AE VISA JCB.
***The Conservatory* : Meals** 22.50/28.50 – 16.00 – **86 rm** 175.00/310.00 **s.**, 9 suites.

**Halkin** p. 32 AV **a**
5 Halkin St. SW1X 7DJ ✆ 333 1000, Fax 333 1100
« Contemporary interior design » – rm – 25. AE VISA JCB.
**Meals** - Italian *(closed lunch Saturday and Sunday)* 23.00 **st.** and a la carte 30.00/42.00 **st.** 9.50 – 13.50 – **36 rm** 190.00/240.00 **s.**, 5 suites
**Spec.** Duck ravioli with savoy cabbage and foie gras, Ragout of langoustine, rabbit and potato, Tiramisu.

🏨 **Sheraton Belgravia**                                              FR **u**
20 Chesham Pl. SW1X 8HQ ✆ 235 6040, Telex 919020, Fax 259 6243
📶 ✕ rm ☰ 📺 ☎ 🅿 – ♨ 40. 🅰 🆎 ⑩ *VISA* JCB. ✗
*closed Christmas-New Year* – **Meals** *(closed lunch Saturday and Sunday)* 10.00 **t.** (dinner)and a la carte 19.00/25.00 **t.** – ☷ 10.50 – **82 rm** 195.00/265.00 **s.**, 7 suites.

🏨 **Lowndes** (Hyatt)                                                  FR **i**
21 Lowndes St. SW1X 9ES ✆ 823 1234, Telex 919065, Fax 235 1154
♨, ☎ – 📶 ✕ rm ☰ 📺 ☎ – ♨ 25. 🅰 🆎 ⑩ *VISA* JCB. ✗
**Brasserie 21 : Meals** 11.95 – ☷ 12.00 – **77 rm** 160.00/185.00 **s.**, 1 suite.

🏨 **Diplomat**                                                         FR **a**
2 Chesham St. SW1X 8DT ✆ 235 1544, Fax 259 6153
without rest. – 📺 ☎. 🅰 🆎 ⑩ *VISA*. ✗
**27 rm** ☷ 65.00/130.00 **t.**

XXX **Al Bustan**                                                      FR **z**
27 Motcomb St. SW1X 8JU ✆ 235 8277
☰. 🅰 🆎 ⑩ *VISA*
**Meals** - Lebanese a la carte 24.00/35.00 **t.**

XX **Motcombs**                                                       FR **z**
26 Motcomb St. SW1X 8JU ✆ 235 6382, Fax 245 6351
☰. 🅰 🆎 ⑩ *VISA*
*closed Saturday lunch, Sunday dinner and Bank Holidays* – **Meals** 14.75/28.95 **t.** and a la carte ⓘ 5.50.

**Hyde Park and Knightsbridge** – ✉ SW1/SW7 – ☎ 0171 – pp. 30 and 31.

🏨 **Hyde Park** (Forte)                                               FQ **x**
66 Knightsbridge SW1Y 7LA ✆ 235 2000, Fax 235 4552
≼, ♨ – 📶 ✕ rm ☰ 📺 ☎ ♿ – ♨ 250. 🅰 🆎 ⑩ *VISA* JCB. ✗
**Park Room : Meals** - Italian 25.00/29.50
(see also **The Restaurant, Marco Pierre White** below) – ☷ 15.00 – **166 rm** 199.00/275.00 **s.**, 19 suites – SB.

🏨 **Knightsbridge Green**                                            EQ **z**
159 Knightsbridge SW1X 7PD ✆ 584 6274, Fax 225 1635
without rest. – 📶 📺 ☎. 🅰 🆎 *VISA*. ✗
*closed 4 days at Christmas* – ☷ 8.50 – **10 rm** 75.00/100.00 **st.**, **14 suites** 115.00 **st.**

XXXX **The Restaurant, Marco Pierre White**                           FQ **x**
❀❀❀ (at Hyde Park H.), 66 Knightsbridge SW1Y 7LA ✆ 259 5380, Fax 235 4552
☰. 🅰 🆎 *VISA*
*closed Saturday lunch, Sunday, last week December, first week January and Bank Holidays* – **Meals** (booking essential) 25.00/65.00 **t.**
**Spec.** Millefeuille of crab and tomatoes with a tomato vinaigrette, Tronçonettes of turbot with grilled sea scallops and a Sauternes sauce, Caramelised apple tart with vanilla ice cream and caramel sauce.

XXX **Pearl of Knightsbridge**                                        EQ **e**
22 Brompton Rd SW1X 7QN ✆ 225 3888, Fax 225 0252
☰. 🅰 🆎 *VISA*
*closed 25 and 26 December* – **Meals** - Chinese 20.00/30.00 **t.** and a la carte ⓘ 7.00.

*When visiting London use the Green Guide **"London"***

– *Detailed descriptions of places of interest*

– *Useful local information*

– *A section on the historic square-mile of the City of London with a detailed fold-out plan*

– *The lesser known London boroughs – their people, places and sights*

– *Plans of selected areas and important buildings.*

**Mayfair** – ✉ W1 – ☎ 0171 – pp. 28 and 29.

**Dorchester** BN **a**
Park Lane W1A 2HJ ☎ 629 8888, Telex 887704, Fax 409 0114
– 500. AE VISA JCB.
***Grill* : Meals** 23.50/28.00 **st.** and a la carte 29.30/40.30
***Terrace* : Meals** *(dinner Friday and Saturday only)*
(see also ***Oriental*** below) – 14.50 – **194 rm** 195.00/255.00 **s.**, 53 suites – SB.

**Claridge's** BL **c**
Brook St. W1A 2JQ ☎ 629 8860, Telex 21872, Fax 499 2210
– 60. AE VISA JCB.
***Restaurant* : Meals** *(closed Saturday lunch)* 26.00/36.00 **st.** and a la carte
***Causerie* : Meals** *(closed Saturday dinner and Sunday)* 16.00/30.00 – 17.00 – **137 rm** 180.00/290.00 **s.**, 53 suites – SB.

**Four Seasons** BP **a**
Hamilton Pl., Park Lane W1A 1AZ ☎ 499 0888, Telex 22771, Fax 493 1895
– rm – 500. AE VISA JCB.
***Lanes* : Meals** 22.75/25.00 **st.** and dinner a la carte 22.00/38.00
(see also ***Four Seasons*** below) – 14.75 – **201 rm** 210.00/265.00 **s.**, 26 suites.

**Le Meridien Piccadilly** EM **a**
21 Piccadilly W1V 0BH ☎ 734 8000, Telex 25795, Fax 437 3574
, squash – rm – 260. AE VISA JCB.
***Terrace Garden* : Meals** 18.50/21.00 **t.** and a la carte
(see also ***Oak Room*** below) – 12.50 – **247 rm** 200.00/275.00, 18 suites.

**Grosvenor House** (Forte) AM **a**
Park Lane W1A 3AA ☎ 499 6363, Telex 24871, Fax 493 3341
– rm – 1500. AE VISA JCB.
***Pavilion* : Meals** 13.50/21.50 **t.** and a la carte
***Pasta Vino* : Meals** *(closed Saturday lunch and Sunday)* a la carte 21.50/33.00
(see also ***Chez Nico at Ninety Park Lane*** below) – 14.50 – **383 rm** 180.00/225.00 **s.**, 71 suites – SB.

**Connaught** ✿ BM **e**
Carlos Pl. W1Y 6AL ☎ 499 7070, Fax 495 3262
rest. AE VISA.
***The Restaurant*** and ***Grill Room* : Meals** (booking essential) 25.00/35.00 **t.** and a la carte 24.60/63.10 – **66 rm**, 24 suites
Spec. Galette Connaught aux 'diamants noirs', salade Aphrodite, Homard et langoustines grillés aux herbes, Crème brûlée d'un soir.

**47 Park Street** AM **c**
47 Park St. W1Y 4EB ☎ 491 7282, Telex 22116, Fax 491 7281
AE VISA JCB.
**Meals** (room service)(see also ***Le Gavroche*** below) – 17.00 – **52 suites** 235.00/380.00 **s.**

**London Hilton on Park Lane** BP **e**
22 Park Lane W1Y 4BE ☎ 493 8000, Telex 24873, Fax 493 4957
« London from rooftop restaurant », – rm – 1250. AE VISA JCB.
***Windows* : Meals** *(closed Sunday dinner)* 30.95/44.00 **t.** and a la carte
***Trader Vics* : Meals** *(closed Saturday lunch)* a la carte 23.00/30.50 – 14.95 – **395 rm** 195.00/300.00 **s.**, 52 suites.

Brown's (Forte) DM **e**
29-34 Albemarle St. W1A 4SW ☎ 493 6020, Fax 493 9381
rm – 70
**112 rm**, 6 suites.

**Park Lane** BP **x**
Piccadilly W1Y 8BX ☎ 499 6321, Telex 21533, Fax 499 1965
– rm – 300. AE VISA JCB.
***Bracewells* : Meals** *(closed Saturday lunch and Sunday)* 19.50/35.00 **st.** and a la carte
***Brasserie on the Park* : Meals** 10.95 **st.** and a la carte – 12.95 – **278 rm** 165.00/185.00 **s.**, 30 suites.

**Britannia** (Inter-Con) BM **x**
Grosvenor Sq. W1A 3AN ✆ 629 9400, Telex 23941, Fax 629 7736
rm TV ☎ – 100. AE VISA JCB.
***Adam Room* : Meals** *(closed Saturday and Sunday)* 23.00/26.00 **st.** and a la carte (see also ***Shogun*** below) – 14.95 – **305 rm** 145.00/220.00, 12 suites.

**Inter-Continental** BP **o**
1 Hamilton Pl., Hyde Park Corner W1V 0QY ✆ 409 3131, Telex 25853, Fax 409 7461
– rm TV ☎ – 1000. AE VISA JCB.
**Meals** 21.00/24.50 **t.** and a la carte 7.00 : (see also ***Le Soufflé*** below) – 16.00 – **433 rm** 195.00/270.00 **s.**, 34 suites.

**May Fair Inter-Continental** DN **z**
Stratton St. W1A 2AN ✆ 629 7777, Telex 262526, Fax 629 1459
– rm TV ☎ – 300. AE VISA JCB.
**Meals** (see ***The Chateau*** below) – 14.50 – **262 rm** 190.00/250.00, 25 suites.

**Athenaeum** CP **s**
116 Piccadilly W1V 0BJ ✆ 499 3464, Fax 493 1860
– rm TV ☎ – 55. AE VISA JCB.
***Bulloch's* : Meals** *(closed lunch Saturday and Sunday)* a la carte 24.50/31.50 **t.** – 14.50 – **111 rm** 165.00/230.00, 33 suites.

**Marriott** BL **a**
Duke St., Grosvenor Sq. W1A 4AW ✆ 493 1232, Telex 268101, Fax 491 3201
– rm TV ☎ – 600. AE VISA JCB.
***Diplomat* : Meals** 18.00/23.00 **st.** and a la carte – 12.25 – **212 rm** 180.00/220.00 **s.**, 11 suites – SB.

**Westbury** (Forte) DM **a**
Conduit St. W1A 4UH ✆ 629 7755, Telex 24378, Fax 495 1163
rm TV ☎ – 120. AE VISA JCB
**Meals** *(closed lunch Saturday and Sunday)* 21.50/25.00 **st.** and a la carte 10.75 – 13.00 – **231 rm** 145.00/215.00 **st.**, 13 suites – SB.

**Washington** CN **s**
5-7 Curzon St. W1Y 8DT ✆ 499 7000, Telex 24540, Fax 495 6172
TV ☎ – 80. AE VISA JCB.
**Meals** *(closed lunch Saturday and Sunday)* 19.95 **st.** and a la carte 6.95 – 9.95 – **169 rm** 148.00/258.00 **st.**, 4 suites.

**Holiday Inn** DN **r**
3 Berkeley St. W1X 6NE ✆ 493 8282, Telex 24561, Fax 629 2827
rm TV ☎ – 70. AE VISA JCB.
**Meals** *(closed Saturday lunch)* 15.75 **t.** and a la carte 12.00 – 10.95 – **183 rm** 140.00/190.00 **st.**, 2 suites – SB.

**Chesterfield** CN **c**
35 Charles St. W1X 8LX ✆ 491 2622, Telex 269394, Fax 491 4793
rm rest TV ☎ – 110. AE VISA JCB.
**Meals** *(closed Saturday lunch)* 7.50/18.50 **t.** and a la carte 7.50 – 10.95 – **106 rm** 120.00/170.00 **st.**, 4 suites.

**Green Park** CN **a**
Half Moon St. W1Y 8BP ✆ 629 7522, Telex 28856, Fax 491 8971
rm rest TV ☎ – 70. AE VISA JCB.
**Meals** *(closed lunch Saturday and Sunday)* 9.75/12.00 **st.** and a la carte 5.00 – 9.75 – **161 rm** 104.00/174.00 **st.**

**Flemings** CN **z**
7-12 Half Moon St. W1Y 7RA ✆ 499 2964, Fax 499 1817
rest TV ☎ – 45. AE VISA JCB.
**Meals** 14.00/20.00 **st.** and a la carte 7.50 – 10.25 – **121 rm** 115.00/150.00 **st.**, 11 suites.

**London Mews Hilton** BP **u**
2 Stanhope Row W1Y 7HE ✆ 493 7222, Fax 629 9423
rm TV ☎ – 50. AE VISA JCB
**Meals** (light meals only) a la carte 14.45/24.20 **st.** 8.50 – 10.95 – **71 rm** 141.00/175.00 **st.**, 1 suite.

XXXXX ✿ **Oak Room** (at Le Meridien Piccadilly H.) EM **a**
21 Piccadilly W1V 0BH ✆ 734 8000, Telex 25795, Fax 437 3574
*closed Saturday lunch, Sunday and 1 to 21 August* – **Meals** - French 24.50/46.00 **t.** and a la carte 38.50/46.50 **t.** 7.75
**Spec.** Salade de lapereau et grenouilles aux champignons des bois, Suprême de bar cuit à la vapeur au beurre de truffe, Pigeon fermier et artichauts poivrades, chutney aux pommes acides.

XXXXX ✿✿✿ **Chez Nico at Ninety Park Lane** (Ladenis) (at Grosvenor House H.) AM **e**
Park Lane W1A 3AA ✆ 409 1290, Fax 355 4877
*closed lunch Saturday and Bank Holiday Mondays, Sunday, 4 days at Easter and 10 days at Christmas* – **Meals** - French (booking essential) 25.00/54.00 **st.**
**Spec.** Salad of crisp guinea fowl with french beans, truffle oil and truffles, Grilled scallops with sesame seeds and fresh vermicelli, Milk-fed veal cutlet with rosemary and sweet garlic.

XXXX ✿✿ **Le Gavroche** (Roux) AM **c**
43 Upper Brook St. W1Y 1PF ✆ 408 0881, Fax 409 0939
*closed Saturday, Sunday, 24 December-3 January and Bank Holidays* – **Meals** - French (booking essential) 36.00/75.00 **st.** and a la carte 47.50/87.60 **st.** 10.00
**Spec.** Soufflé suissesse, L'Assiette du boucher, Omelette Rothschild.

XXXX ✿ **Oriental** (at Dorchester H.) BN **a**
Park Lane W1A 2HJ ✆ 629 8888, Telex 887704, Fax 409 0114
*closed Saturday lunch, Sunday and August* – **Meals** - Chinese (Canton) 20.00/28.00 **st.** and a la carte 28.00/60.50 **st.** 11.00
**Spec.** Deep fried mixed seafood with mango wrapped in rice paper, Braised shark's fin soup with mixed seafood, Roasted Peking duck.

XXXX ✿ **Four Seasons** (at Four Seasons H.) BP **a**
Hamilton Pl., Park Lane W1A 1AZ ✆ 499 0888, Telex 22771, Fax 493 1895
**Meals** - French 25.00/45.00 **st.** and a la carte 34.50/48.75 **st.** 7.00
**Spec.** Pan fried fillet of red mullet with an orange powder coat and baby carrots, Saddle of rabbit wrapped in lettuce with Spring broad beans, Hot bitter chocolate cake with white chocolate ice cream.

XXXX ✿ **Les Saveurs** BN **o**
37a Curzon St. W1Y 8EY ✆ 491 8919, Fax 491 3658
*closed Saturday, Sunday, 2 weeks August, 2 weeks Christmas-New Year and Bank Holidays* – **Meals** - French 21.00/39.00 **t.** 8.00
**Spec.** Foie gras Aubergine, Roast guinea fowl with tapenade, Café irlandais glacé.

XXXX **Le Soufflé** (at Inter-Continental H.) BP **o**
1 Hamilton Pl., Hyde Park Corner W1V 0QY ✆ 409 3131, Telex 25853, Fax 409 7461
*closed Saturday lunch, Sunday dinner, Monday, August and 2 weeks Christmas-New Year* – **Meals** 27.50/45.00 **t.** and a la carte 34.50/44.50 **t.** 9.00.

XXX **Princess Garden** AL **z**
8-10 North Audley St. W1Y 1WF ✆ 493 3223, Fax 491 2655
*closed 1 week Christmas* – **Meals** - Chinese (Peking, Szechuan) 33.00 **t.** (lunch) and a la carte 22.00/39.00 **t.** 8.00.

XXX **Zen Central** CN **x**
20 Queen St. W1X 7PJ ✆ 629 8089
**Meals** - Chinese 28.00/50.00 **t.** and a la carte 19.50/35.50 **t.**

XXX **The Chateau** (at May Fair Inter-Continental H.) DN **z**
Stratton St. W1A 2AN ✆ 915 2842, Fax 629 1459
▤. AE VISA JCB
**Meals** 22.00/29.50 **t.** and a la carte 4.50.

XXX **Scotts** BM **a**
20 Mount St. W1Y 6HE ✆ 629 5248, Fax 499 8246
▤. AE VISA JCB
*closed Saturday lunch, Sunday and 24 to 26 December* – **Meals** - Seafood a la carte 29.25/50.00 **t.**

XX **Greenhouse** BN **e**
27a Hay's Mews W1X 7RJ ✆ 499 3331, Fax 225 0011
▤. AE VISA
*closed Saturday lunch, 1 to 7 January and Bank Holidays* – **Meals** a la carte 22.75/33.75 **t.** 7.50.

XX **Bentley's** EM **i**
11-15 Swallow St. W1R 7HD ✆ 734 4756, Fax 287 2972
▤. AE VISA JCB
*closed Sunday and Bank Holidays* – **Meals** - Seafood 19.50 **t.** and a la carte.

XX **Langan's Brasserie** DN **e**
Stratton St. W1X 5FD ✆ 491 8822
▤. AE VISA
*closed Saturday lunch, Sunday and Bank Holidays* – **Meals** (booking essential) a la carte 19.05/30.45 **t.**

XX **Mulligans** DM **c**
13-14 Cork St. W1X 1PF ✆ 409 1370, Fax 409 2732
▤. AE VISA
*closed Saturday lunch, Sunday, 25 December-1 January and Bank Holidays* – **Meals** - Irish a la carte 16.75/30.00 **t.** 4.25.

XX **Shogun** (at Britannia H.) BM **x**
Adams Row W1Y 5DE ✆ 493 1255
▤. AE VISA JCB
*closed Monday* – **Meals** - Japanese (dinner only) 30.00 **t.** and a la carte.

X **Ikeda** CKL **a**
30 Brook St. W1Y 1AG ✆ 629 2730, Fax 628 6982
▤. AE VISA JCB
*closed Saturday lunch and Sunday* – **Meals** - Japanese 15.00/38.00 **t.** and a la carte.

X **O'Keefe's** CK **e**
19 Dering St. W1R 9AA ✆ 495 0878, Fax 629 7082
*closed Saturday dinner and Sunday* – **Meals** a la carte approx. 14.00 **t.** 6.50.

**Regent's Park and Marylebone** – ✉ NW1/NW6/NW8/W1 – ✆ 0171 – Except where otherwise stated see pp. 28 and 29 – Basement Services Arcade, Selfridges Store, Oxford St., W1 ✆ 730 3488/824 8000.

**Regent London** p. 21 HU **a**
222 Marylebone Rd NW1 6JQ ✆ 631 8000, Telex 8813733, Fax 631 8080
« Victorian Gothic architecture, atrium and winter garden », – rm ▤ TV – 350. AE VISA JCB.
***The Dining Room :*** **Meals** 21.50/29.00 **st.** and a la carte – 13.25 – **307 rm** 160.00/255.00 **s.**, 2 suites.

**Churchill Inter-Continental** AJ **x**
30 Portman Sq. W1A 4ZX ✆ 486 5800, Telex 264831, Fax 486 1255
– rm ▤ TV – 200. AE VISA JCB.
**Meals** *(closed Saturday lunch)* a la carte 17.00/31.00 **t.** – 14.50 – **406 rm** 190.00/250.00, 37 suites.

**Langham Hilton** p. 21 JU **e**
1 Portland Pl. W1N 3AA ✆ 636 1000, Fax 323 2340
– rm ▤ TV – 320. AE VISA JCB.
***Memories of the Empire :*** **Meals** 21.25/29.75 **st.** and a la carte – 14.75 – **364 rm** 180.00/275.00 **s.**, 20 suites – SB.

**Selfridge** (Mt. Charlotte Thistle) AK **e**
Orchard St. W1H 0JS 408 2080, Fax 629 8849
rm – 220. AE VISA JCB.
***Fletchers* : Meals** *(closed Sunday)* 16.95/24.50 **st.** and a la carte
***Orchard* : Meals** 16.95/19.50 – 10.25 – **293 rm** 145.00/160.00 **st.**, 2 suites.

**SAS Portman** AJ **o**
22 Portman Sq. W1H 9FL 486 5844, Telex 261526, Fax 935 0537
– rm – 350. AE VISA JCB.
**Meals** 15.00/31.00 **st.** 6.00 – 12.50 – **259 rm** 130.00/170.00 **s.**, 13 suites.

**Berkshire** (Radisson Edwardian) BK **n**
350 Oxford St. W1N 0BY 629 7474, Telex 22270, Fax 629 8156
rm – 40. AE VISA JCB.
**Meals** *(closed Saturday, Sunday and Bank Holiday lunch)* 23.40 **st.** and a la carte 7.00 – 13.50 – **145 rm** 158.00/245.00 **st.**, 2 suites.

**London Regent's Park Hilton** p. 21 GT **v**
18 Lodge Rd NW8 7JT 722 7722, Telex 23101, Fax 483 2408
– 150. AE VISA JCB.
***Minsky's* : Meals** 14.95/19.95 **t.** and a la carte
***Kashinoki* : Meals** - Japanese *(closed Monday, 25 to 26 December and 1 to 3 January)* 9.00/30.00 – 11.30 – **374 rm** 115.00/130.00 **st.**, 3 suites.

Clifton Ford BH **a**
47 Welbeck St. W1M 8DN 486 6600, Telex 22569, Fax 486 7492
– 150
**198 rm**, 2 suites.

**Montcalm** p. 33 EZ **x**
Great Cumberland Pl. W1A 2LF 402 4288, Telex 28710, Fax 724 9180
– rm – 80. AE VISA JCB.
**Meals** *(closed Saturday lunch and Sunday)* 20.00/25.00 **t.** and a la carte 8.00 – 14.00 – **105 rm** 160.00/200.00, 11 suites.

**Marble Arch Marriott** p. 33 EZ **i**
134 George St. W1H 6DN 723 1277, Fax 402 0666
, , – rm – 150. AE VISA JCB.
**Meals** 17.95/24.95 **st.** and a la carte 7.00 – 11.85 – **237 rm** 135.00/145.00 **s.**, 2 suites – SB.

**Berners Park Plaza** EJ **r**
10 Berners St. W1A 3BE 636 1629, Telex 25759, Fax 580 3972
rm rest – 150. AE VISA JCB.
**Meals** 15.95 **st.** and a la carte – 10.75 – **227 rm** 120.00/140.00 **st.**, 3 suites.

St. George's (Forte) p. 21 JU **a**
Langham Pl. W1N 8QS 580 0111, Fax 436 7997
– rm – 35
**83 rm**, 3 suites.

Forte Crest Regents Park p. 21 JU **i**
Carburton St. W1P 8EE 388 2300, Telex 22453, Fax 387 2806
rm rest – 600
**315 rm**, 2 suites.

**Rathbone** p. 22 KU **x**
Rathbone St. W1P 1AJ 636 2001, Telex 28728, Fax 636 3882
rm . AE VISA JCB.
**Meals** *(closed lunch Saturday and Sunday)* 15.00 **t.** 4.50 – 8.50 – **72 rm** 120.00/145.00 **st.** – SB.

**Dorset Square** p. 21 HU **s**
39-40 Dorset Sq. NW1 6QN 723 7874, Fax 724 3328
« Attractively furnished Regency town houses », – . AE VISA.
**Meals** *(closed Sunday lunch and Saturday)* a la carte 17.00/23.75 **t.** – 9.50 – **37 rm** 95.00/165.00 **t.**

**25 Dorset Square** HU **e**
25 Dorset Sq. NW1 6QN 262 7505, Fax 723 0194
without rest., « Regency town houses » – . AE VISA.
8.50 – **12 suites** 170.00/250.00 **st.**

**Durrants** AH **e**
26-32 George St. W1H 6BJ ✆ 935 8131, Fax 487 3510
« Converted Georgian houses with Regency façade » – 🅱 TV ☎ – 60. AE VISA. 
**Meals** 19.00 **t.** and a la carte 6.75 – 8.25 – **93 rm** 85.00/105.00 **st.**, 3 suites.

**Savoy Court** AK **i**
Granville Pl. W1H 0EH ✆ 408 0130, Fax 493 2070
rest TV ☎. AE VISA JCB.
**Meals** (buffet lunch)/dinner 13.50 – 9.00 – **94 rm** 81.00/118.00.

**Langham Court** p. 21 JU **z**
31-35 Langham St. W1N 5RE ✆ 436 6622, Fax 436 2303
TV ☎ – 80. AE VISA JCB.
**Meals** *(closed lunch Saturday, Sunday and Bank Holidays)* 16.95/17.95 **t.** and a la carte 4.95 – 9.50 – **60 rm** 115.00/139.00 **st.**

**Holiday Inn Garden Court** BJ **c**
57-59 Welbeck St. W1M 8HS ✆ 935 4442, Telex 894630, Fax 487 3782
rm rest TV ☎ – 180. AE VISA JCB.
**Meals** *(closed lunch Saturday and Sunday)* 12.95/13.95 6.00 – 9.00 – **138 rm** 100.00/130.00 **st.**

**Harewood** p. 21 HU **x**
Harewood Row NW1 6SE ✆ 262 2707, Fax 262 2975
rest TV ☎. AE VISA JCB
**Meals** (dinner only) 16.50 **st.** 4.95 – 8.50 – **92 rm** 65.00/89.00 **st.** – SB.

**Hart House** AH **a**
51 Gloucester Pl. W1H 3PE ✆ 935 2288, Fax 935 8516
without rest. – TV ☎. AE VISA.
**16 rm** 45.00/75.00 **st.**

Regents Park HT **a**
156 Gloucester Pl. NW1 6DT ✆ 258 1911, Fax 258 0288
rest TV ☎
***Singapore Garden* : Meals** - South East Asian – **29 rm.**

**Bryanston Court** p. 33 EZ **z**
56-60 Great Cumberland Pl. W1H 7FD ✆ 262 3141, Fax 262 7248
without rest. – TV ☎. AE VISA JCB.
**54 rm** 70.00/90.00 **st.**

**Lincoln House** AJ **c**
33 Gloucester Pl. W1H 3PD ✆ 486 7630, Fax 486 0166
without rest. – TV ☎. AE VISA.
**22 rm** 39.00/65.00 **st.**

**Walsh's** p. 22 KU **r**
5 Charlotte St. W1P 1HD ✆ 637 0222, Fax 637 0224
. AE VISA JCB
*closed Saturday lunch, Sunday and Bank Holidays* – **Meals** - Seafood a la carte 23.00/35.00 **st.**

**Hudson's** HU **r**
221b Baker St. NW1 ✆ 935 3130
AE VISA
*closed 25 December* – **Meals** - English 12.50/15.00 **t.** and a la carte 4.50.

**Nico Central** DJ **c**
35 Great Portland St. W1N 5DD ✆ 436 8846
. AE VISA
*closed Saturday lunch, Sunday, 4 days Easter, 10 days Christmas and Bank Holiday Mondays* – **Meals** 21.00/25.00 **st.** 9.00.

**Caldesi** BJ **e**
15-17 Marylebone Lane W1M 5FE ✆ 935 9226
. AE VISA JCB
*closed Saturday lunch, Sunday and Bank Holidays* – **Meals** - Italian 10.95 **t.** and a la carte 3.75.

XX **Gaylord** p. 22 KU **o**
79-81 Mortimer St. W1N 7TB ✆ 580 3615
▤. AE VISA JCB
**Meals** - Indian 11.95/13.95 **t.** and a la carte.

XX **Maroush III** EZ **r**
62 Seymour St. W1H 5AF ✆ 724 5024
▤. AE VISA
*closed Christmas Day* – **Meals** - Lebanese 12.00/50.00 **t.** and a la carte 🍷 7.00.

XX **Stephen Bull** BH **e**
5-7 Blandford St. W1H 3AA ✆ 486 9696
▤. AE VISA
*closed Saturday lunch, Sunday, 1 week Christmas and Bank Holidays* – **Meals** a la carte 20.00/27.50 **t.** 🍷 5.50.

XX **Baboon** BJ **x**
76 Wigmore St. W1H 9DQ ✆ 224 2992, Fax 935 9588
▤. AE VISA JCB
*closed Saturday lunch, Sunday and Bank Holidays* – **Meals** 12.50 **t.** and a la carte.

XX **Sampan's** (at Cumberland H.) AK **n**
Marble Arch W1A 4RF ✆ 262 1234
AE VISA JCB
*closed Sunday, 1 week Christmas and Bank Holidays* – **Meals** - Chinese (Canton) (dinner only) 15.50 and a la carte 🍷 6.50.

XX **Asuka** p. 21 HU **u**
Berkeley Arcade, 209a Baker St. NW1 6AB ✆ 486 5026
AE VISA JCB
*closed Saturday lunch, Sunday and Bank Holidays* – **Meals** - Japanese 12.50/23.90 **st.** and a la carte.

XX **La Loggia** p. 33 EZ **a**
68 Edgware Rd W2 2EQ ✆ 723 0554
▤. AE VISA JCB
*closed Saturday lunch, Sunday and Bank Holidays* – **Meals** - Italian 13.80/15.50 **st.** and a la carte 🍷 4.80.

X **Le Muscadet** HU **v**
25 Paddington St. W1M 3RF ✆ 935 2883
▤. VISA
*closed Saturday lunch, Sunday, last 3 weeks August and 2 weeks Christmas-New Year* – **Meals** - French a la carte 21.60/26.00 **t.** 🍷 8.20.

X **L'Aventure** p. 20 FS **s**
3 Blenheim Terr. NW8 0EH ✆ 624 6232
AE VISA
*closed Saturday lunch, 4 days Easter, 1 week Christmas and Bank Holidays* – **Meals** - French 18.50/25.00 **t.** 🍷 7.25.

X **Nakamura** BJ **i**
31 Marylebone Lane W1M 5FH ✆ 935 2931
AE VISA JCB
*closed Sunday lunch and Saturday* – **Meals** - Japanese 6.00/37.90 **t.** and a la carte.

X **Langan's Bistro** p. 21 IU **e**
26 Devonshire St. W1N 1RJ ✆ 935 4531
▤. AE VISA
*closed Saturday lunch, Sunday and Bank Holidays* – **Meals** 16.95 **t.**

X **Zoe** BJ **a**
3-5 Barrett St., St. Christopher's Pl. W1M 5HH ✆ 224 1122, Fax 935 5444
▤. AE VISA
*closed Sunday and Bank Holidays* – **Meals** 10.00 **t.** and a la carte.

**St. James's** – ✉ W1/SW1/WC2 – ☎ 0171 – pp. 28 and 29.

**Ritz** DN **a**
Piccadilly W1V 9DG ☎ 493 8181, Telex 267200, Fax 493 2687
« Elegant restaurant in Louis XVI style » – lift ▤ TV ☎ – 50. AE VISA JCB. ✗
**Meals** (dancing Friday and Saturday evenings) 26.00/43.50 **st.** and a la carte approx. 52.00 **st.** 12.50 – ☕ 14.50 – **116 rm** 161.00/251.00 **s.**, 14 suites – SB.

**Dukes** EP **x**
35 St. James's Pl. SW1A 1NY ☎ 491 4840, Fax 493 1264
– lift ▤ rest TV ☎ – 55. AE VISA JCB. ✗
**Meals** *(closed Saturday lunch)* (residents only) a la carte 17.00/35.75 **t.** 6.75 – ☕ 12.50 – **38 rm** 125.00/185.00, **26 suites** 210.00/400.00.

**22 Jermyn Street** FM **e**
22 Jermyn St. SW1Y 6HL ☎ 734 2353, Fax 734 0750
lift TV ☎. AE VISA JCB
**Meals** (restricted room service only) a la carte 22.00/26.50 **t.** 6.35 – ☕ 13.00 – **5 rm** 170.00 **s.**, **13 suites** 220.00/250.00 **s.**

**Stafford** DN **u**
16-18 St. James's Pl. SW1A 1NJ ☎ 493 0111, Telex 28602, Fax 493 7121
– lift ▤ rest TV ☎ – 35. AE VISA JCB. ✗
**Meals** *(closed Saturday lunch)* 22.50/25.00 **st.** and a la carte 7.00 – ☕ 12.00 – **70 rm** 184.00/215.00 **st.**, 4 suites – SB.

**Forte Crest St. James's** EN **i**
81 Jermyn St. SW1Y 6JF ☎ 930 2111, Fax 839 2125
lift rm ▤ rest TV ☎ – 80
**253 rm**, 3 suites.

**Royal Trafalgar Thistle** (Mt. Charlotte Thistle) GM **r**
Whitcomb St. WC2H 7HG ☎ 930 4477, Telex 298564, Fax 925 2149
lift rm TV ☎. AE VISA JCB. ✗
**Meals** 13.75 **st.** and a la carte 6.40 – ☕ 10.50 – **108 rm** 105.00/130.00 **st.** – SB.

**Hospitality Inn Piccadilly** (Mt. Charlotte Thistle) FGM **a**
39 Coventry St. W1V 8EL ☎ 930 4033, Telex 8950058, Fax 925 2586
without rest. – lift rm TV ☎. AE VISA JCB. ✗ – ☕ 9.25 – **92 rm** 115.00/130.00 **t.**

**Pastoria** GM **v**
3-6 St. Martin's St., off Leicester Sq. WC2H 7HL ☎ 930 8641, Telex 25538, Fax 925 0551
lift ▤ rest TV ☎ – 60. AE VISA JCB. ✗
**Meals** *(closed Saturday lunch and Sunday)* 15.00 **t.** and a la carte – ☕ 9.25 – **58 rm** 99.00/119.00 **st.**

**Quaglino's** EN **r**
16 Bury St. SW1Y 6AL ☎ 930 6767, Fax 839 2866
▤. AE VISA
*closed lunch 1 January, dinner 24 December and 25-26 December* – **Meals** (booking essential) 12.95 **t.** (lunch) and a lacarte 20.25/29.50 **t.** 6.95.

**Suntory** EP **z**
72-73 St. James's St. SW1A 1PH ☎ 409 0201, Fax 499 0208
▤. AE VISA JCB
*closed Sunday and Bank Holidays* – **Meals** - Japanese 15.00/90.00 **st.** and a la carte 22.30/83.50 **st.** 7.00.

**Overton's** EP **a**
5 St. James's St. SW1A 1EF ☎ 839 3774, Fax 839 4330
▤. AE VISA JCB
*closed Saturday lunch, Sunday dinner, 10 days Christmas-New Year and Bank Holidays* – **Meals** - Seafood 19.50/27.50 **t.** 5.50.

XXX ✿ **The Square** EN **v**
32 King St. SW1Y 6RJ ☏ 839 8787, Fax 321 2124
▤. AE VISA
*closed lunch Saturday and Sunday* – **Meals** 36.00 **t.** (dinner) and lunch a la carte 25.00/30.00 **t.**
**Spec.** Seared tuna with tartare of vegetables and soy wilted greens, Rump of lamb with aubergine, rosemary and olive oil, Port roasted figs with cinnamon fritters.

XX **Le Caprice** DN **c**
Arlington House, Arlington St. SW1A 1RT ☏ 629 2239, Fax 493 9040
▤. AE VISA
*closed 24 December-2 January* – **Meals** a la carte 22.25/36.00 **t.**

XX **Green's** EN **n**
36 Duke St. SW1Y 6DF ☏ 930 4566, Fax 930 1383
▤. AE VISA JCB
*closed Sunday dinner, 25 to 26 December and 1 January* – **Meals** - English rest. a la carte 24.50/30.50 **t.**

XX **Matsuri** EN **r**
15 Bury St. SW1Y 6AL ☏ 839 1101, Fax 930 7010
▤. AE VISA JCB
*closed Sunday and Bank Holidays* – **Meals** - Japanese (Teppan-Yaki, Sushi) 12.00/49.50 **t.** and a la carte.

X **Criterion** FM **c**
224 Piccadilly W1V 9LB ☏ 925 0909, Fax 839 1494
« 19C Neo-Byzantine decor » – AE VISA
*closed Sunday dinner, 25-26 December and 1 January* – **Meals** - Brasserie a la carte 14.00/21.45 **t.**

**Soho** – ✉ W1/WC2 – ☎ 0171 – pp. 28 and 29.

**Hampshire** (Radisson Edwardian) GM **s**
Leicester Sq. WC2H 7LH ☏ 839 9399, Telex 914848, Fax 930 8122
rm ▤ TV ☎ – 80. AE VISA JCB.
**Meals** 19.50/27.50 **st.** and a la carte – 13.50 – **119 rm** 184.00/220.00 **st.**, 5 suites – SB.

**Hazlitt's** FK **u**
6 Frith St. W1V 5TZ ☏ 434 1771, Fax 439 1524
without rest. – TV ☎. AE VISA JCB.
*closed Christmas* – **22 rm** 98.00/122.00 **s.**, 1 suite.

XXXX ✿ **Grill Room at the Café Royal** (Forte) EM **e**
68 Regent St. W1R 6EL ☏ 437 9090, Fax 439 7672
« Rococo decoration » – ▤. AE VISA JCB
*closed Saturday lunch, Sunday and Bank Holidays* – **Meals** 22.50/39.00 **st.** and a la carte 35.00/55.00 **st.** 9.00.
**Spec.** Escalopes of fresh foie gras with a ragout of celeriac and truffle sauce, Roasted fillet of sea bass with fennel, sundried tomatoes and saffron, Pyramid of walnut ganache with vanilla sauce.

XXX **Au Jardin des Gourmets** GJ **a**
5 Greek St. W1V 5LA ☏ 437 1816, Fax 437 0043
▤. AE VISA
*closed lunch Saturday and Bank Holidays, Sunday and 25-26 December* – ***Restaurant :*** **Meals** - French a la carte 23.50/32.45 **t.**

XX ***Brasserie*** *closed lunch Saturday and Sunday* – **Meals** 10.95/17.50 **st.** 5.75.

XXX **Lindsay House** GL **i**
21 Romilly St. W1V 5TG ☏ 439 0450, Fax 581 2848
▤. AE VISA JCB
*closed 25 and 26 December* – **Meals** 10.00 **t.** (lunch) and a la carte 22.75/27.50 **t.** 4.50.

XX **L'Escargot** GK **e**
48 Greek St. W1V 5LQ ✆ 437 2679, Fax 437 0790
▤. AE ⓓ VISA
*closed Saturday lunch and Sunday* – **Meals** a la carte approx. 23.50 **t.** 🍾 5.25.

XX **Lexington** EK **e**
45 Lexington St. W1R 3LG ✆ 434 3401, Fax 287 2997
▤. AE ⓓ VISA
*closed Saturday lunch, Sunday, 1 week Christmas and Bank Holidays* – **Meals** 16.00 **t.** (dinner) and a la carte 19.00/24.25 **t.**

XX **Red Fort** FJK **r**
77 Dean St. W1V 5HA ✆ 437 2115, Fax 434 0721
▤. AE ⓓ VISA
**Meals** - Indian (buffet lunch) 12.50 **t.** and dinner a la carte 20.85/25.85 **t.**

XX **Brasserie at the Café Royal** (Forte) EM **e**
68 Regent St. W1R 6EL ✆ 437 9090, Fax 439 7672
▤. AE ⓓ VISA JCB
*closed Sunday dinner* – **Meals** 15.50/17.50 **st.** and a la carte 🍾 6.50.

XX **Soho Soho** (first floor) FK **s**
11-13 Frith St. W1 ✆ 494 3491, Fax 437 3091
▤. AE ⓓ VISA
*closed Saturday lunch and Sunday* – **Meals** a la carte approx. 35.00 **st.**

XX **Ming** GK **c**
35-36 Greek St. W1V 5LN ✆ 734 2721
▤. AE ⓓ VISA JCB
*closed Sunday and Bank Holiday lunch* – **Meals** - Chinese 10.00/19.50 **t.** and a la carte 🍾 6.00.

XX **Gopal's** FK **e**
12 Bateman St. W1V 5TD ✆ 434 0840
▤. AE VISA
*closed 25 and 26 December* – **Meals** - Indian 13.00/19.50 **t.** and a la carte.

XX **Gay Hussar** GJ **c**
2 Greek St. W1V 6NB ✆ 437 0973, Fax 437 9920
▤. AE ⓓ VISA
*closed Sunday and Bank Holidays* – **Meals** - Hungarian 16.00 **t.** (lunch) and a la carte 17.85/26.10 **t.** 🍾 7.50.

X **dell 'Ugo** FK **z**
56 Frith St. W1V 5TA ✆ 734 8300, Fax 734 8784
AE ⓓ VISA
*closed Sunday and Bank Holidays* – **Meals** 10.00 **t.** and a la carte 16.40/20.70 **t.**

X **Sri Siam** GK **r**
14 Old Compton St. W1V 5PE ✆ 434 3544
▤. AE ⓓ VISA
*closed Sunday lunch* – **Meals** - Thai 9.50/14.95 **t.** and a la carte 🍾 4.60.

X **Alastair Little** FK **o**
49 Frith St. W1V 5TE ✆ 734 5183
AE VISA
*closed Saturday lunch, Sunday, 25 to 26 December and Bank Holidays* – **Meals** (booking essential) 25.00 **t.** (lunch) and a la carte 35.00/44.50 **t.** 🍾 6.00.

X **Bistrot Bruno** FK **z**
63 Frith St. W1V 5TA ✆ 734 4545, Fax 287 1027
▤. AE ⓓ VISA
*closed Saturday lunch, Sunday and Christmas to New Year* – **Meals** a la carte 18.00/26.00 **t.** 🍾 4.75.

X **Poons** GM **e**
4 Leicester St., Leicester Sq. WC2 7BL ✆ 437 1528
▤. AE VISA
*closed 24 to 28 December* – **Meals** - Chinese 7.50/20.00 **t.** and a la carte.

**Andrew Edmunds** EK **c**
44 Lexington St. W1R 3LH ✆ 437 5708
VISA
**Meals** a la carte 11.15/17.85 **t.** 4.00.

**Fung Shing** GL **a**
15 Lisle St. WC2H 7BE ✆ 437 1539
AE VISA
**Meals** - Chinese (Canton) 12.50/40.00 **t.** and a la carte 4.25.

**Saigon** FGK **x**
45 Frith St. W1V 5TE ✆ 437 7109
AE VISA
*closed Sunday and Bank Holidays* – **Meals** - Vietnamese 15.80/19.50 **t.**

**Strand and Covent Garden** – ✉ WC2 – 0171 – Except where otherwise stated see p. 33.

**Savoy** DEY **a**
Strand WC2R 0EU ✆ 836 4343, Telex 24234, Fax 240 6040
rm – 500. AE VISA JCB.
*Grill* : **Meals** *(closed Saturday lunch, Sunday, August and Bank Holidays)* 31.00 **st.** (dinner) and a la carte 26.65/43.40
*River* : **Meals** 26.50/39.50 **st.** and a la carte 26.50/58.50 – 15.75 – **154 rm** 180.00/275.00 **s.**, 48 suites.

**Howard** EX **e**
12 Temple Pl. WC2R 2PR ✆ 836 3555, Telex 268047, Fax 379 4547
rm – 100. AE VISA.
**Meals** 25.00 **st.** and a la carte 4.75 – 15.50 – **133 rm** 190.00/226.00 **st.**, 2 suites.

**Waldorf** (Forte) EX **x**
Aldwych WC2B 4DD ✆ 836 2400, Telex 24574, Fax 836 7244
rm rm – 450. AE VISA JCB.
**Meals** (in bar Sunday lunch) 25.00/28.00 **t.** and a la carte 7.00 – 12.95 – **285 rm** 160.00/200.00 **st.**, 7 suites – SB.

**Simpson's-in-the-Strand** EX **o**
100 Strand WC2R 0EW ✆ 836 9112, Fax 836 1381
AE VISA JCB
*closed 25 to 26 December* – **Meals** - English (booking essential) 10.00 **t.** and a la carte 15.00/30.25 **t.** 4.95.

**Ivy** p. 29 GK **z**
1 West St. WC2H 9NE ✆ 836 4751, Fax 497 3644
AE VISA
*closed August Bank Holiday* – **Meals** 14.00 **t.** (lunch) and a la carte 19.75/37.25 **t.**

**Now and Zen** DX **x**
4a Upper St. Martin's Lane WC2H 9EA ✆ 497 0376, Fax 497 0378
AE VISA
*closed 25 December* – **Meals** - Chinese a la carte approx. 16.00.

**Christopher's** EX **z**
18 Wellington St. WC2E 7DD ✆ 240 4222, Fax 240 3357
AE VISA
*closed 24 December-2 January and Bank Holidays* – **Meals** a la carte 19.50/35.50 10.00.

**Orso** EX **z**
27 Wellington St. WC2E 7DA ✆ 240 5269, Fax 497 2148
– *closed 24 and 25 December* – **Meals** - Italian (booking essential) a la carte 19.50/25.50 **t.** 5.00.

**Rules** DX **n**
35 Maiden Lane WC2E 7LB ✆ 836 5314, Fax 497 1081
« London's oldest restaurant with antique collection of drawings, paintings and cartoons » – AE VISA
*closed 23 to 26 December* – **Meals** - English 12.95/15.95 **t.** anda la carte 20.65/22.20 **t.** 4.60.

XX **L'Estaminet** DX **a**
14 Garrick St., off Floral St. WC2 9BJ ✆ 379 1432
AE VISA
*closed Sunday* – **Meals** - French a la carte 21.00/24.00 **t.**

XX **Sheekey's** DX **z**
28-32 St. Martin's Court WC2N 4AL ✆ 240 2565, Fax 240 0545
AE VISA
**Meals** - Seafood 17.95/19.95 **t.** and a la carte.

XX **Bertorelli's** DX **c**
44a Floral St. WC2E 9DA ✆ 836 3969, Fax 836 1868
AE VISA JCB
*closed Sunday and 25-26 December* – **Meals** - Italian a la carte 14.00/20.50 **t.**

X **Le Cafe du Jardin** EX **a**
28 Wellington St. WC2E 7BD ✆ 836 8769, Fax 836 4123
AE VISA
**Meals** a la carte 16.70/25.95 **t.** 4.50.

X **Magno's Brasserie** DV **e**
65a Long Acre WC2E 9JH ✆ 836 6077, Fax 379 6184
AE VISA JCB
*closed Saturday lunch, Sunday, Christmas and Bank Holidays* – **Meals** - French 13.50/16.50 **t.** and a la carte 6.75.

X **Joe Allen** EX **c**
13 Exeter St. WC2E 7DT ✆ 836 0651, Fax 497 2148
*closed 24 and 25 December* – **Meals** a la carte 16.50/22.00 **t.**

## Victoria – ✉ SW1 – ☎ 0171 – Except where otherwise stated see p. 32.

**i** Victoria Station Forecourt, SW1V 1JU ✆ 730 3488/824 8000.

**St. James Court** CX **i**
Buckingham Gate SW1E 6AF ✆ 834 6655, Fax 630 7587
– rm – 180. AE VISA JCB.
***Mediterranée* : Meals** a la carte approx. 15.00
(see also ***Auberge de Provence*** and ***Inn of Happiness*** below) – 13.20 – **375 rm** 140.00/175.00 **s.**, 18 suites – SB.

**Royal Horseguards Thistle** (Mt. Charlotte Thistle) p. 26 LX **a**
2 Whitehall Court SW1A 2EJ ✆ 839 3400, Telex 917096, Fax 925 2263
rm rest – 60. AE.
**Meals** 19.50 **t.** and a la carte – **368 rm**, 8 suites.

**Stakis London St. Ermin's** CX **a**
Caxton St. SW1H 0QW ✆ 222 7888, Fax 222 6914
rm rest – 150. AE VISA JCB.
**Meals** *(closed Saturday and Sunday lunch)* (carving rest.) 12.75/16.50 **t.** and a la carte – 9.75 – **283 rm** 115.00/129.00 **t.**, 7 suites – SB.

**Goring** BX **a**
15 Beeston Pl., Grosvenor Gdns SW1W 0JW ✆ 396 9000, Telex 919166, Fax 834 4393
– 50. AE VISA.
**Meals** 17.50/32.00 **t.** 7.50 – 12.00 – **73 rm** 125.00/155.00 **s.**, 5 suites – SB.

**Royal Westminster Thistle** (Mt. Charlotte Thistle) BX **z**
49 Buckingham Palace Rd SW1W 0QT ✆ 834 1821, Telex 916821, Fax 931 7542
rm – 160. AE VISA.
**Meals** *(closed Sunday and Bank Holidays)* (bar lunch)/dinner 19.50 **st.** and a la carte 5.20 – 10.25 – **134 rm** 122.00/145.00 **st.** – SB.

**Grosvenor Thistle** (Mt. Charlotte Thistle) BX **e**
101 Buckingham Palace Rd SW1W 0SJ ✆ 834 9494, Telex 916006, Fax 630 1978
rm – 200. AE VISA JCB.
**Meals** (carving rest.) 16.35 **st.** and a la carte 6.00 – 8.95 – **360 rm** 98.00/130.00 **st.**, 6 suites.

**Dolphin Square** KZ **a**
Dolphin Sq. SW1V 3LX ✆ 834 3800, Fax 798 8735
squash – rest – 50.
**Meals** 11.95/17.95 **st.** and dinner a la carte 5.50 – 9.95 – **14 rm** 101.00/121.00 **st.**, **137 suites** 126.00/147.00 **st.**

**Scandic Crown** BY **i**
2 Bridge Pl. SW1V 1QA ✆ 834 8123, Fax 828 1099
– rm – 180.
**Meals** 12.95/17.95 **st.** and a la carte 5.00 – 10.50 – **205 rm** 115.00/145.00 **st.**, 5 suites – SB.

**Rubens** BX **n**
39-41 Buckingham Palace Rd SW1W 0PS ✆ 834 6600, Fax 828 5401
rm rest – 75.
**Meals** *(closed Saturday and Sunday lunch)* (carving rest.) 14.95 **st.** and a la carte 6.00 – 8.95 – **188 rm** 97.00/123.00 **st.**, 1 suite.

**Rochester** CY **e**
69 Vincent Sq. SW1P 2PA ✆ 828 6611, Fax 233 6724
rest – 80.
**Meals** 16.95/17.95 **st.** and a la carte 5.00 – 9.50 – **70 rm** 105.00/145.00 **st.**

**Tophams Ebury Court** AX **i**
28 Ebury St. SW1W 0LU ✆ 730 8147, Fax 823 5966
– 30.
**Meals** (in bar Saturday lunch and Sunday) a la carte 16.70/24.85 **t.** 5.95 – **42 rm** 70.00/120.00 **t.**

**Winchester** BY **s**
17 Belgrave Rd SW1V 1RB ✆ 828 2972, Fax 828 5191
without rest. –
**18 rm** 58.00/65.00 **st.**

**Hamilton House** BY **n**
60 Warwick Way SW1V 1SA ✆ 821 7113, Fax 630 0806
without rest. –
**40 rm** 40.00/65.00 **st.**

**Collin House** AY **r**
104 Ebury St. SW1W 9QD ✆ 730 8031, Fax 730 8031
without rest. –
*closed 2 weeks Christmas* – **13 rm** 34.00/56.00 **st.**

**Inn of Happiness** (at St. James Court H.) CX **i**
Buckingham Gate SW1E 6AF ✆ 821 1931, Fax 630 7587
*closed Saturday lunch* – **Meals** - Chinese (buffet lunch Sunday) 15.50/25.00 **t.** and a la carte 6.25.

**Auberge de Provence** (at St. James Court H.) CX **i**
Buckingham Gate SW1E 6AF ✆ 821 1899, Fax 630 7587
*closed Saturday lunch, Sunday, 1 week January, 2 weeks August and Bank Holidays* – **Meals** - French 24.50/42.00 **t.** and a la carte.

**L'Incontro** p. 31 FT **u**
87 Pimlico Rd SW1W 8PH ✆ 730 6327, Fax 730 5062
*closed lunch Saturday and Sunday, 25 to 26 December and Bank Holidays* – **Meals** - Italian 16.50 **st.** (lunch) and a la carte 25.90/41.00 **st.** 7.50.

**Santini** ABX **v**
29 Ebury St. SW1W 0NZ ✆ 730 4094, Fax 730 0544
*closed lunch Saturday and Sunday, 25 to 26 December and Bank Holidays* – **Meals** - Italian a la carte 23.40/42.50 **t.** 7.00.

**Shepherds** p. 26 LZ **z**
Marsham Court, Marsham St. SW1P 4LA ✆ 834 9552, Fax 233 6047
*closed Saturday, Sunday and Bank Holidays* – **Meals** - English 19.95 **t.**

XX **Simply Nico** CY **a**
48a Rochester Row SW1P 1JU ✆ 630 8061
▤. AE VISA
*closed Saturday lunch, Sunday, 4 days at Easter, 10 days Christmas-New Year and Bank Holidays* – **Meals** (booking essential) 23.50 **st.** 9.00.

XX **Mijanou** AY **n**
143 Ebury St. SW1W 9QN ✆ 730 4099, Fax 823 6402
▤. AE VISA
*closed Saturday, Sunday, 1 week Easter, 3 weeks August, 2 weeks Christmas-New Year and Bank Holidays* – **Meals** 16.50/38.50 **t.** and a la carte.

XX **Ken Lo's Memories of China** AY **u**
67-69 Ebury St. SW1W 0NZ ✆ 730 7734, Fax 730 2992
▤. AE VISA JCB
*closed Sunday lunch and Bank Holidays* – **Meals** - Chinese 15.00 **t.** and a la carte.

XX **L'Amico** p. 26 LY **e**
44 Horseferry Rd SW1P 2AF ✆ 222 4680
AE VISA
*closed Saturday and Sunday* – **Meals** - Italian (booking essential) 14.00/26.00 **t.** and a la carte 4.25.

XX **Hunan** p. 25 IZ **a**
51 Pimlico Rd SW1W 8NE ✆ 730 5712
AE VISA
*closed Sunday lunch, 24 to 26 December and 1 January* – **Meals** - Chinese (Hunan) 19.80 **t.** (dinner) and a la carte 13.10/50.80 **t.** 4.50.

XX **Tate Gallery** p. 26 LZ **c**
Tate Gallery, Millbank SW1P 4RG ✆ 887 8877, Fax 887 8007
« Rex Whistler murals » – ▤
*closed Sunday* – **Meals** (booking essential) (lunch only) a la carte 16.55/25.85 **t.** 6.75.

XX **Gran Paradiso** BY **a**
52 Wilton Rd SW1V 1DE ✆ 828 5818, Fax 828 3608
AE VISA JCB
*closed Saturday lunch, Sunday and last 2 weeks August* – **Meals** - Italian a la carte 16.50/20.50 **t.** 3.50.

XX **La Fontana** p. 31 FT **o**
101 Pimlico Rd SW1W 8PH ✆ 730 6630
AE VISA
*closed Bank Holidays* – **Meals** - Italian a la carte 18.50/28.00 **t.** 6.00.

X **Olivo** AY **z**
21 Eccleston St. SW1W 9LX ✆ 730 2505
▤. AE VISA
*closed lunch Saturday and Sunday, 1 week August and Bank Holidays* – **Meals** - Italian 15.50 **t.** (lunch) and a la carte 18.05/22.30 **t.**

X **La Poule au Pot** p. 25 IZ **e**
231 Ebury St. SW1W 8UT ✆ 730 7763
▤. AE VISA
*closed Bank Holidays* – **Meals** - French 13.50 **t.** (lunch) and dinner a la carte 20.00/25.00 **t.**

X **Mimmo d'Ischia** AY **o**
61 Elizabeth St. SW1W 9PP ✆ 730 5406, Fax 730 9439
▤. AE VISA
*closed Sunday and Bank Holidays* – **Meals** - Italian a la carte approx. 30.00 **t.**

X **Villa Medici** BY **c**
35 Belgrave Rd SW1 5AX ✆ 834 4932
AE VISA JCB
*closed Saturday lunch, Sunday and Bank Holidays* – **Meals** - Italian 12.90 **t.** and a la carte 3.80.

# European dialling codes
## Indicatifs téléphoniques européens
## Indicativi telefonici dei paesi europei
## Telefon-Vorwahlnummern europäischer Länder

| from/de/dal/von | | | to/en/en/nach |
|---|---|---|---|
| AND | Andorra | 1944 | **Great Britain** |
| A | Austria | 0044 | » |
| B | Belgium | 0044 | » |
| BG | Bulgaria | 0044 | » |
| CZ | Czech Republic | 0044 | » |
| DK | Denmark | 00944 | » |
| FIN | Finland | 99044 | » |
| F | France | 1944 | » |
| D | Germany | 0044 | » |
| GR | Greece | 0044 | » |
| H | Hungary | 0044 | » |
| I | Italy | 0044 | » |
| FL | Liechtenstein | 0044 | » |
| L | Luxembourg | 0044 | » |
| M | Malta | 0044 | » |
| MC | Monaco | 1944 | » |
| NL | Netherlands | 0944 | » |
| N | Norway | 09544 | » |
| PL | Poland | 0044 | » |
| P | Portugal | 0044 | » |
| IRL | Rep. of Ireland | 0044 | » |
| RO | Romania | - | » |
| SK | Slovak Republic | 0044 | » |
| E | Spain | 0744 | » |
| S | Sweden | 00944 | » |
| CH | Switzerland | 0044 | » |

| from/de/dal/von | | to/en/en/nach |
|---|---|---|
| **Great Britain** | 0033 | Andorra |
| » | 0043 | Austria |
| » | 0032 | Belgium |
| » | 00359 | Bulgaria |
| » | 0042 | Czech Republic |
| » | 0045 | Denmark |
| » | 00358 | Finland |
| » | 0033 | France |
| » | 0049 | Germany |
| » | 0030 | Greece |
| » | 0036 | Hungary |
| » | 0039 | Italy |
| » | 0041 | Liechtenstein |
| » | 00352 | Luxembourg |
| » | 00356 | Malta |
| » | 003393 | Monaco |
| » | 0031 | Netherlands |
| » | 0047 | Norway |
| » | 0048 | Poland |
| » | 00351 | Portugal |
| » | 00353 | Rep. of Ireland |
| » | 0040 | Romania |
| » | 0042 | Slovak Republic |
| » | 0034 | Spain |
| » | 0046 | Sweden |
| » | 0041 | Switzerland |

# Underground

## Métro

## Metropolitana

## U-Bahn

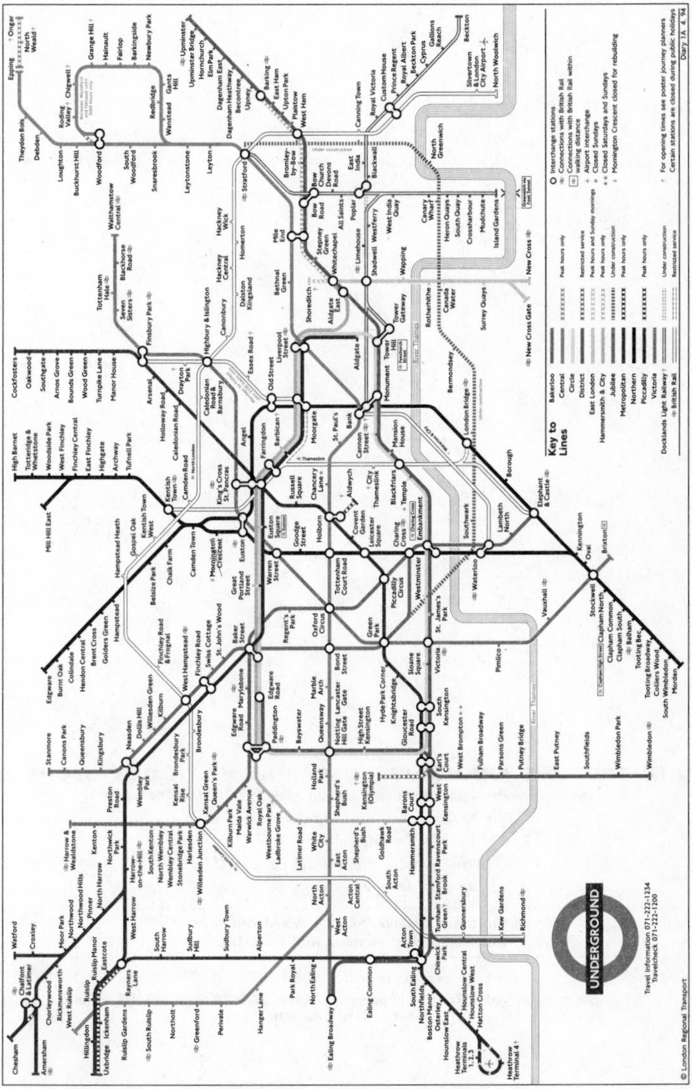


LRT Registered user No 94/2082

**MANUFACTURE FRANÇAISE DES PNEUMATIQUES MICHELIN**
Société en commandite par actions au capital de 2 000 000 000 de francs
Place des Carmes-Déchaux - 63 Clermont-Ferrand (France)
R.C.S. Clermont-Fd B 855 200 507

Dépôt légal Janvier 95 - ISBN 2-06-006659-X

Printed in France 12-94-20
Photocomposition : APS, Tours - Impression : KAPP, LAHURE & JOMBART, Evreux
Reliure : N.R.I., Auxerre

Illustrations Rodolphe Corbel, pages : 3 - 47 - 96
Illustrations Narratif Systèmes/Genclo, pages : 14 - 24 - 34 - 44 - 87 - 89.

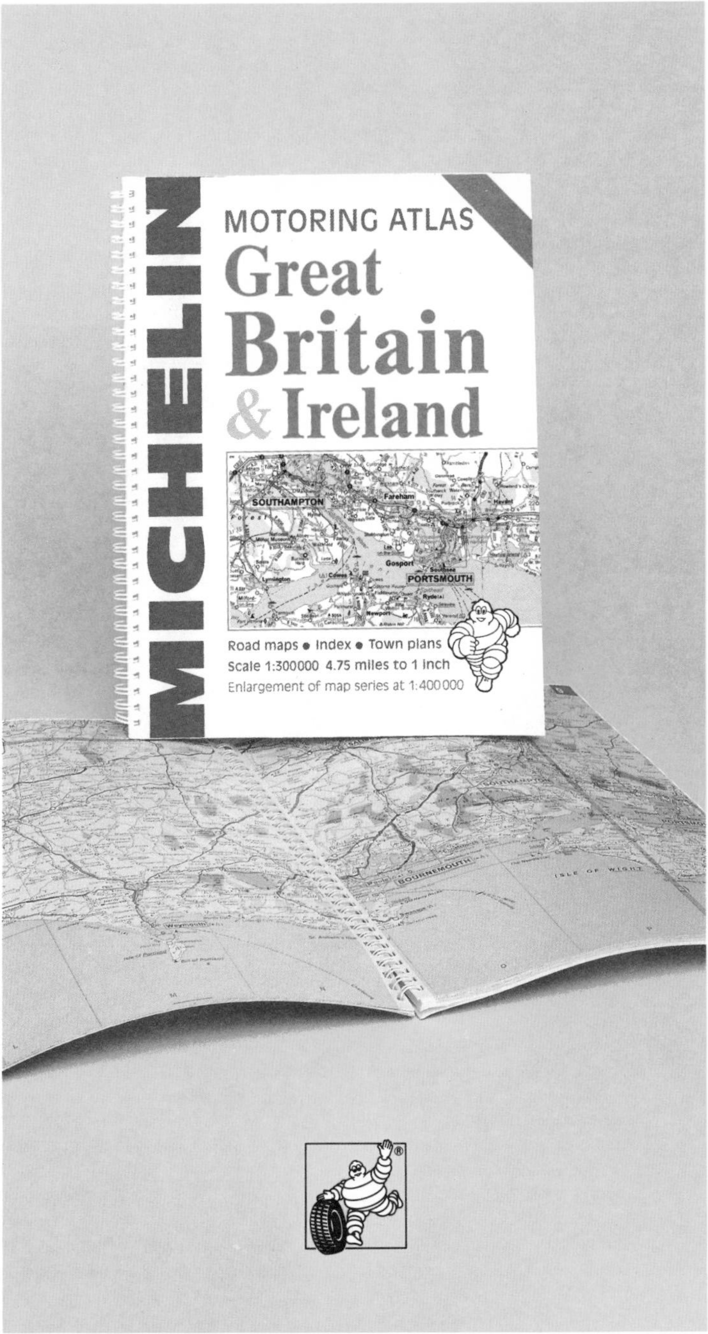
MICHELIN
MOTORING ATLAS
Great Britain
& Ireland
SOUTHAMPTON
Fareham
Gosport
PORTSMOUTH
Road maps • Index • Town plans
Scale 1:300000 4.75 miles to 1 inch
Enlargement of map series at 1:400 000
BOURNEMOUTH
ISLE OF WIGHT

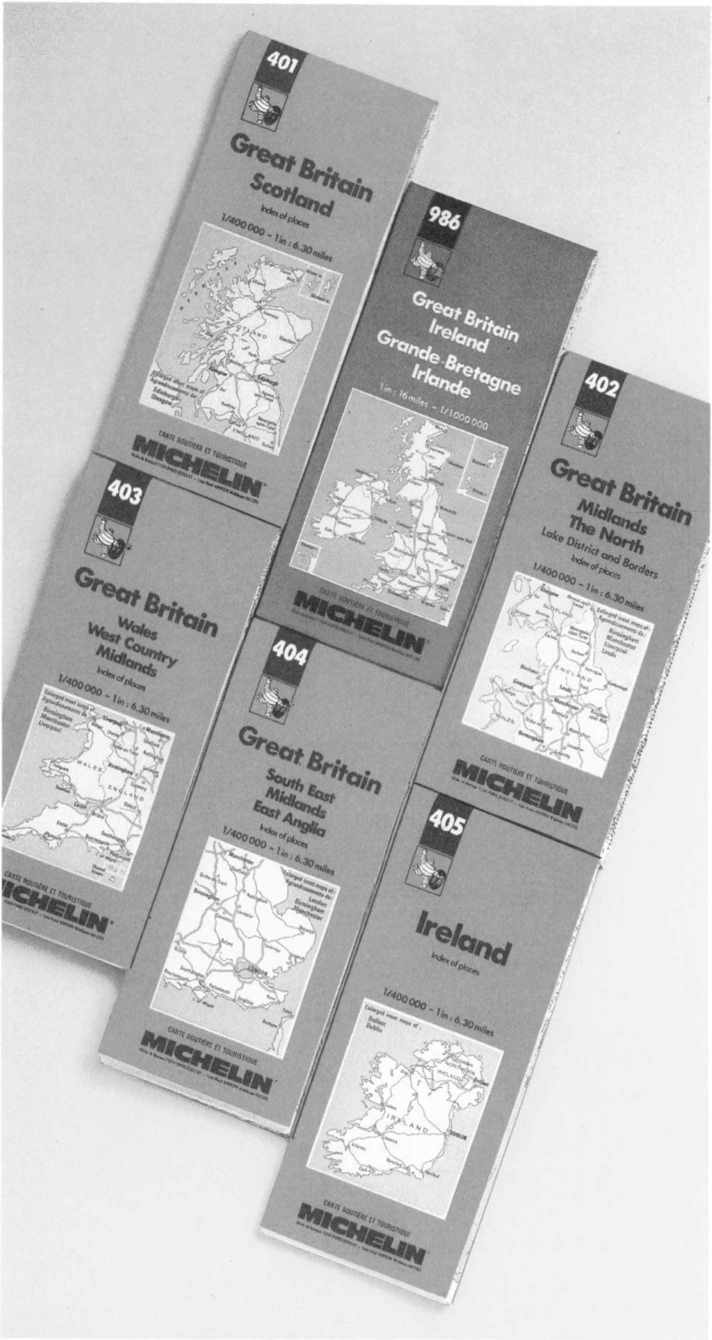
401
Great Britain
Scotland
Index of places
1/400 000 - 1 in : 6.30 miles
CARTE ROUTIÈRE ET TOURISTIQUE
MICHELIN
986
Great Britain
Ireland
Grande-Bretagne
Irlande
1 in : 16 miles - 1/1 000 000
CARTE ROUTIÈRE ET TOURISTIQUE
MICHELIN
402
Great Britain
Midlands
The North
Lake District and Borders
Index of places
1/400 000 - 1 in : 6.30 miles
CARTE ROUTIÈRE ET TOURISTIQUE
MICHELIN
403
Great Britain
Wales
West Country
Midlands
Index of places
1/400 000 - 1 in : 6.30 miles
CARTE ROUTIÈRE ET TOURISTIQUE
MICHELIN
404
Great Britain
South East
Midlands
East Anglia
Index of places
1/400 000 - 1 in : 6.30 miles
CARTE ROUTIÈRE ET TOURISTIQUE
MICHELIN
405
Ireland
Index of places
1/400 000 - 1 in : 6.30 miles
CARTE ROUTIÈRE ET TOURISTIQUE
MICHELIN